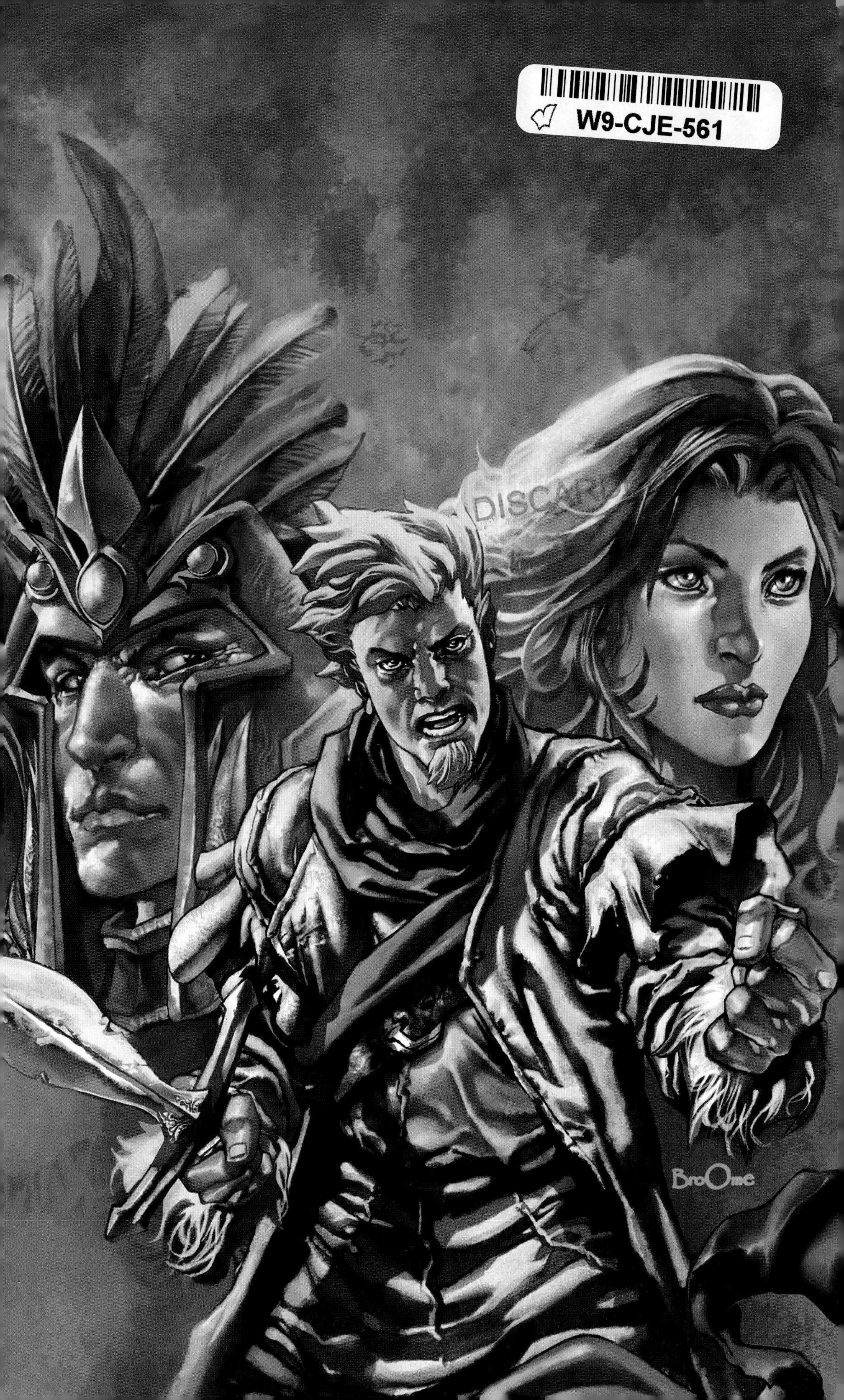
BroOme

The Wood Boy

PART ONE

Raymond E Feist
WRITER

Sean J Jordan
ADAPTATION

Mat Broome
ARTWORK

Stephen Broome
COLORS

Dave Lanphear
LETTERING

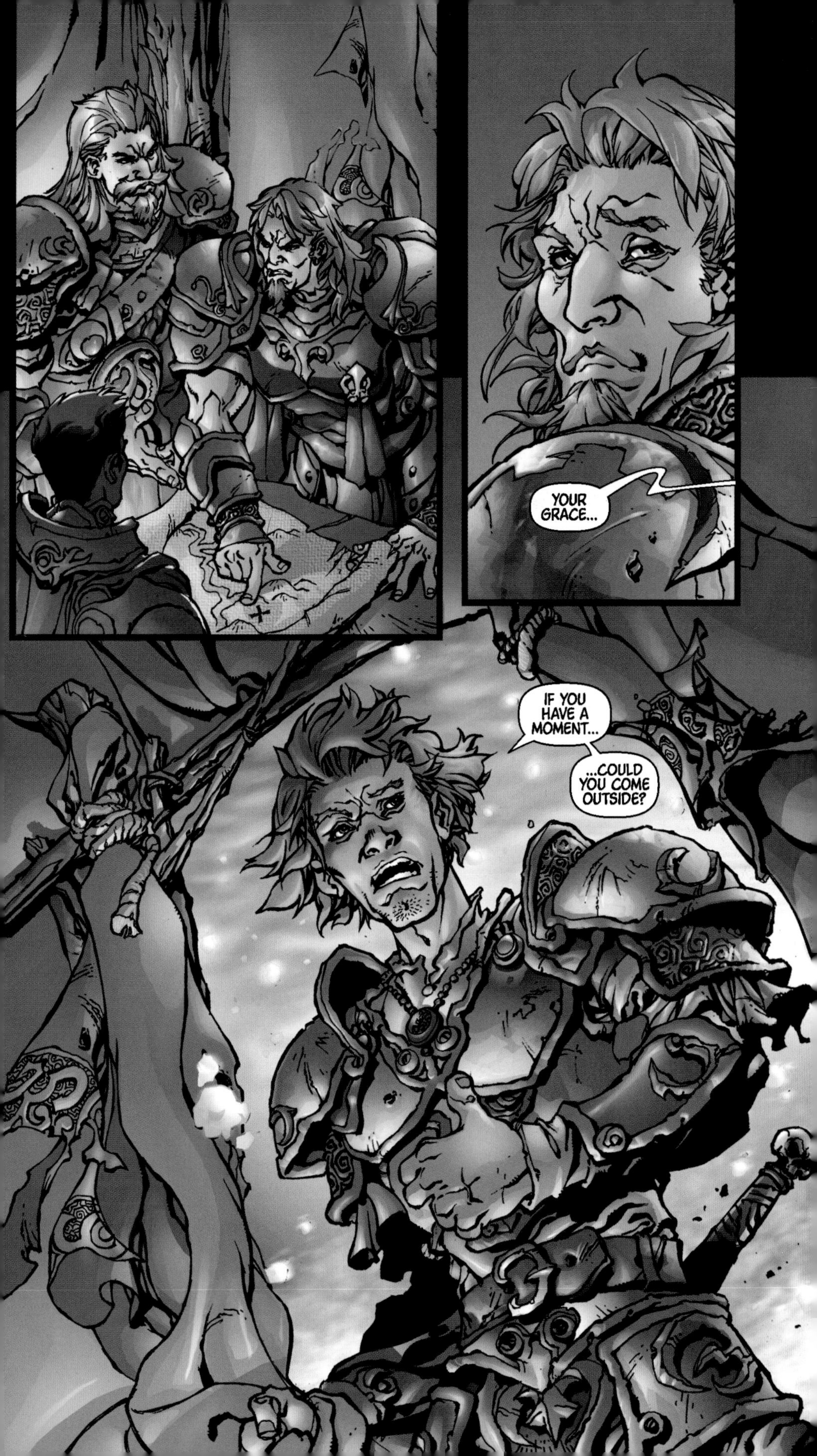
YOUR GRACE...
IF YOU HAVE A MOMENT...
...COULD YOU COME OUTSIDE?

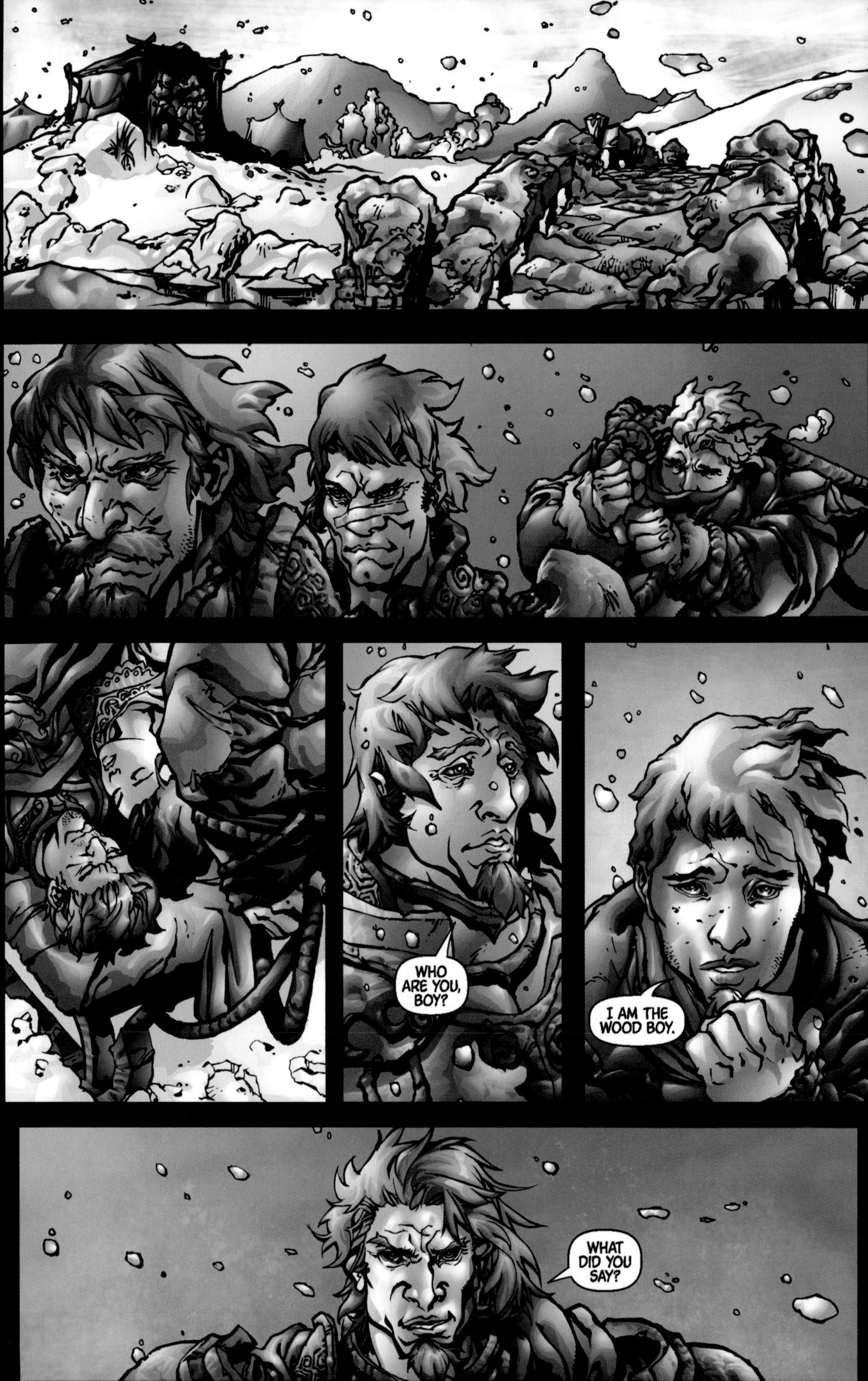
WHO ARE YOU, BOY?
I AM THE WOOD BOY.
WHAT DID YOU SAY?

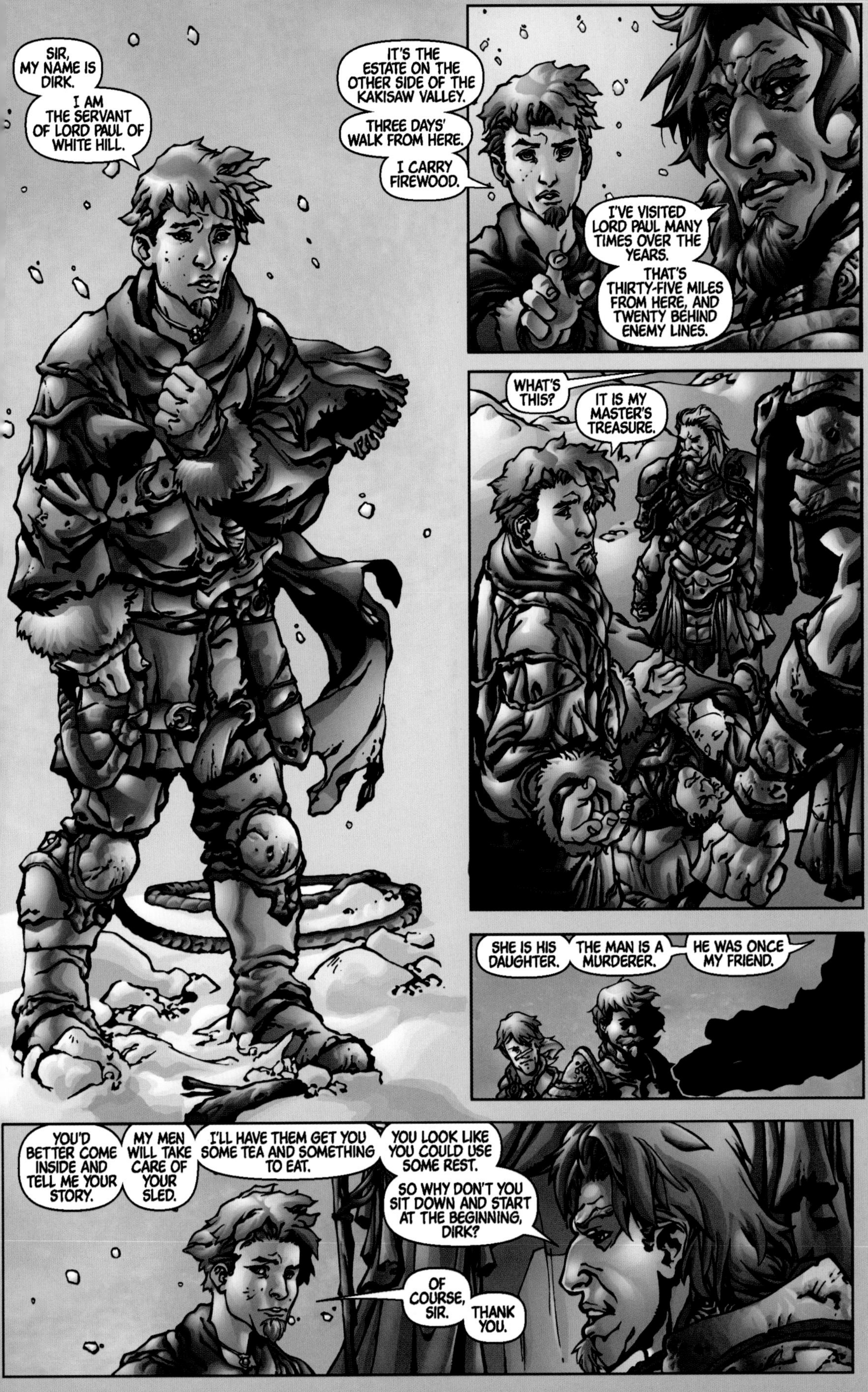
SIR, MY NAME IS DIRK.
I AM THE SERVANT OF LORD PAUL OF WHITE HILL.
IT'S THE ESTATE ON THE OTHER SIDE OF THE KAKISAW VALLEY.
THREE DAYS' WALK FROM HERE.
I CARRY FIREWOOD.
I'VE VISITED LORD PAUL MANY TIMES OVER THE YEARS.
THAT'S THIRTY-FIVE MILES FROM HERE, AND TWENTY BEHIND ENEMY LINES.
WHAT'S THIS?
IT IS MY MASTER'S TREASURE.
SHE IS HIS DAUGHTER.
THE MAN IS A MURDERER.
HE WAS ONCE MY FRIEND.
YOU'D BETTER COME INSIDE AND TELL ME YOUR STORY.
MY MEN WILL TAKE CARE OF YOUR SLED.
I'LL HAVE THEM GET YOU SOME TEA AND SOMETHING TO EAT.
YOU LOOK LIKE YOU COULD USE SOME REST.
SO WHY DON'T YOU SIT DOWN AND START AT THE BEGINNING, DIRK?
OF COURSE, SIR.
THANK YOU.

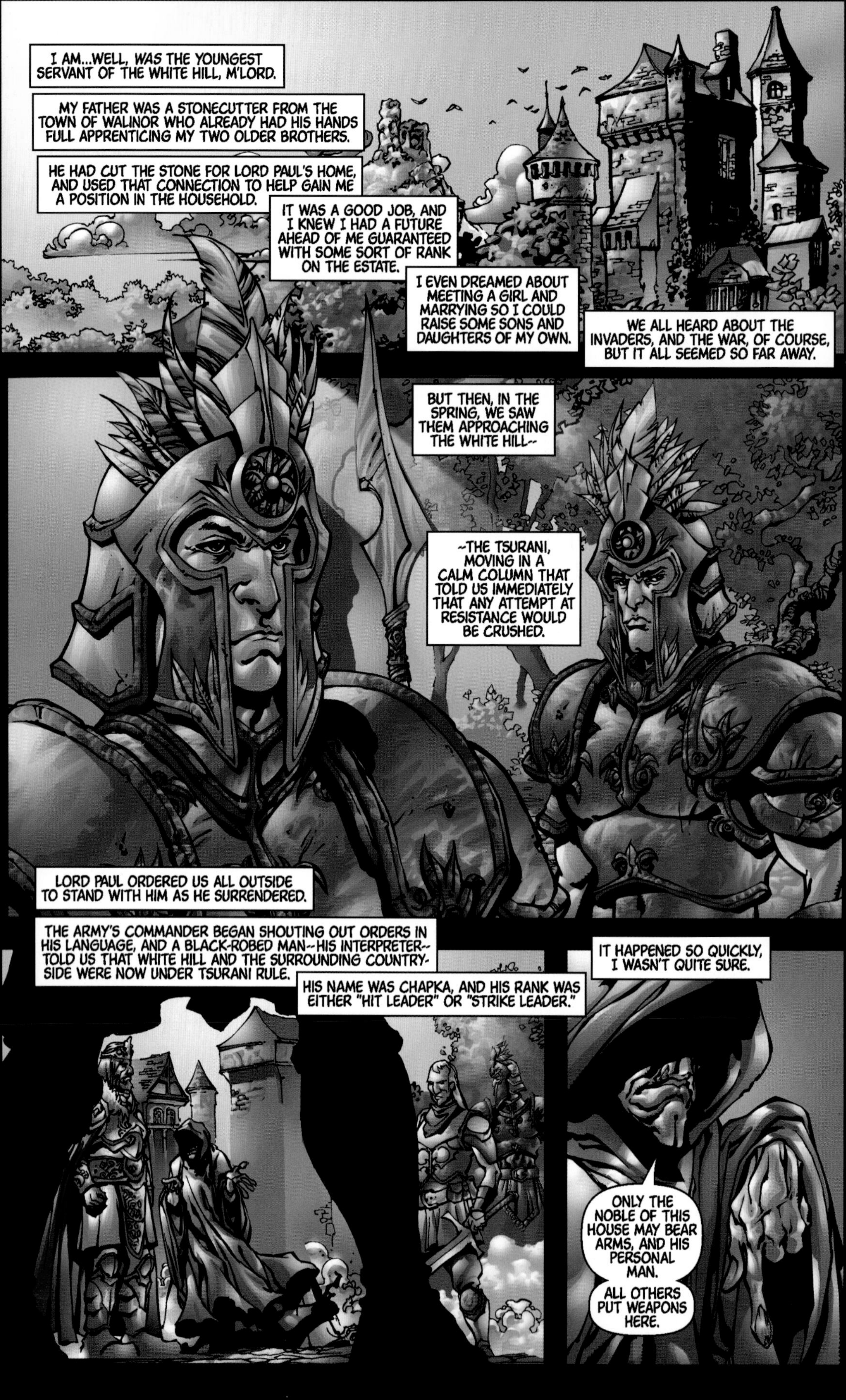
I AM...WELL, *WAS* THE YOUNGEST SERVANT OF THE WHITE HILL, M'LORD.
MY FATHER WAS A STONECUTTER FROM THE TOWN OF WALINOR WHO ALREADY HAD HIS HANDS FULL APPRENTICING MY TWO OLDER BROTHERS.
HE HAD CUT THE STONE FOR LORD PAUL'S HOME, AND USED THAT CONNECTION TO HELP GAIN ME A POSITION IN THE HOUSEHOLD.
IT WAS A GOOD JOB, AND I KNEW I HAD A FUTURE AHEAD OF ME GUARANTEED WITH SOME SORT OF RANK ON THE ESTATE.
I EVEN DREAMED ABOUT MEETING A GIRL AND MARRYING SO I COULD RAISE SOME SONS AND DAUGHTERS OF MY OWN.
WE ALL HEARD ABOUT THE INVADERS, AND THE WAR, OF COURSE, BUT IT ALL SEEMED SO FAR AWAY.
BUT THEN, IN THE SPRING, WE SAW THEM APPROACHING THE WHITE HILL--
--THE TSURANI, MOVING IN A CALM COLUMN THAT TOLD US IMMEDIATELY THAT ANY ATTEMPT AT RESISTANCE WOULD BE CRUSHED.
LORD PAUL ORDERED US ALL OUTSIDE TO STAND WITH HIM AS HE SURRENDERED.
THE ARMY'S COMMANDER BEGAN SHOUTING OUT ORDERS IN HIS LANGUAGE, AND A BLACK-ROBED MAN--HIS INTERPRETER--TOLD US THAT WHITE HILL AND THE SURROUNDING COUNTRY-SIDE WERE NOW UNDER TSURANI RULE.
HIS NAME WAS CHAPKA, AND HIS RANK WAS EITHER "HIT LEADER" OR "STRIKE LEADER."
IT HAPPENED SO QUICKLY, I WASN'T QUITE SURE.
ONLY THE NOBLE OF THIS HOUSE MAY BEAR ARMS, AND HIS PERSONAL MAN.
ALL OTHERS PUT WEAPONS HERE.

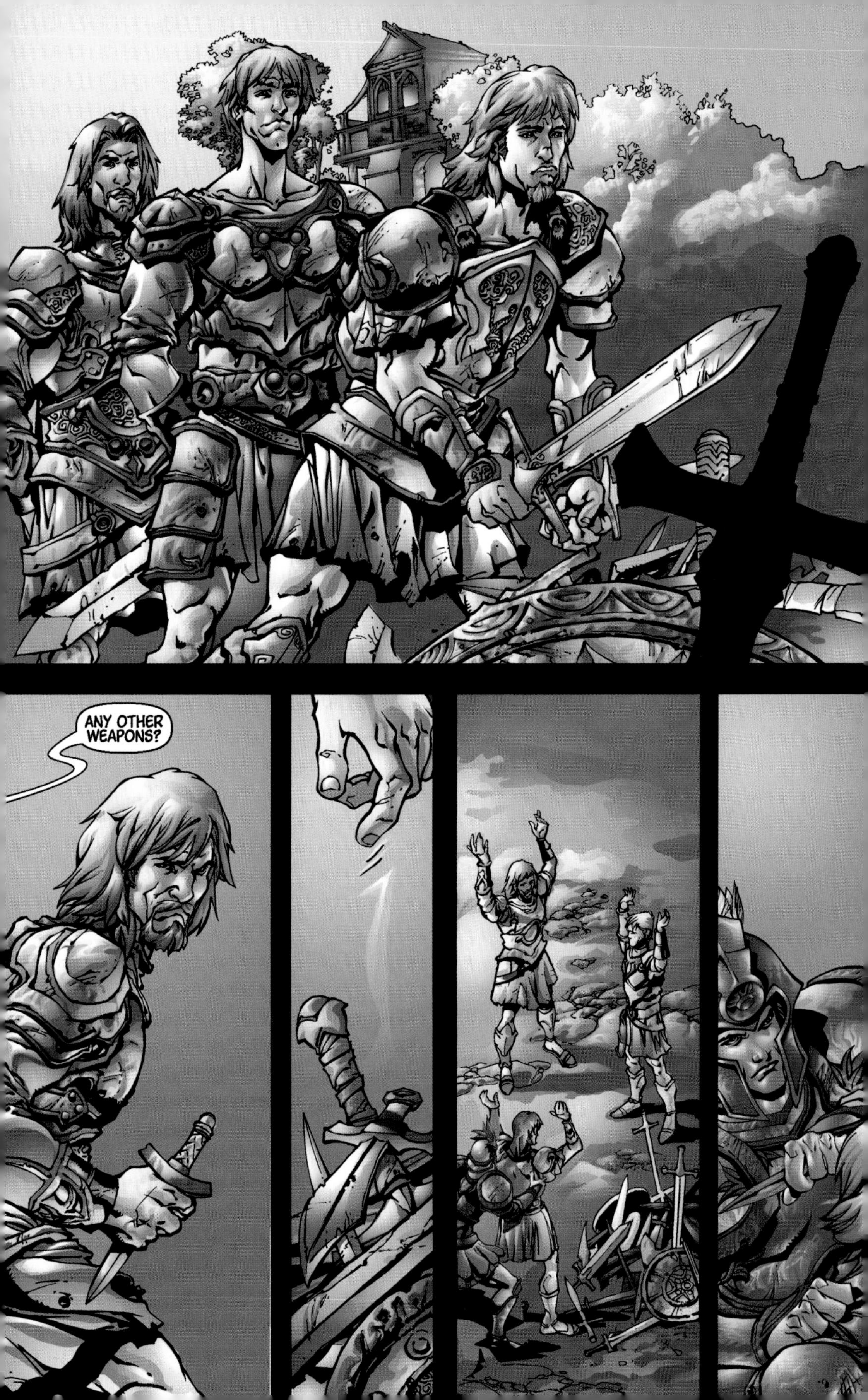
ANY OTHER WEAPONS?

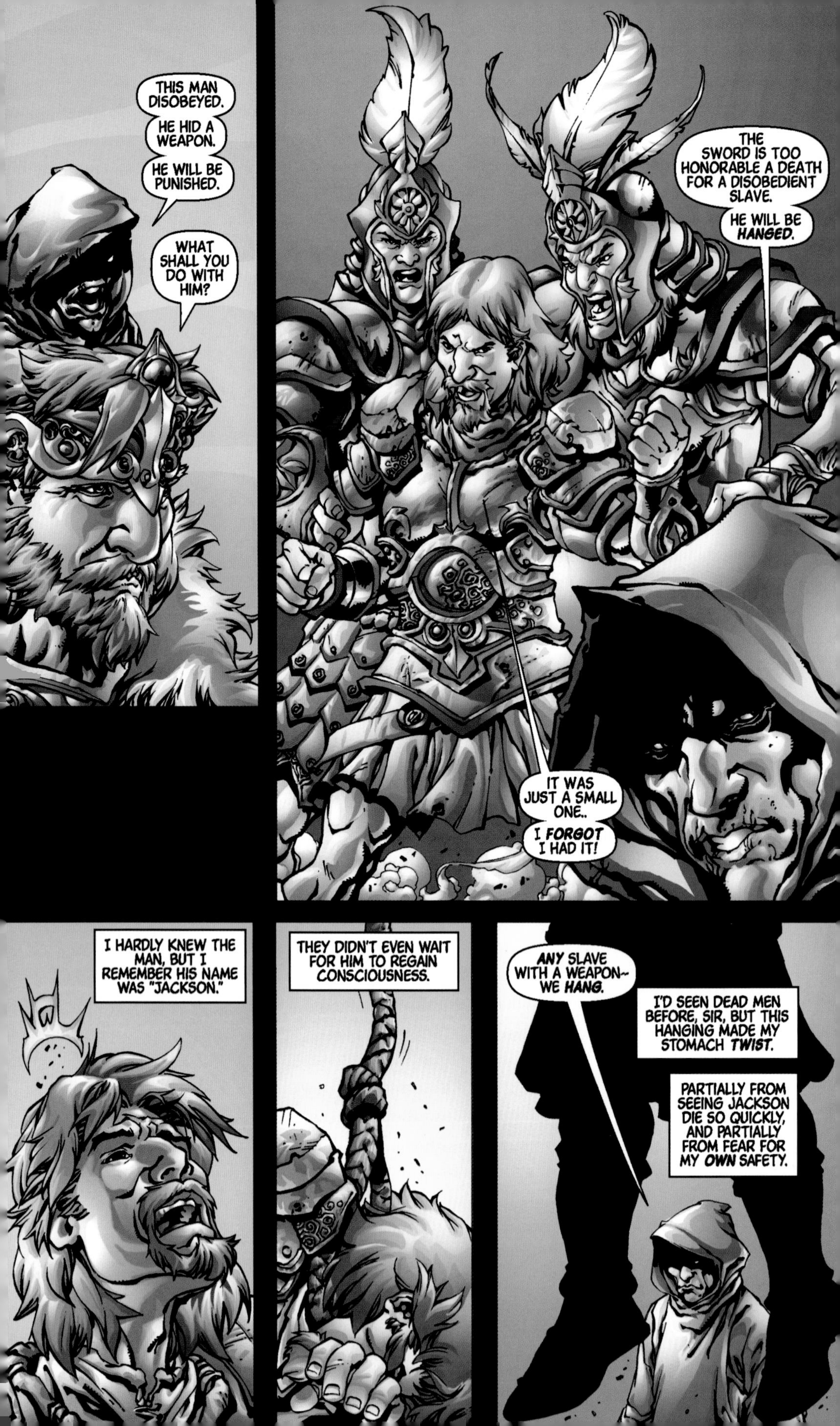
THIS MAN DISOBEYED.
HE HID A WEAPON.
HE WILL BE PUNISHED.
WHAT SHALL YOU DO WITH HIM?
THE SWORD IS TOO HONORABLE A DEATH FOR A DISOBEDIENT SLAVE.
HE WILL BE HANGED.
IT WAS JUST A SMALL ONE..
I FORGOT I HAD IT!
I HARDLY KNEW THE MAN, BUT I REMEMBER HIS NAME WAS "JACKSON."
THEY DIDN'T EVEN WAIT FOR HIM TO REGAIN CONSCIOUSNESS.
ANY SLAVE WITH A WEAPON~ WE HANG.
I'D SEEN DEAD MEN BEFORE, SIR, BUT THIS HANGING MADE MY STOMACH TWIST.
PARTIALLY FROM SEEING JACKSON DIE SO QUICKLY, AND PARTIALLY FROM FEAR FOR MY OWN SAFETY.

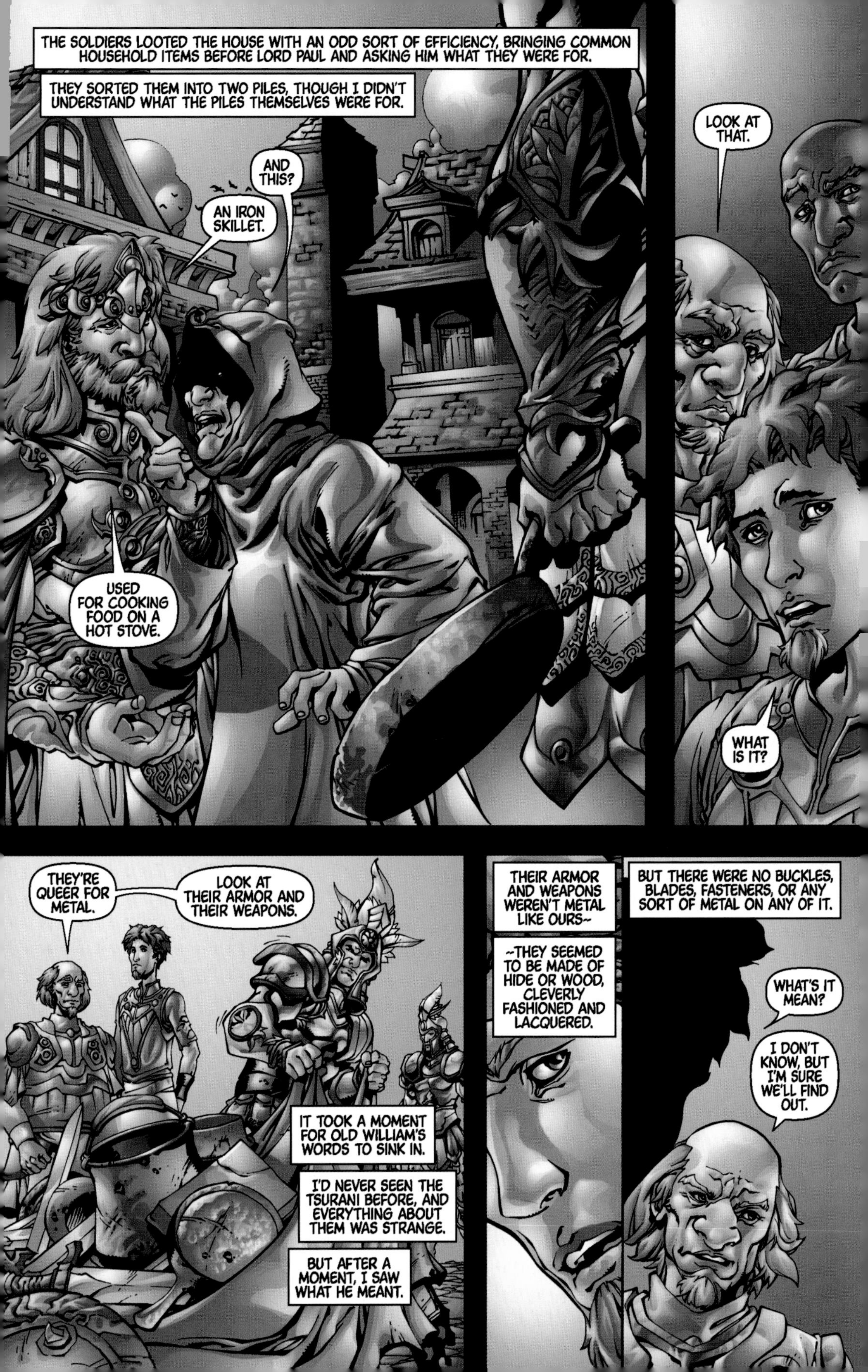
THE SOLDIERS LOOTED THE HOUSE WITH AN ODD SORT OF EFFICIENCY, BRINGING COMMON HOUSEHOLD ITEMS BEFORE LORD PAUL AND ASKING HIM WHAT THEY WERE FOR.
THEY SORTED THEM INTO TWO PILES, THOUGH I DIDN'T UNDERSTAND WHAT THE PILES THEMSELVES WERE FOR.
AND THIS?
AN IRON SKILLET.
USED FOR COOKING FOOD ON A HOT STOVE.
LOOK AT THAT.
WHAT IS IT?
THEY'RE QUEER FOR METAL.
LOOK AT THEIR ARMOR AND THEIR WEAPONS.
IT TOOK A MOMENT FOR OLD WILLIAM'S WORDS TO SINK IN.
I'D NEVER SEEN THE TSURANI BEFORE, AND EVERYTHING ABOUT THEM WAS STRANGE.
BUT AFTER A MOMENT, I SAW WHAT HE MEANT.
THEIR ARMOR AND WEAPONS WEREN'T METAL LIKE OURS~
~THEY SEEMED TO BE MADE OF HIDE OR WOOD, CLEVERLY FASHIONED AND LACQUERED.
BUT THERE WERE NO BUCKLES, BLADES, FASTENERS, OR ANY SORT OF METAL ON ANY OF IT.
WHAT'S IT MEAN?
I DON'T KNOW, BUT I'M SURE WE'LL FIND OUT.

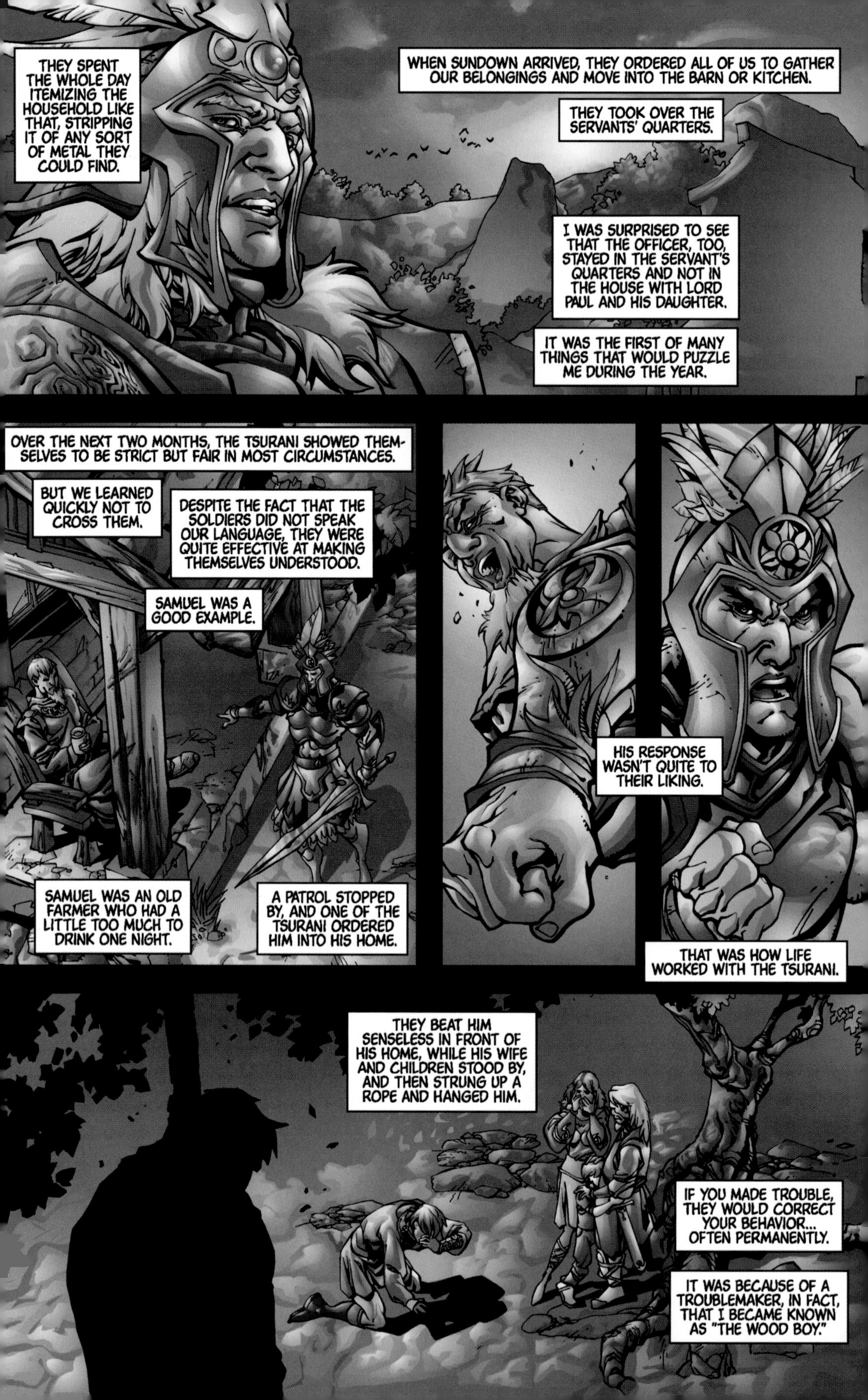
THEY SPENT THE WHOLE DAY ITEMIZING THE HOUSEHOLD LIKE THAT, STRIPPING IT OF ANY SORT OF METAL THEY COULD FIND.
WHEN SUNDOWN ARRIVED, THEY ORDERED ALL OF US TO GATHER OUR BELONGINGS AND MOVE INTO THE BARN OR KITCHEN.
THEY TOOK OVER THE SERVANTS' QUARTERS.
I WAS SURPRISED TO SEE THAT THE OFFICER, TOO, STAYED IN THE SERVANT'S QUARTERS AND NOT IN THE HOUSE WITH LORD PAUL AND HIS DAUGHTER.
IT WAS THE FIRST OF MANY THINGS THAT WOULD PUZZLE ME DURING THE YEAR.
OVER THE NEXT TWO MONTHS, THE TSURANI SHOWED THEMSELVES TO BE STRICT BUT FAIR IN MOST CIRCUMSTANCES.
BUT WE LEARNED QUICKLY NOT TO CROSS THEM.
DESPITE THE FACT THAT THE SOLDIERS DID NOT SPEAK OUR LANGUAGE, THEY WERE QUITE EFFECTIVE AT MAKING THEMSELVES UNDERSTOOD.
SAMUEL WAS A GOOD EXAMPLE.
SAMUEL WAS AN OLD FARMER WHO HAD A LITTLE TOO MUCH TO DRINK ONE NIGHT.
A PATROL STOPPED BY, AND ONE OF THE TSURANI ORDERED HIM INTO HIS HOME.
HIS RESPONSE WASN'T QUITE TO THEIR LIKING.
THAT WAS HOW LIFE WORKED WITH THE TSURANI.
THEY BEAT HIM SENSELESS IN FRONT OF HIS HOME, WHILE HIS WIFE AND CHILDREN STOOD BY, AND THEN STRUNG UP A ROPE AND HANGED HIM.
IF YOU MADE TROUBLE, THEY WOULD CORRECT YOUR BEHAVIOR... OFTEN PERMANENTLY.
IT WAS BECAUSE OF A TROUBLEMAKER, IN FACT, THAT I BECAME KNOWN AS "THE WOOD BOY."

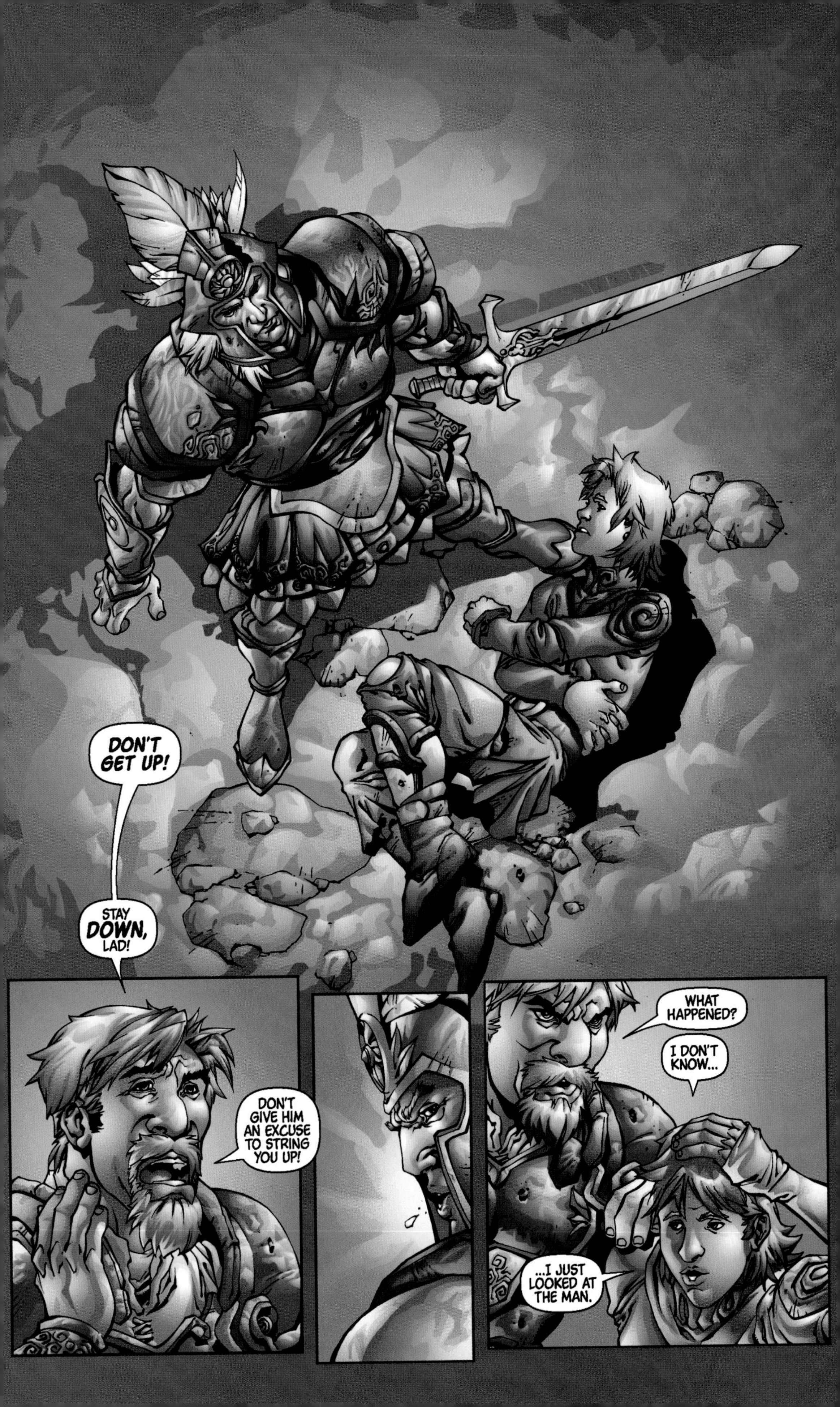
DON'T GET UP!
STAY DOWN, LAD!
DON'T GIVE HIM AN EXCUSE TO STRING YOU UP!
WHAT HAPPENED?
I DON'T KNOW...
...I JUST LOOKED AT THE MAN.

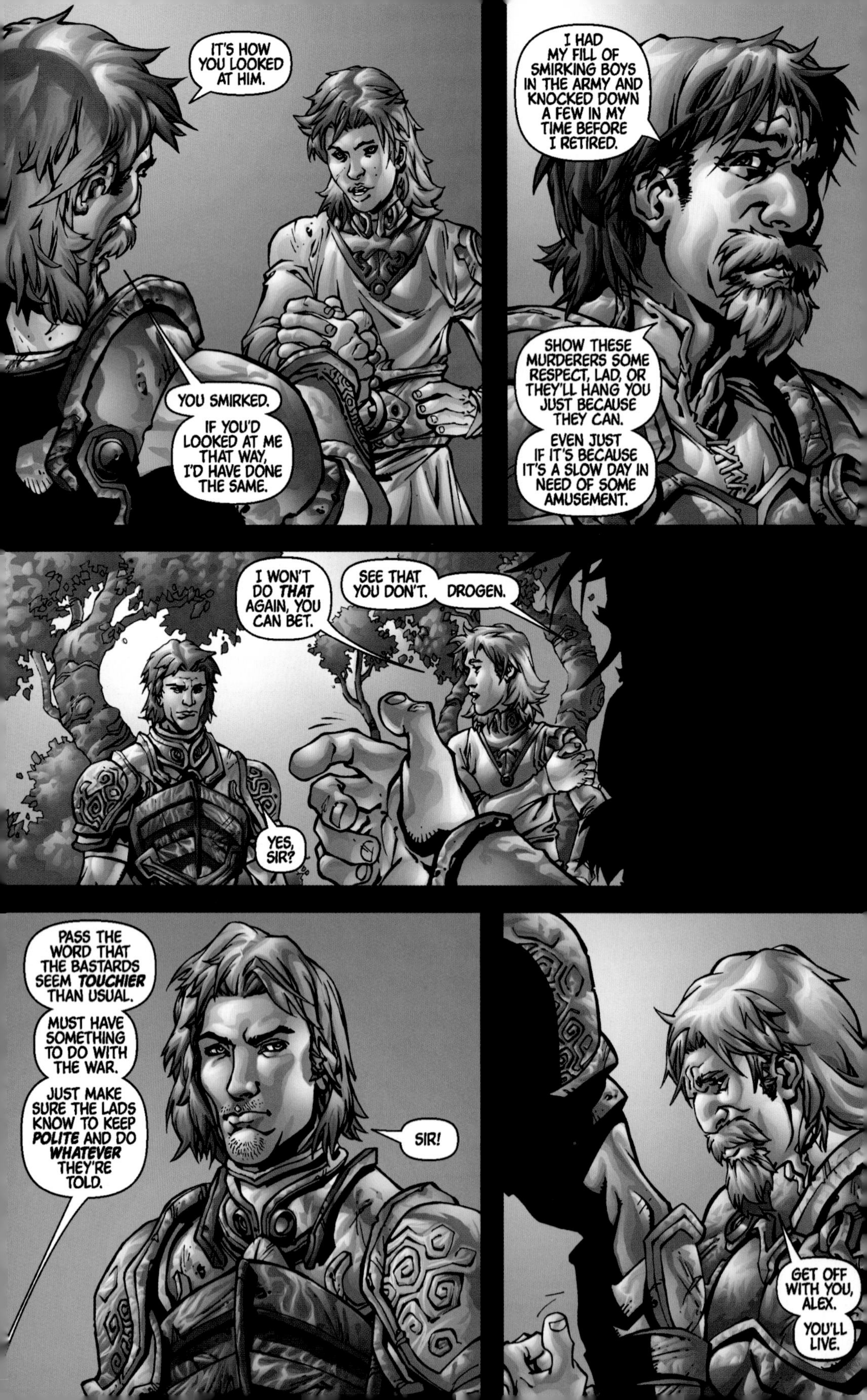
IT'S HOW YOU LOOKED AT HIM.
YOU SMIRKED.
IF YOU'D LOOKED AT ME THAT WAY, I'D HAVE DONE THE SAME.
I HAD MY FILL OF SMIRKING BOYS IN THE ARMY AND KNOCKED DOWN A FEW IN MY TIME BEFORE I RETIRED.
SHOW THESE MURDERERS SOME RESPECT, LAD, OR THEY'LL HANG YOU JUST BECAUSE THEY CAN.
EVEN JUST IF IT'S BECAUSE IT'S A SLOW DAY IN NEED OF SOME AMUSEMENT.
I WON'T DO *THAT* AGAIN, YOU CAN BET.
SEE THAT YOU DON'T.
DROGEN.
YES, SIR?
PASS THE WORD THAT THE BASTARDS SEEM *TOUCHIER* THAN USUAL.
MUST HAVE SOMETHING TO DO WITH THE WAR.
JUST MAKE SURE THE LADS KNOW TO KEEP *POLITE* AND DO *WHATEVER* THEY'RE TOLD.
SIR!
GET OFF WITH YOU, ALEX.
YOU'LL LIVE.

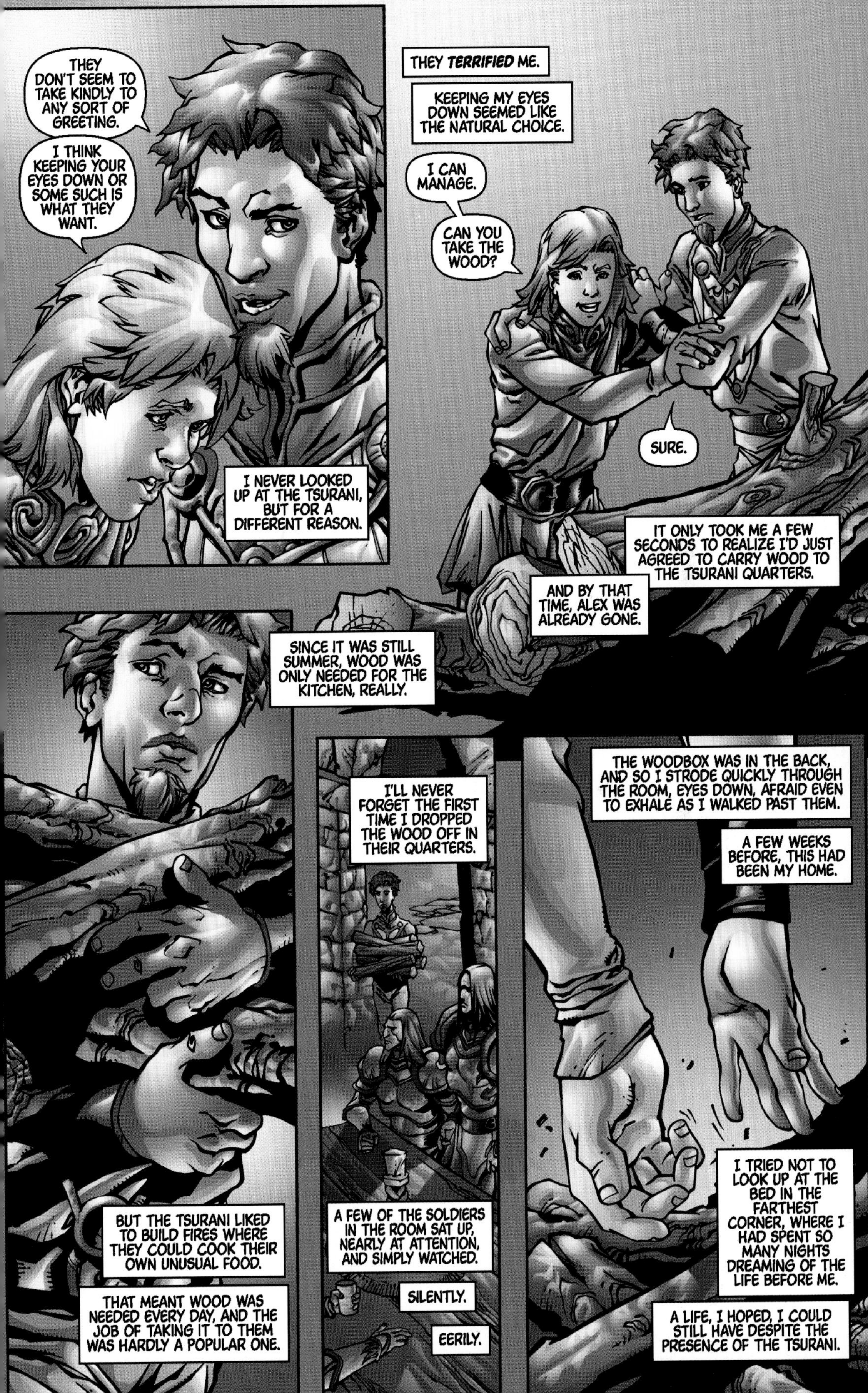
THEY DON'T SEEM TO TAKE KINDLY TO ANY SORT OF GREETING.
I THINK KEEPING YOUR EYES DOWN OR SOME SUCH IS WHAT THEY WANT.
I NEVER LOOKED UP AT THE TSURANI, BUT FOR A DIFFERENT REASON.
THEY *TERRIFIED* ME.
KEEPING MY EYES DOWN SEEMED LIKE THE NATURAL CHOICE.
I CAN MANAGE.
CAN YOU TAKE THE WOOD?
SURE.
IT ONLY TOOK ME A FEW SECONDS TO REALIZE I'D JUST AGREED TO CARRY WOOD TO THE TSURANI QUARTERS.
AND BY THAT TIME, ALEX WAS ALREADY GONE.
SINCE IT WAS STILL SUMMER, WOOD WAS ONLY NEEDED FOR THE KITCHEN, REALLY.
BUT THE TSURANI LIKED TO BUILD FIRES WHERE THEY COULD COOK THEIR OWN UNUSUAL FOOD.
THAT MEANT WOOD WAS NEEDED EVERY DAY, AND THE JOB OF TAKING IT TO THEM WAS HARDLY A POPULAR ONE.
I'LL NEVER FORGET THE FIRST TIME I DROPPED THE WOOD OFF IN THEIR QUARTERS.
A FEW OF THE SOLDIERS IN THE ROOM SAT UP, NEARLY AT ATTENTION, AND SIMPLY WATCHED.
SILENTLY.
EERILY.
THE WOODBOX WAS IN THE BACK, AND SO I STRODE QUICKLY THROUGH THE ROOM, EYES DOWN, AFRAID EVEN TO EXHALE AS I WALKED PAST THEM.
A FEW WEEKS BEFORE, THIS HAD BEEN MY HOME.
I TRIED NOT TO LOOK UP AT THE BED IN THE FARTHEST CORNER, WHERE I HAD SPENT SO MANY NIGHTS DREAMING OF THE LIFE BEFORE ME.
A LIFE, I HOPED, I COULD STILL HAVE DESPITE THE PRESENCE OF THE TSURANI.

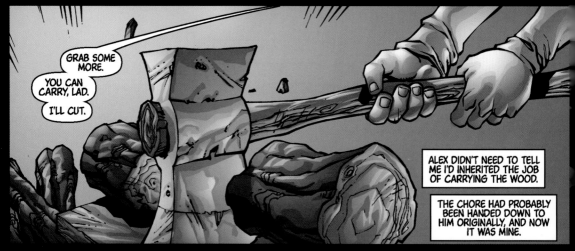

GRAB SOME MORE.

YOU CAN CARRY, LAD.

I'LL CUT.

ALEX DIDN'T NEED TO TELL ME I'D INHERITED THE JOB OF CARRYING THE WOOD.

THE CHORE HAD PROBABLY BEEN HANDED DOWN TO HIM ORIGINALLY, AND NOW IT WAS MINE.

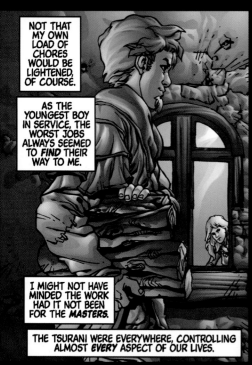

NOT THAT MY OWN LOAD OF CHORES WOULD BE LIGHTENED, OF COURSE.

AS THE YOUNGEST BOY IN SERVICE, THE WORST JOBS ALWAYS SEEMED TO *FIND* THEIR WAY TO ME.

I MIGHT NOT HAVE MINDED THE WORK HAD IT NOT BEEN FOR THE *MASTERS*.

THE TSURANI WERE EVERYWHERE, CONTROLLING ALMOST *EVERY* ASPECT OF OUR LIVES.

I OFTEN WONDERED IF ONE DAY, THEY WOULD BE DRIVEN FROM WHITE HILL.

BUT NEWS OF THE WAR NEVER REACHED US, AND THE TSURANI BEGAN TO SETTLE AS IF THEY WERE NEVER LEAVING.

THE DAYS WORE ON, AND LIFE BECAME MORE AND MORE ROUTINE.

AND WHILE OUR ENSLAVEMENT TO THE TSURANI DID NOT *GROW* ANY EASIER, WE EVENTUALLY BECAME BETTER ACCUSTOMED TO IT.

FALL CAME QUICKLY, AND BY THAT TIME, I WAS RESPONSIBLE FOR KEEPING *ALL* OF THE WOODBOXES ON THE PROPERTY FILLED.

AS THE DAYS GREW COOLER AND SNOW COVERED THE GROUND, MY WORKLOAD INCREASED.

ALEX DID THE *CHOPPING,* AND THE "WOOD BOY" *HAULED* THE LOAD.

SOON, THAT WAS THE *ONLY* NAME ANYONE WOULD CALL ME.

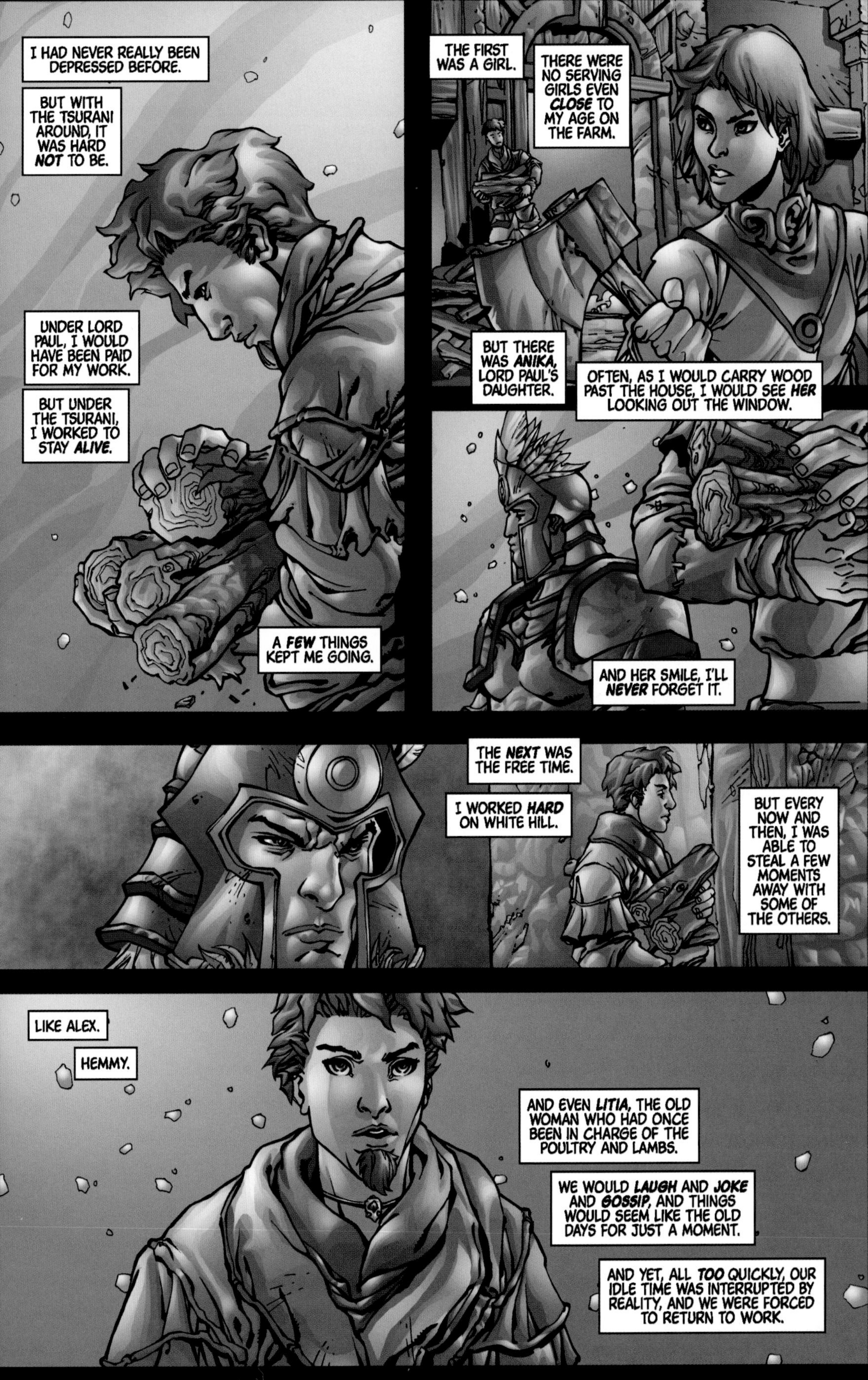
I HAD NEVER REALLY BEEN DEPRESSED BEFORE.
BUT WITH THE TSURANI AROUND, IT WAS HARD *NOT* TO BE.
UNDER LORD PAUL, I WOULD HAVE BEEN PAID FOR MY WORK.
BUT UNDER THE TSURANI, I WORKED TO STAY *ALIVE*.
A *FEW* THINGS KEPT ME GOING.
THE FIRST WAS A GIRL.
THERE WERE NO SERVING GIRLS EVEN *CLOSE* TO MY AGE ON THE FARM.
BUT THERE WAS *ANIKA*, LORD PAUL'S DAUGHTER.
OFTEN, AS I WOULD CARRY WOOD PAST THE HOUSE, I WOULD SEE *HER* LOOKING OUT THE WINDOW.
AND HER SMILE, I'LL *NEVER* FORGET IT.
THE *NEXT* WAS THE FREE TIME.
I WORKED *HARD* ON WHITE HILL.
BUT EVERY NOW AND THEN, I WAS ABLE TO STEAL A FEW MOMENTS AWAY WITH SOME OF THE OTHERS.
LIKE ALEX.
HEMMY.
AND EVEN *LITIA*, THE OLD WOMAN WHO HAD ONCE BEEN IN CHARGE OF THE POULTRY AND LAMBS.
WE WOULD *LAUGH* AND *JOKE* AND *GOSSIP*, AND THINGS WOULD SEEM LIKE THE OLD DAYS FOR JUST A MOMENT.
AND YET, ALL *TOO* QUICKLY, OUR IDLE TIME WAS INTERRUPTED BY REALITY, AND WE WERE FORCED TO RETURN TO WORK.

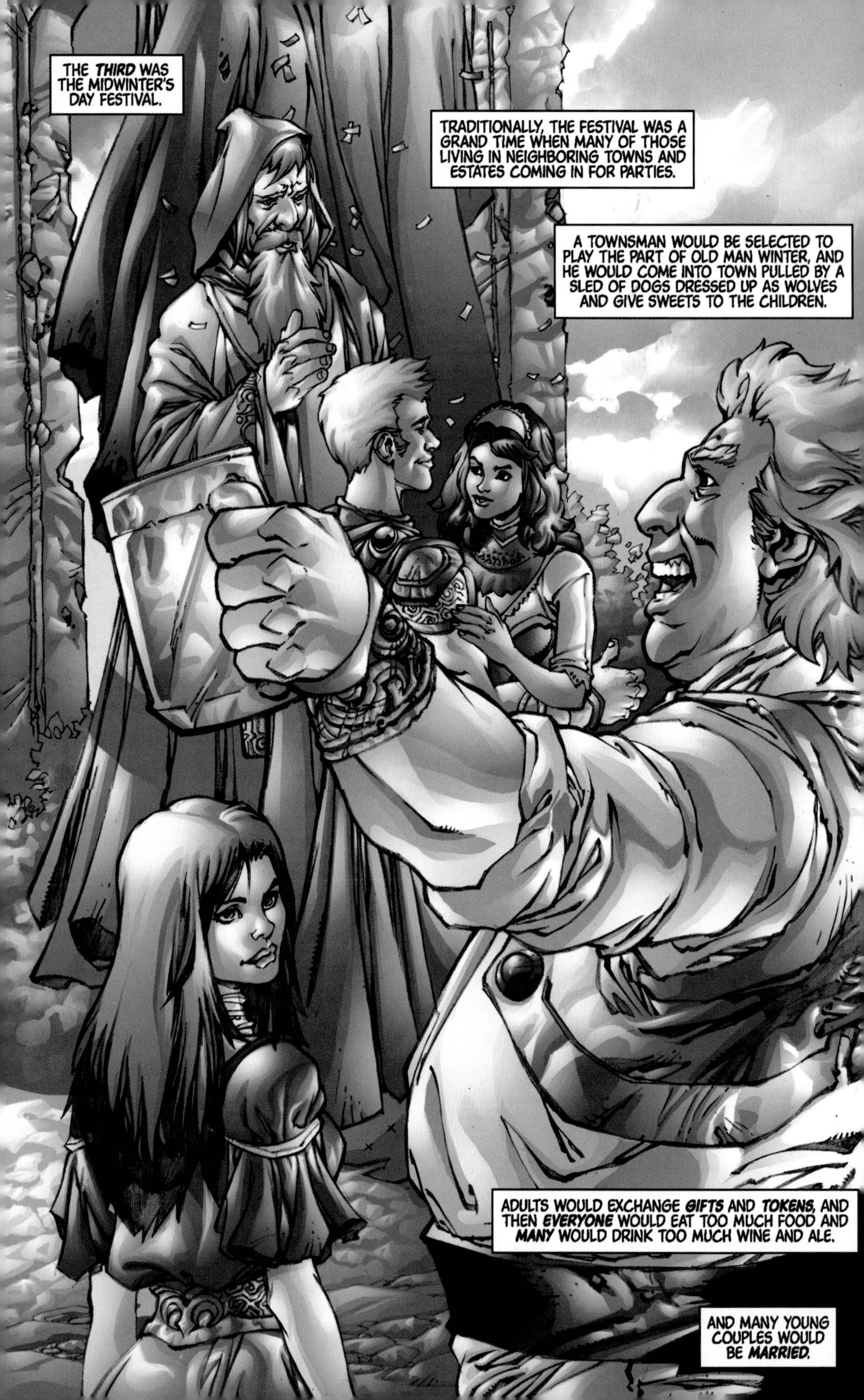
THE *THIRD* WAS THE MIDWINTER'S DAY FESTIVAL.
TRADITIONALLY, THE FESTIVAL WAS A GRAND TIME WHEN MANY OF THOSE LIVING IN NEIGHBORING TOWNS AND ESTATES COMING IN FOR PARTIES.
A TOWNSMAN WOULD BE SELECTED TO PLAY THE PART OF OLD MAN WINTER, AND HE WOULD COME INTO TOWN PULLED BY A SLED OF DOGS DRESSED UP AS WOLVES AND GIVE SWEETS TO THE CHILDREN.
ADULTS WOULD EXCHANGE *GIFTS* AND *TOKENS*, AND THEN *EVERYONE* WOULD EAT TOO MUCH FOOD AND *MANY* WOULD DRINK TOO MUCH WINE AND ALE.
AND MANY YOUNG COUPLES WOULD BE *MARRIED*.

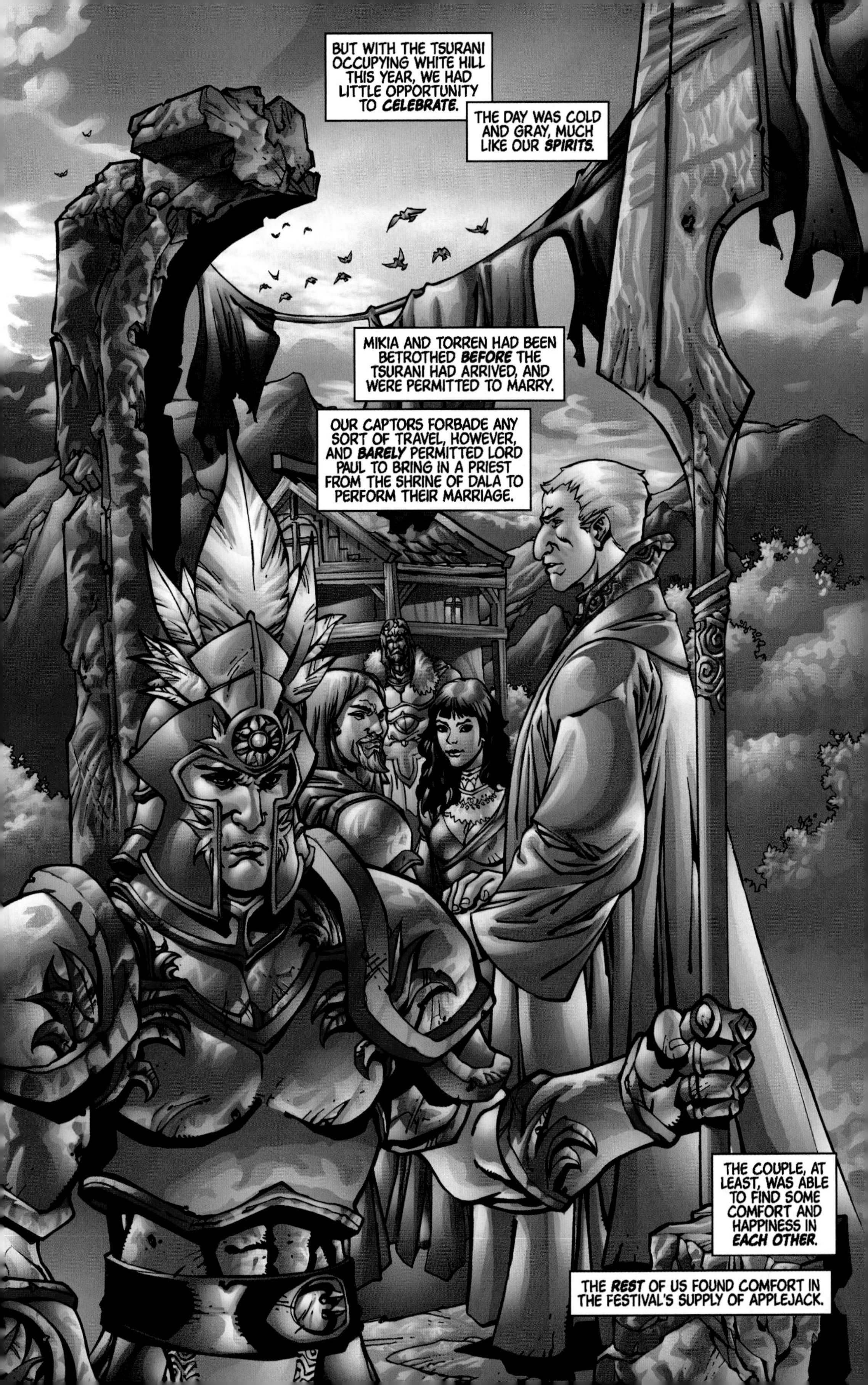
BUT WITH THE TSURANI OCCUPYING WHITE HILL THIS YEAR, WE HAD LITTLE OPPORTUNITY TO *CELEBRATE*.
THE DAY WAS COLD AND GRAY, MUCH LIKE OUR *SPIRITS*.
MIKIA AND TORREN HAD BEEN BETROTHED *BEFORE* THE TSURANI HAD ARRIVED, AND WERE PERMITTED TO MARRY.
OUR CAPTORS FORBADE ANY SORT OF TRAVEL, HOWEVER, AND *BARELY* PERMITTED LORD PAUL TO BRING IN A PRIEST FROM THE SHRINE OF DALA TO PERFORM THEIR MARRIAGE.
THE COUPLE, AT LEAST, WAS ABLE TO FIND SOME COMFORT AND HAPPINESS IN *EACH OTHER*.
THE *REST* OF US FOUND COMFORT IN THE FESTIVAL'S SUPPLY OF APPLEJACK.

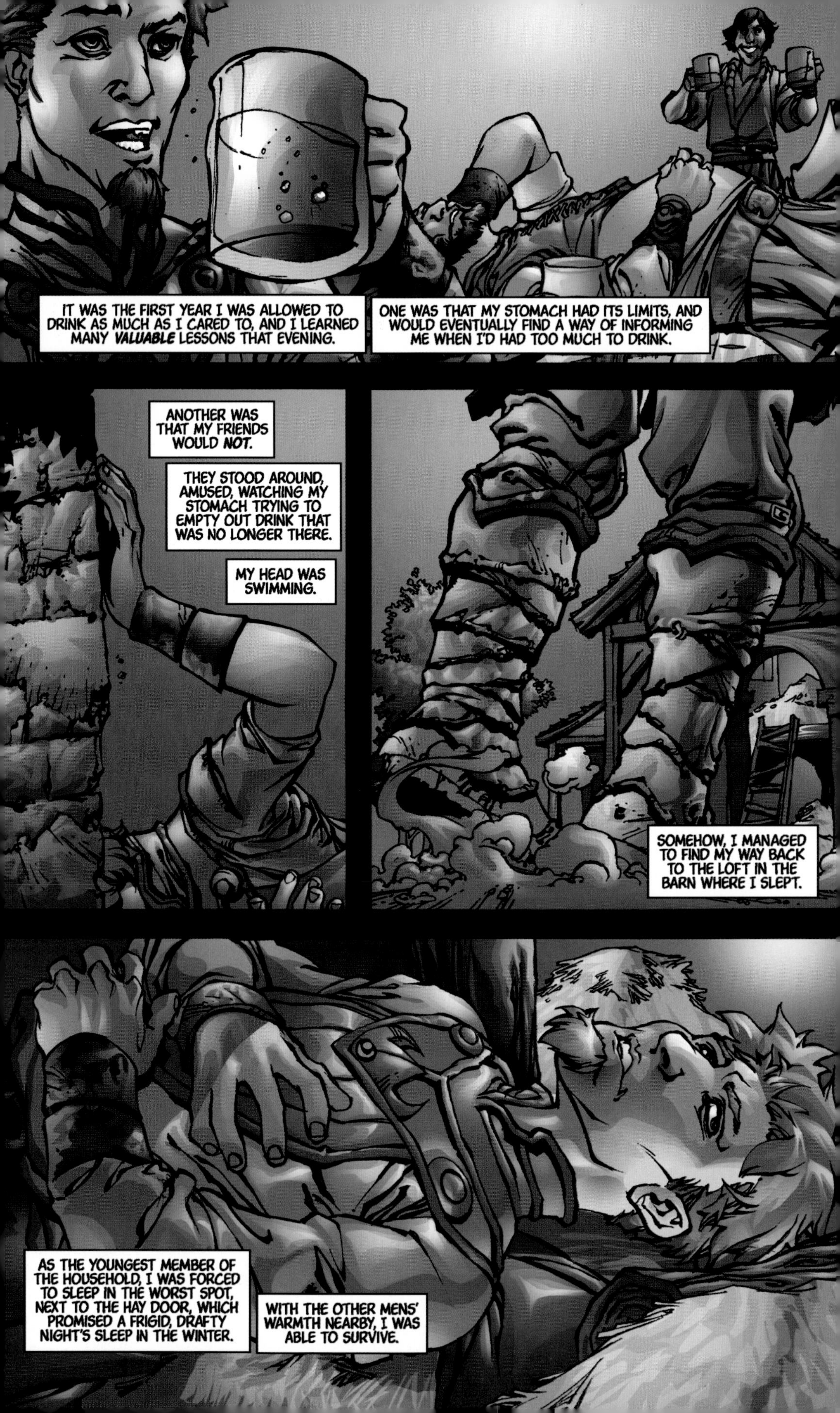
IT WAS THE FIRST YEAR I WAS ALLOWED TO DRINK AS MUCH AS I CARED TO, AND I LEARNED MANY *VALUABLE* LESSONS THAT EVENING.
ONE WAS THAT MY STOMACH HAD ITS LIMITS, AND WOULD EVENTUALLY FIND A WAY OF INFORMING ME WHEN I'D HAD TOO MUCH TO DRINK.
ANOTHER WAS THAT MY FRIENDS WOULD *NOT.*
THEY STOOD AROUND, AMUSED, WATCHING MY STOMACH TRYING TO EMPTY OUT DRINK THAT WAS NO LONGER THERE.
MY HEAD WAS SWIMMING.
SOMEHOW, I MANAGED TO FIND MY WAY BACK TO THE LOFT IN THE BARN WHERE I SLEPT.
AS THE YOUNGEST MEMBER OF THE HOUSEHOLD, I WAS FORCED TO SLEEP IN THE WORST SPOT, NEXT TO THE HAY DOOR, WHICH PROMISED A FRIGID, DRAFTY NIGHT'S SLEEP IN THE WINTER.
WITH THE OTHER MENS' WARMTH NEARBY, I WAS ABLE TO SURVIVE.

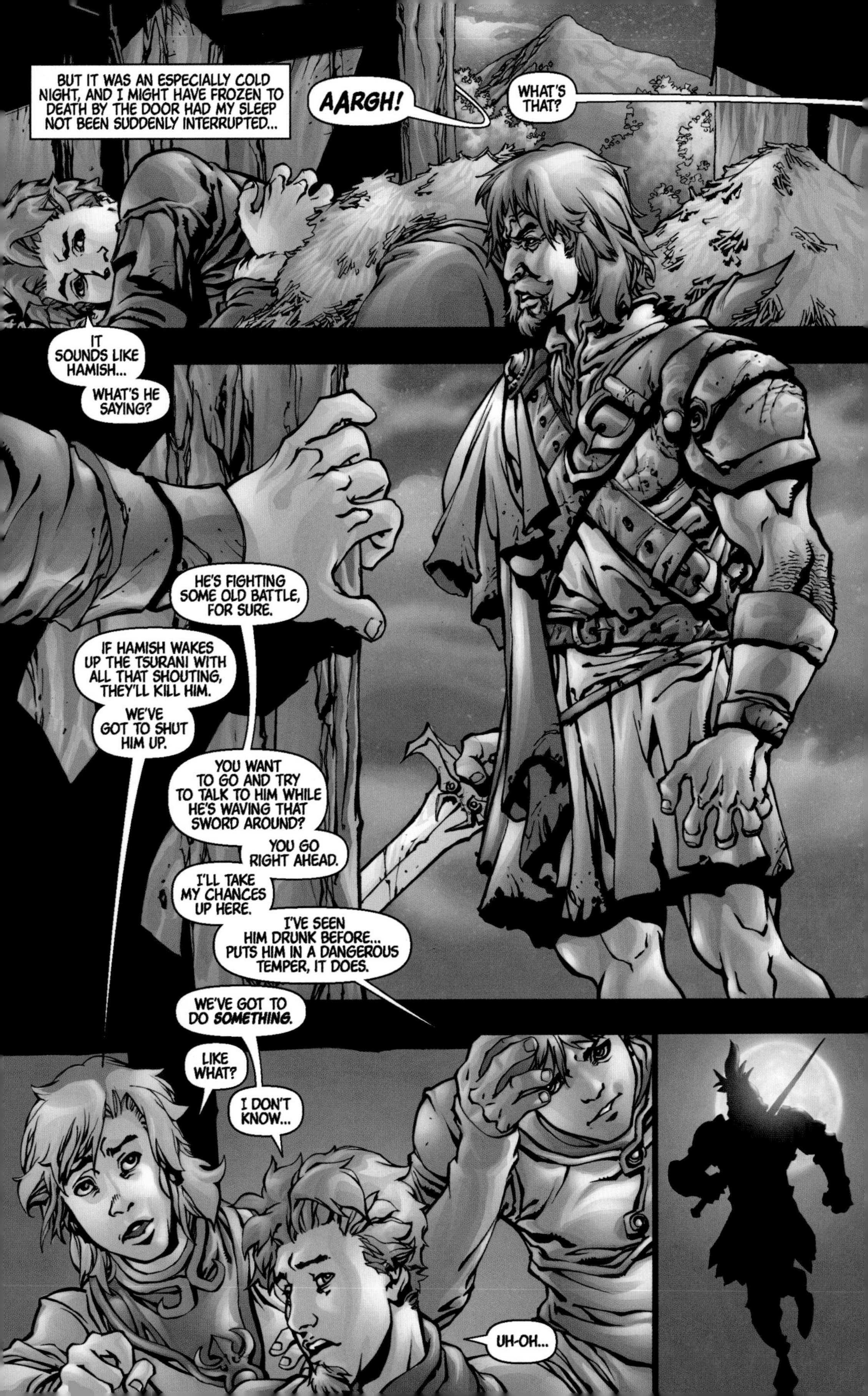

BUT IT WAS AN ESPECIALLY COLD NIGHT, AND I MIGHT HAVE FROZEN TO DEATH BY THE DOOR HAD MY SLEEP NOT BEEN SUDDENLY INTERRUPTED...
AARGH!
WHAT'S THAT?
IT SOUNDS LIKE HAMISH...
WHAT'S HE SAYING?
HE'S FIGHTING SOME OLD BATTLE, FOR SURE.
IF HAMISH WAKES UP THE TSURANI WITH ALL THAT SHOUTING, THEY'LL KILL HIM.
WE'VE GOT TO SHUT HIM UP.
YOU WANT TO GO AND TRY TO TALK TO HIM WHILE HE'S WAVING THAT SWORD AROUND?
YOU GO RIGHT AHEAD.
I'LL TAKE MY CHANCES UP HERE.
I'VE SEEN HIM DRUNK BEFORE... PUTS HIM IN A DANGEROUS TEMPER, IT DOES.
WE'VE GOT TO DO *SOMETHING*.
LIKE WHAT?
I DON'T KNOW...
UH-OH...

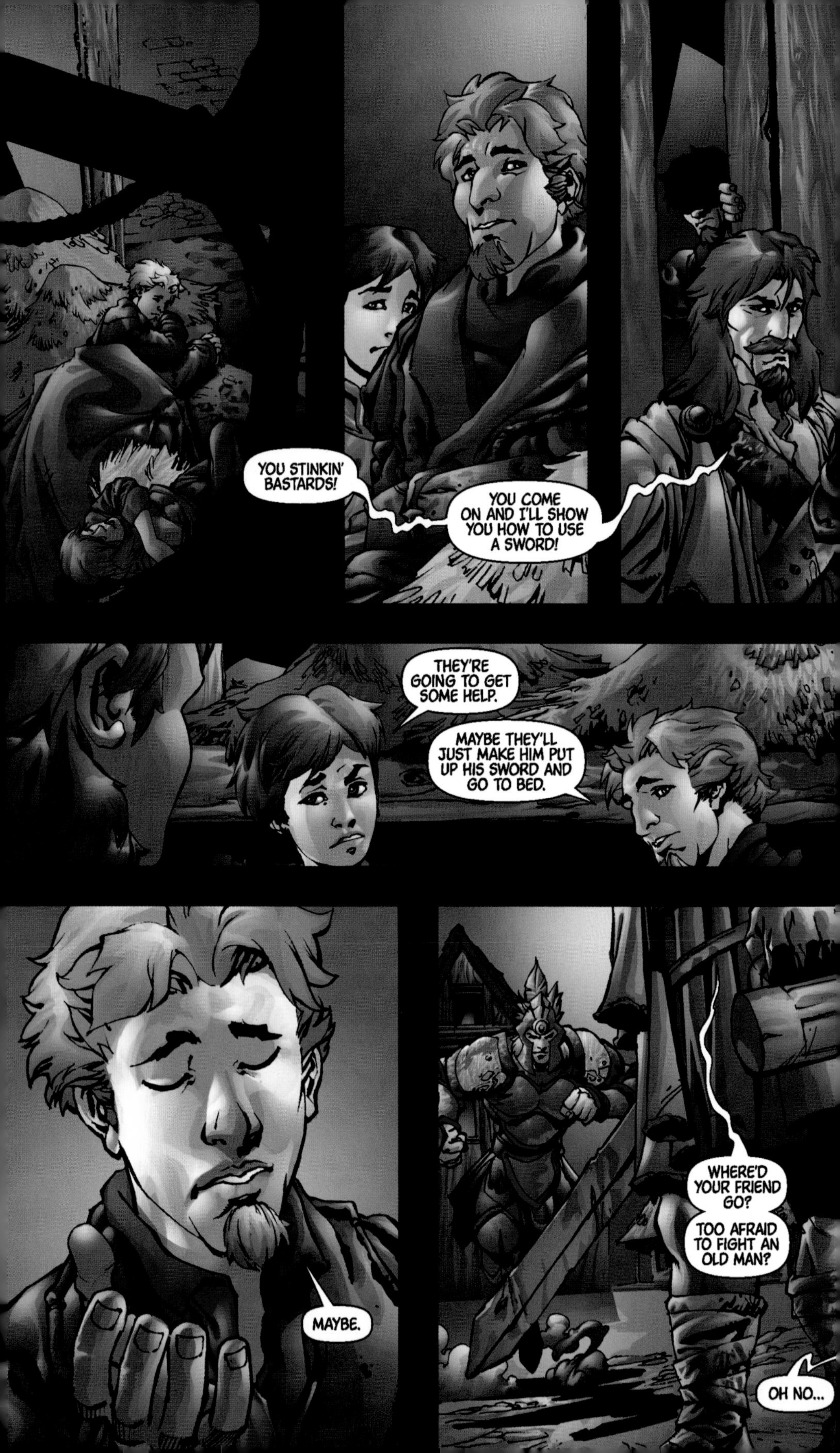
YOU STINKIN' BASTARDS!
YOU COME ON AND I'LL SHOW YOU HOW TO USE A SWORD!
THEY'RE GOING TO GET SOME HELP.
MAYBE THEY'LL JUST MAKE HIM PUT UP HIS SWORD AND GO TO BED.
MAYBE.
WHERE'D YOUR FRIEND GO?
TOO AFRAID TO FIGHT AN OLD MAN?
OH NO...

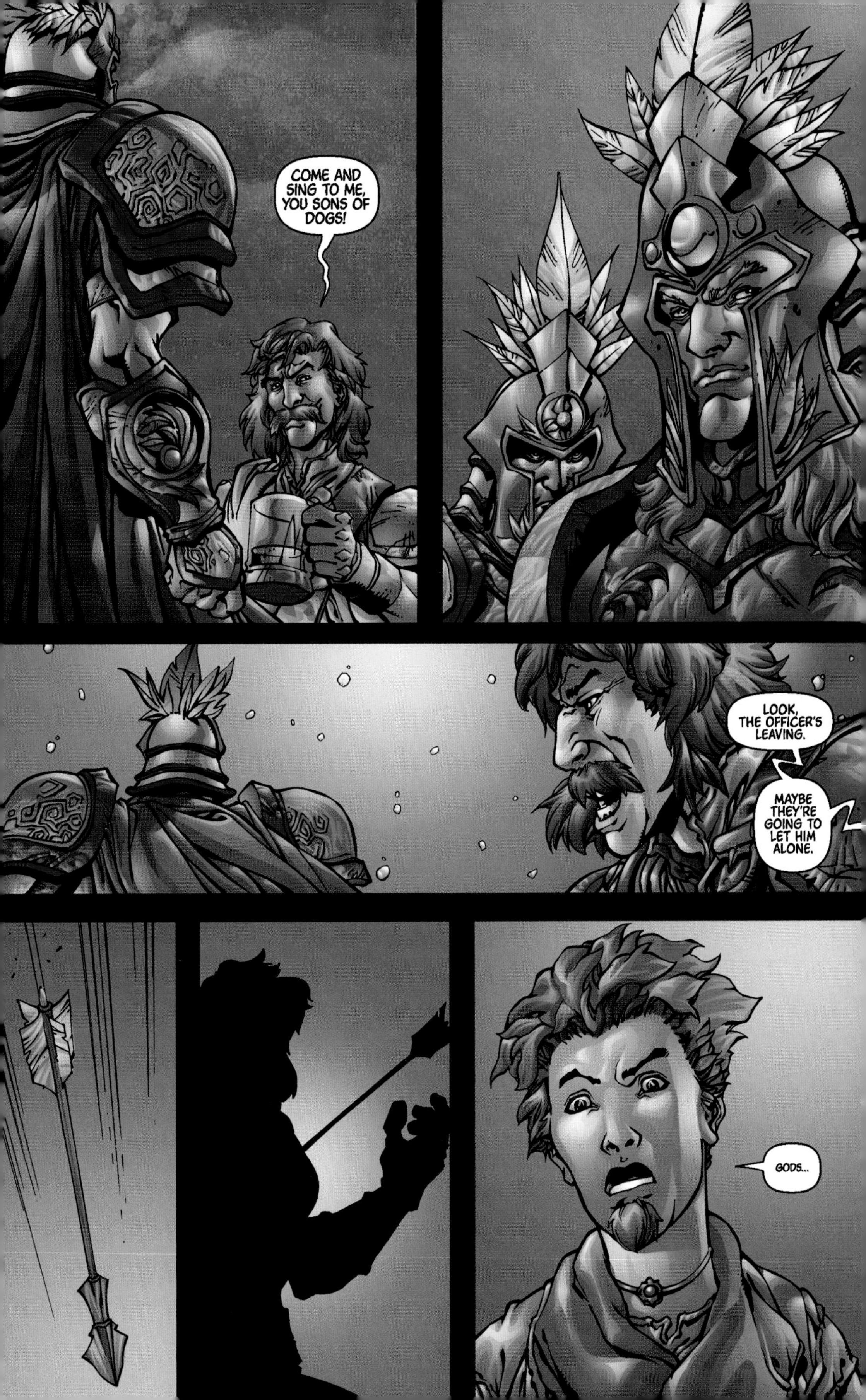
COME AND SING TO ME, YOU SONS OF DOGS!
LOOK, THE OFFICER'S LEAVING.
MAYBE THEY'RE GOING TO LET HIM ALONE.
GODS...

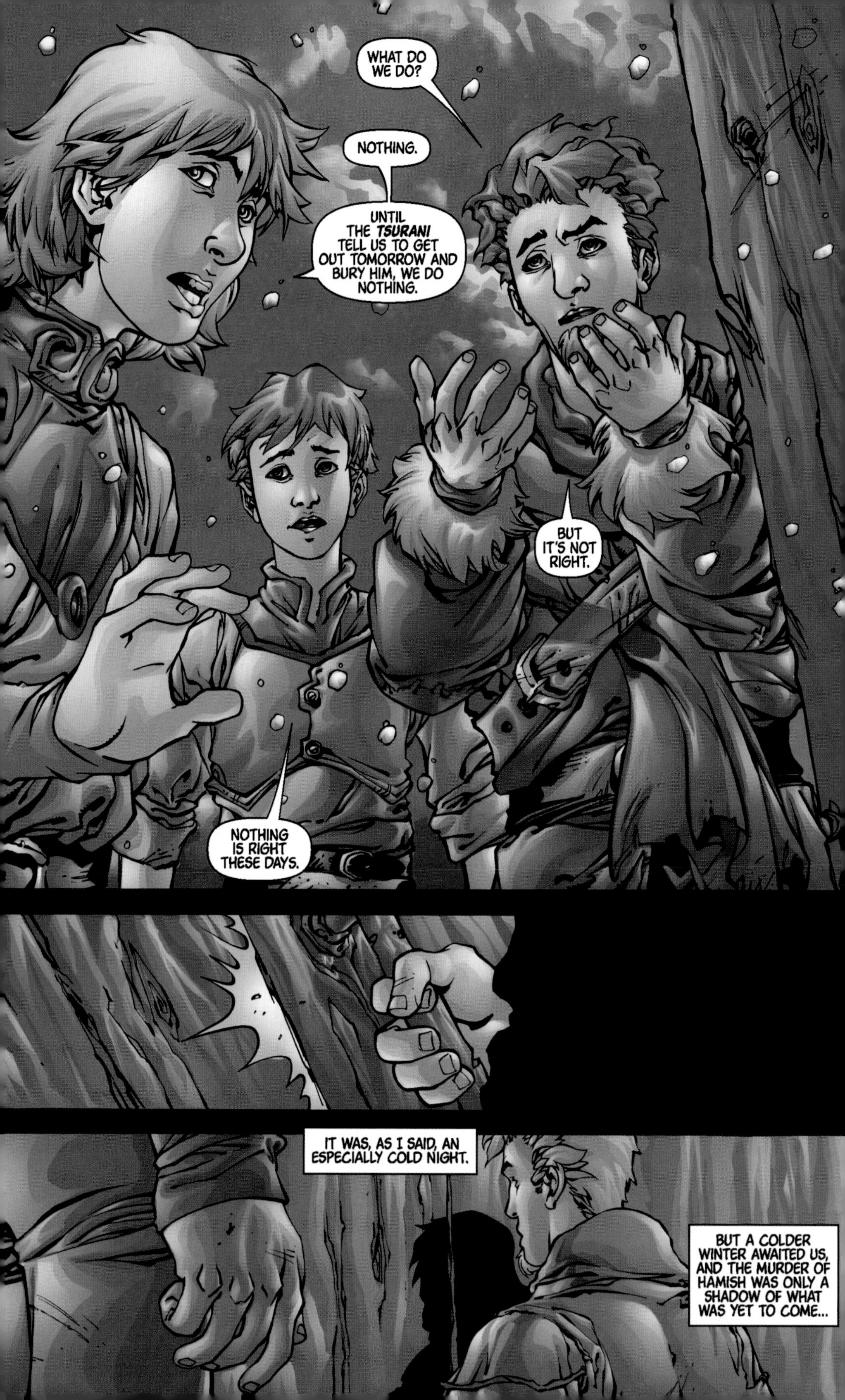
WHAT DO WE DO?
NOTHING.
UNTIL THE TSURANI TELL US TO GET OUT TOMORROW AND BURY HIM, WE DO NOTHING.
BUT IT'S NOT RIGHT.
NOTHING IS RIGHT THESE DAYS.
IT WAS, AS I SAID, AN ESPECIALLY COLD NIGHT.
BUT A COLDER WINTER AWAITED US, AND THE MURDER OF HAMISH WAS ONLY A SHADOW OF WHAT WAS YET TO COME...

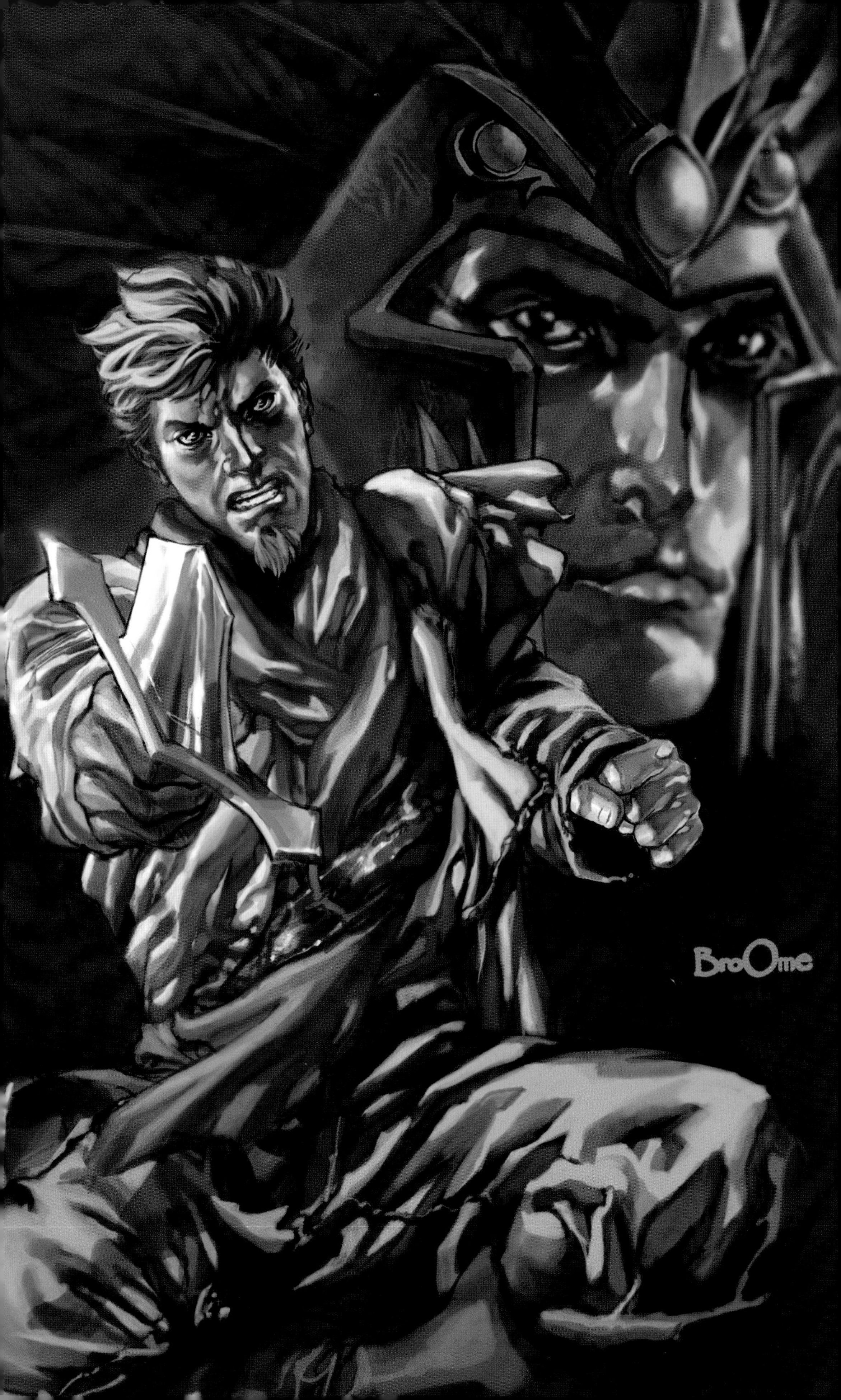
BroOme

The Wood Boy

PART TWO

Raymond E Feist
WRITER

Sean J Jordan
ADAPTATION

Abdul Rashid
ARTWORK

Arif Priyanto
COLORS (Imaginary Friends Studios)

Bill Tortolini
LETTERING (LithiumPro Design)

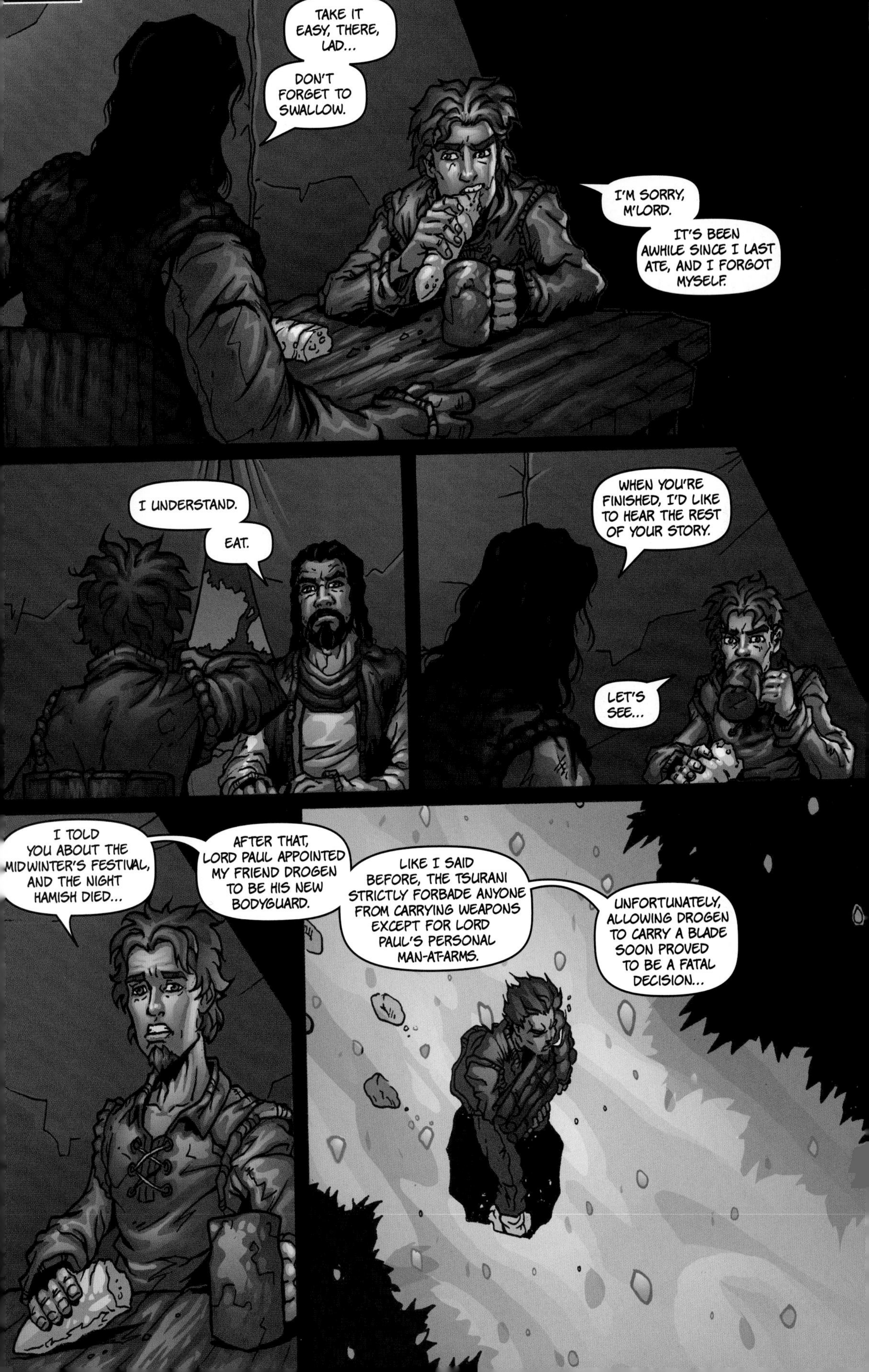
TAKE IT EASY, THERE, LAD...
DON'T FORGET TO SWALLOW.
I'M SORRY, M'LORD.
IT'S BEEN AWHILE SINCE I LAST ATE, AND I FORGOT MYSELF.
I UNDERSTAND.
EAT.
WHEN YOU'RE FINISHED, I'D LIKE TO HEAR THE REST OF YOUR STORY.
LET'S SEE...
I TOLD YOU ABOUT THE MIDWINTER'S FESTIVAL, AND THE NIGHT HAMISH DIED...
AFTER THAT, LORD PAUL APPOINTED MY FRIEND DROGEN TO BE HIS NEW BODYGUARD.
LIKE I SAID BEFORE, THE TSURANI STRICTLY FORBADE ANYONE FROM CARRYING WEAPONS EXCEPT FOR LORD PAUL'S PERSONAL MAN-AT-ARMS.
UNFORTUNATELY, ALLOWING DROGEN TO CARRY A BLADE SOON PROVED TO BE A FATAL DECISION...

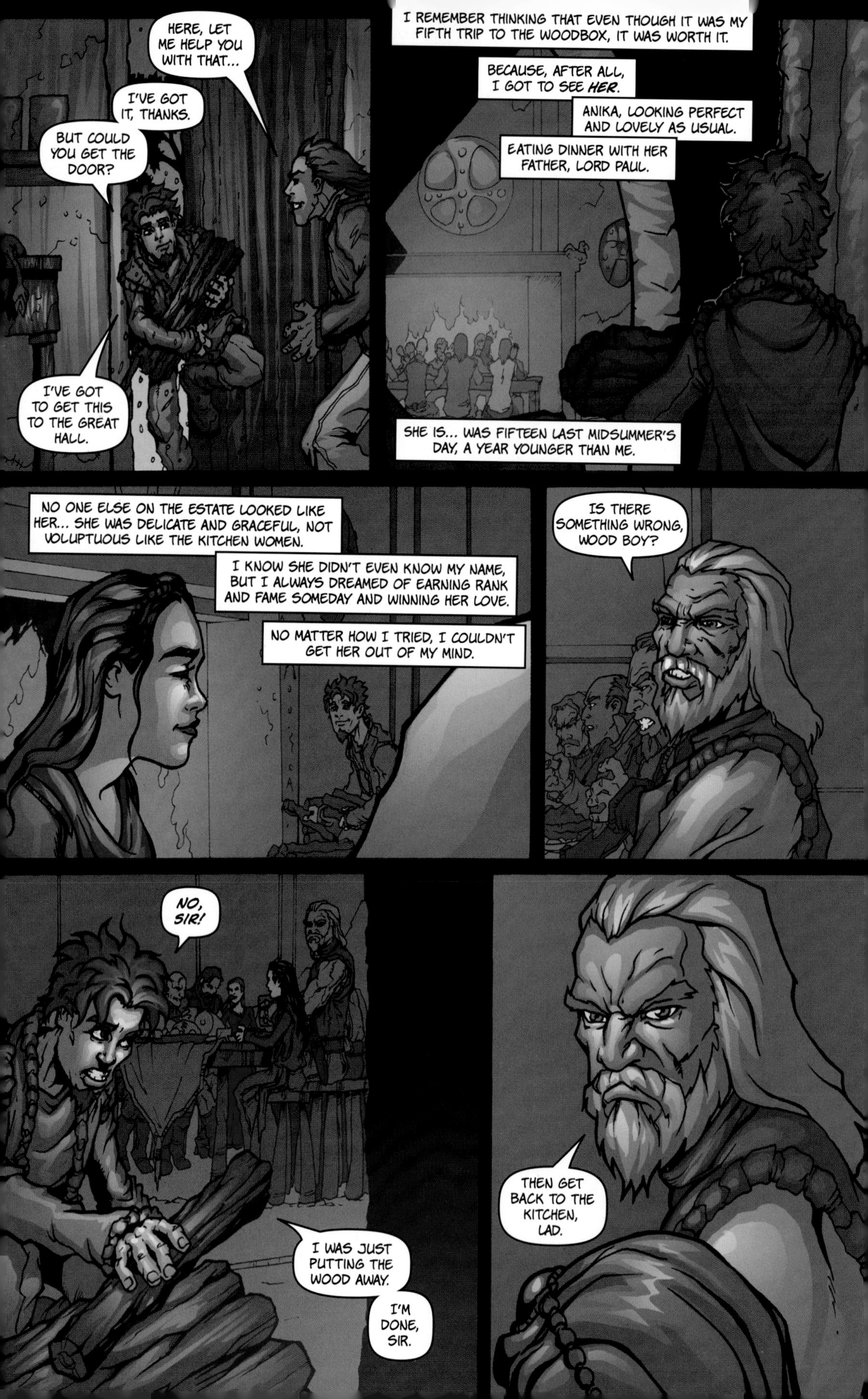
HERE, LET ME HELP YOU WITH THAT...
I'VE GOT IT, THANKS.
BUT COULD YOU GET THE DOOR?
I'VE GOT TO GET THIS TO THE GREAT HALL.
I REMEMBER THINKING THAT EVEN THOUGH IT WAS MY FIFTH TRIP TO THE WOODBOX, IT WAS WORTH IT.
BECAUSE, AFTER ALL, I GOT TO SEE *HER*.
ANIKA, LOOKING PERFECT AND LOVELY AS USUAL.
EATING DINNER WITH HER FATHER, LORD PAUL.
SHE IS... WAS FIFTEEN LAST MIDSUMMER'S DAY, A YEAR YOUNGER THAN ME.
NO ONE ELSE ON THE ESTATE LOOKED LIKE HER... SHE WAS DELICATE AND GRACEFUL, NOT VOLUPTUOUS LIKE THE KITCHEN WOMEN.
I KNOW SHE DIDN'T EVEN KNOW MY NAME, BUT I ALWAYS DREAMED OF EARNING RANK AND FAME SOMEDAY AND WINNING HER LOVE.
NO MATTER HOW I TRIED, I COULDN'T GET HER OUT OF MY MIND.
IS THERE SOMETHING WRONG, WOOD BOY?
NO, SIR!
I WAS JUST PUTTING THE WOOD AWAY.
I'M DONE, SIR.
THEN GET BACK TO THE KITCHEN, LAD.

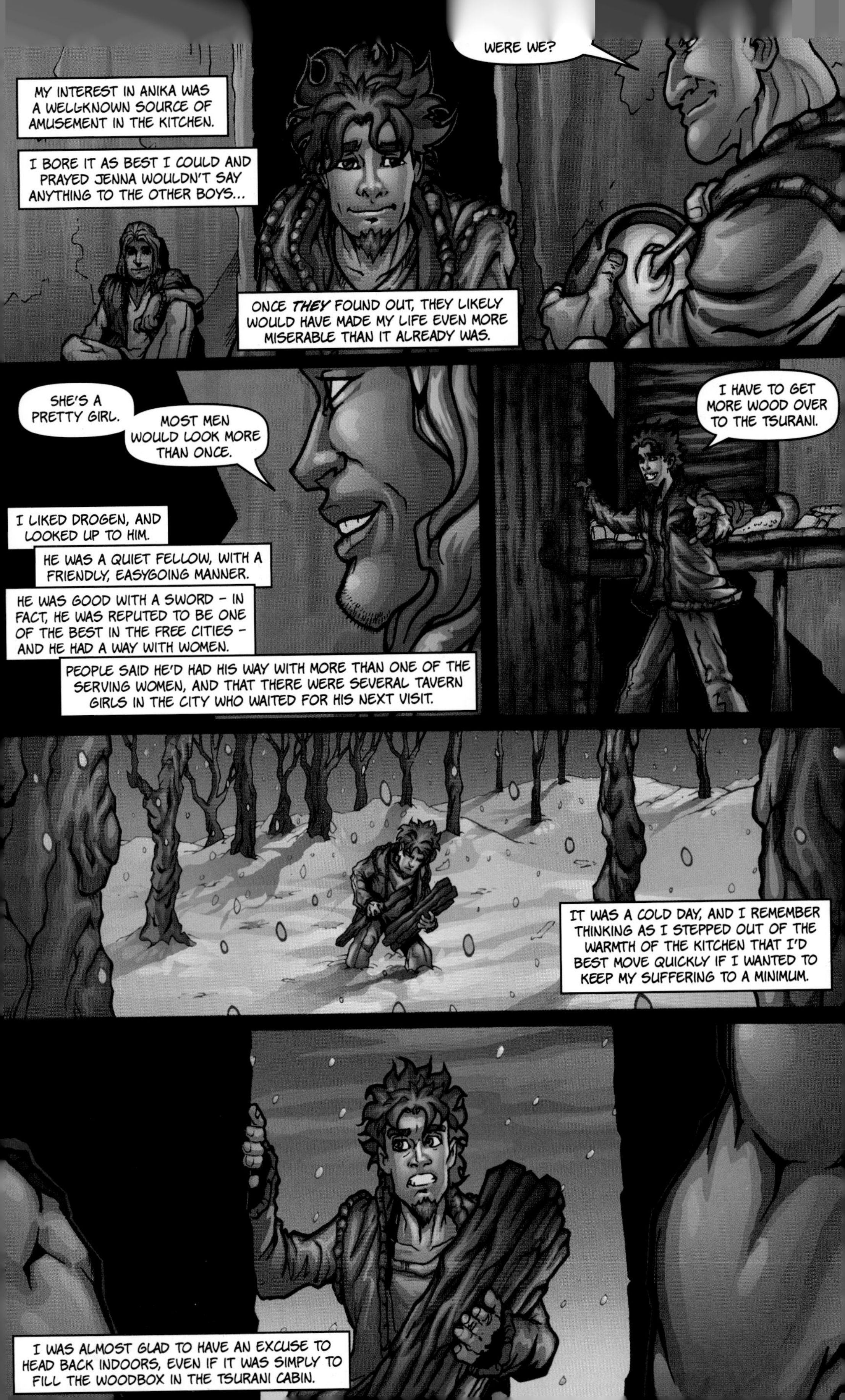
MY INTEREST IN ANIKA WAS A WELL-KNOWN SOURCE OF AMUSEMENT IN THE KITCHEN.
I BORE IT AS BEST I COULD AND PRAYED JENNA WOULDN'T SAY ANYTHING TO THE OTHER BOYS...
ONCE *THEY* FOUND OUT, THEY LIKELY WOULD HAVE MADE MY LIFE EVEN MORE MISERABLE THAN IT ALREADY WAS.
WERE WE?
SHE'S A PRETTY GIRL.
MOST MEN WOULD LOOK MORE THAN ONCE.
I LIKED DROGEN, AND LOOKED UP TO HIM.
HE WAS A QUIET FELLOW, WITH A FRIENDLY, EASYGOING MANNER.
HE WAS GOOD WITH A SWORD – IN FACT, HE WAS REPUTED TO BE ONE OF THE BEST IN THE FREE CITIES – AND HE HAD A WAY WITH WOMEN.
PEOPLE SAID HE'D HAD HIS WAY WITH MORE THAN ONE OF THE SERVING WOMEN, AND THAT THERE WERE SEVERAL TAVERN GIRLS IN THE CITY WHO WAITED FOR HIS NEXT VISIT.
I HAVE TO GET MORE WOOD OVER TO THE TSURANI.
IT WAS A COLD DAY, AND I REMEMBER THINKING AS I STEPPED OUT OF THE WARMTH OF THE KITCHEN THAT I'D BEST MOVE QUICKLY IF I WANTED TO KEEP MY SUFFERING TO A MINIMUM.
I WAS ALMOST GLAD TO HAVE AN EXCUSE TO HEAD BACK INDOORS, EVEN IF IT WAS SIMPLY TO FILL THE WOODBOX IN THE TSURANI CABIN.

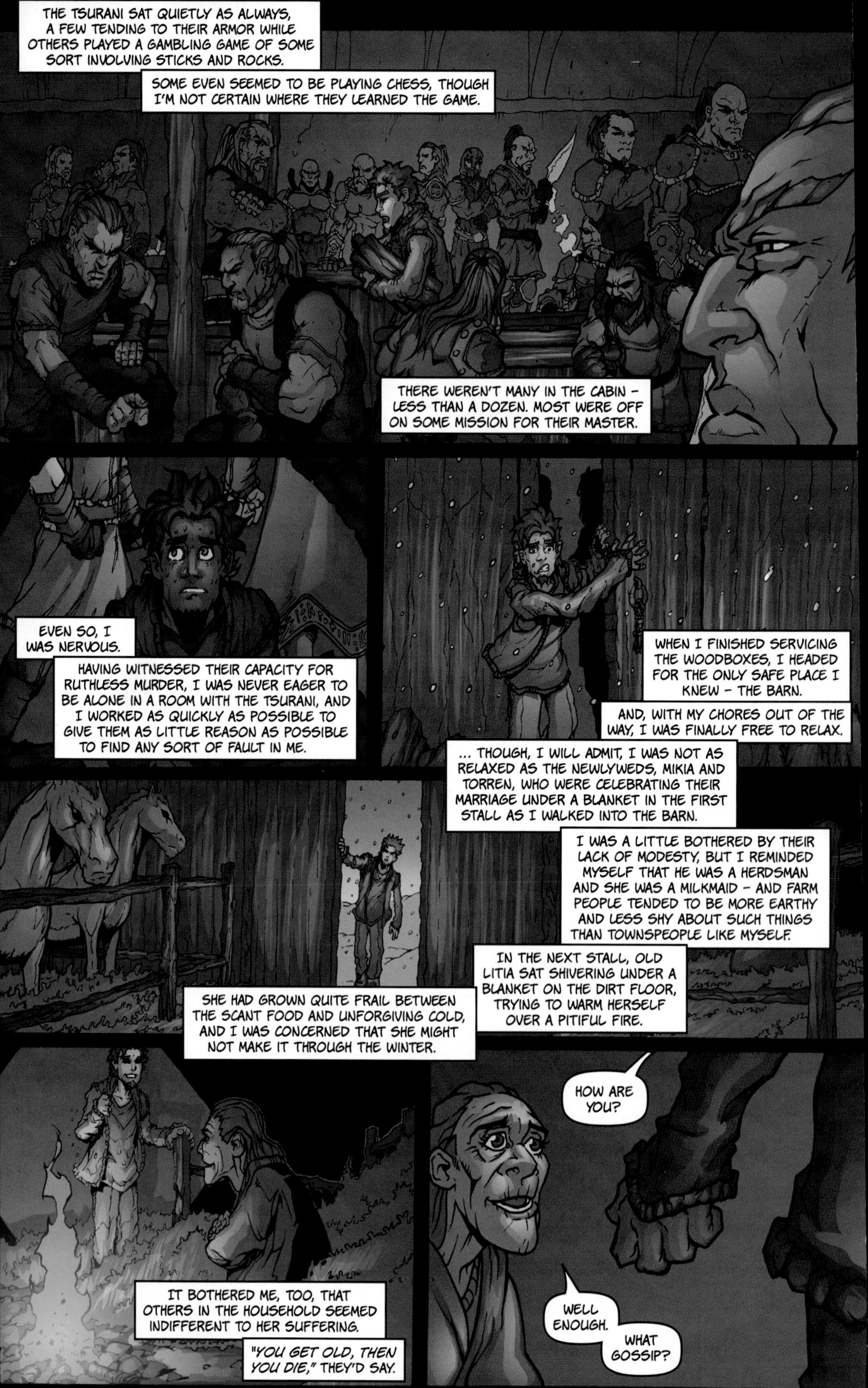
THE TSURANI SAT QUIETLY AS ALWAYS, A FEW TENDING TO THEIR ARMOR WHILE OTHERS PLAYED A GAMBLING GAME OF SOME SORT INVOLVING STICKS AND ROCKS.
SOME EVEN SEEMED TO BE PLAYING CHESS, THOUGH I'M NOT CERTAIN WHERE THEY LEARNED THE GAME.
THERE WEREN'T MANY IN THE CABIN – LESS THAN A DOZEN. MOST WERE OFF ON SOME MISSION FOR THEIR MASTER.
EVEN SO, I WAS NERVOUS.
HAVING WITNESSED THEIR CAPACITY FOR RUTHLESS MURDER, I WAS NEVER EAGER TO BE ALONE IN A ROOM WITH THE TSURANI, AND I WORKED AS QUICKLY AS POSSIBLE TO GIVE THEM AS LITTLE REASON AS POSSIBLE TO FIND ANY SORT OF FAULT IN ME.
WHEN I FINISHED SERVICING THE WOODBOXES, I HEADED FOR THE ONLY SAFE PLACE I KNEW – THE BARN.
AND, WITH MY CHORES OUT OF THE WAY, I WAS FINALLY FREE TO RELAX.
... THOUGH, I WILL ADMIT, I WAS NOT AS RELAXED AS THE NEWLYWEDS, MIKIA AND TORREN, WHO WERE CELEBRATING THEIR MARRIAGE UNDER A BLANKET IN THE FIRST STALL AS I WALKED INTO THE BARN.
I WAS A LITTLE BOTHERED BY THEIR LACK OF MODESTY, BUT I REMINDED MYSELF THAT HE WAS A HERDSMAN AND SHE WAS A MILKMAID – AND FARM PEOPLE TENDED TO BE MORE EARTHY AND LESS SHY ABOUT SUCH THINGS THAN TOWNSPEOPLE LIKE MYSELF.
IN THE NEXT STALL, OLD LITIA SAT SHIVERING UNDER A BLANKET ON THE DIRT FLOOR, TRYING TO WARM HERSELF OVER A PITIFUL FIRE.
SHE HAD GROWN QUITE FRAIL BETWEEN THE SCANT FOOD AND UNFORGIVING COLD, AND I WAS CONCERNED THAT SHE MIGHT NOT MAKE IT THROUGH THE WINTER.
IT BOTHERED ME, TOO, THAT OTHERS IN THE HOUSEHOLD SEEMED INDIFFERENT TO HER SUFFERING.
"YOU GET OLD, THEN YOU DIE," THEY'D SAY.
HOW ARE YOU?
WELL ENOUGH.
WHAT GOSSIP?

AWOKE TO AN ODD SOUND, THOUGH WASN'T QUITE SURE WHAT IT WAS.

IT SOUNDED LIKE A MUFFLED CRY, PERHAPS A GURGLE.

AND, I THOUGHT, MAYBE EVEN A MOAN.

"AHA," I THOUGHT AFTER A MOMENT. "MIKIA AND TORREN ARE AT IT AGAIN."

RELIEVED, I LAID BACK DOWN AND TRIED TO FALL BACK ASLEEP.

AND THEN, JUST AS I BEGAN TO DOZE OFF, I SAW SOMETHING THERE IN THE DARKNESS...

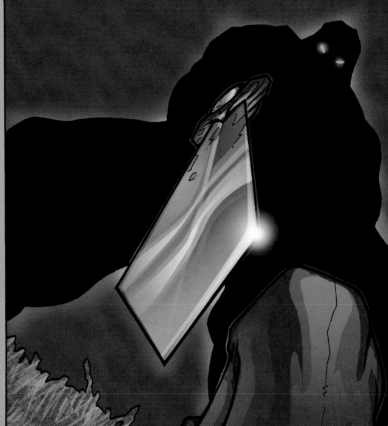

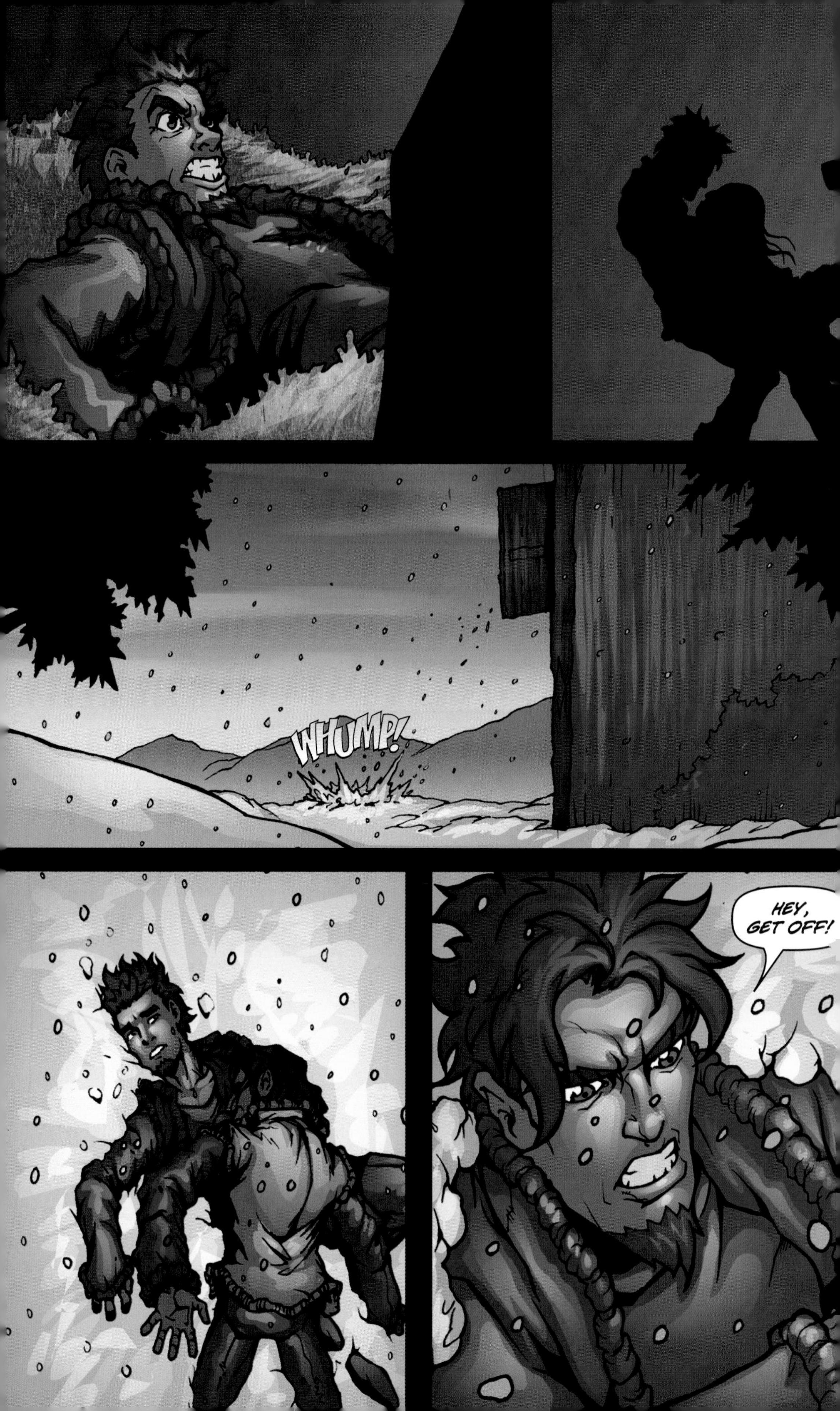
WHUMP!
HEY, GET OFF!

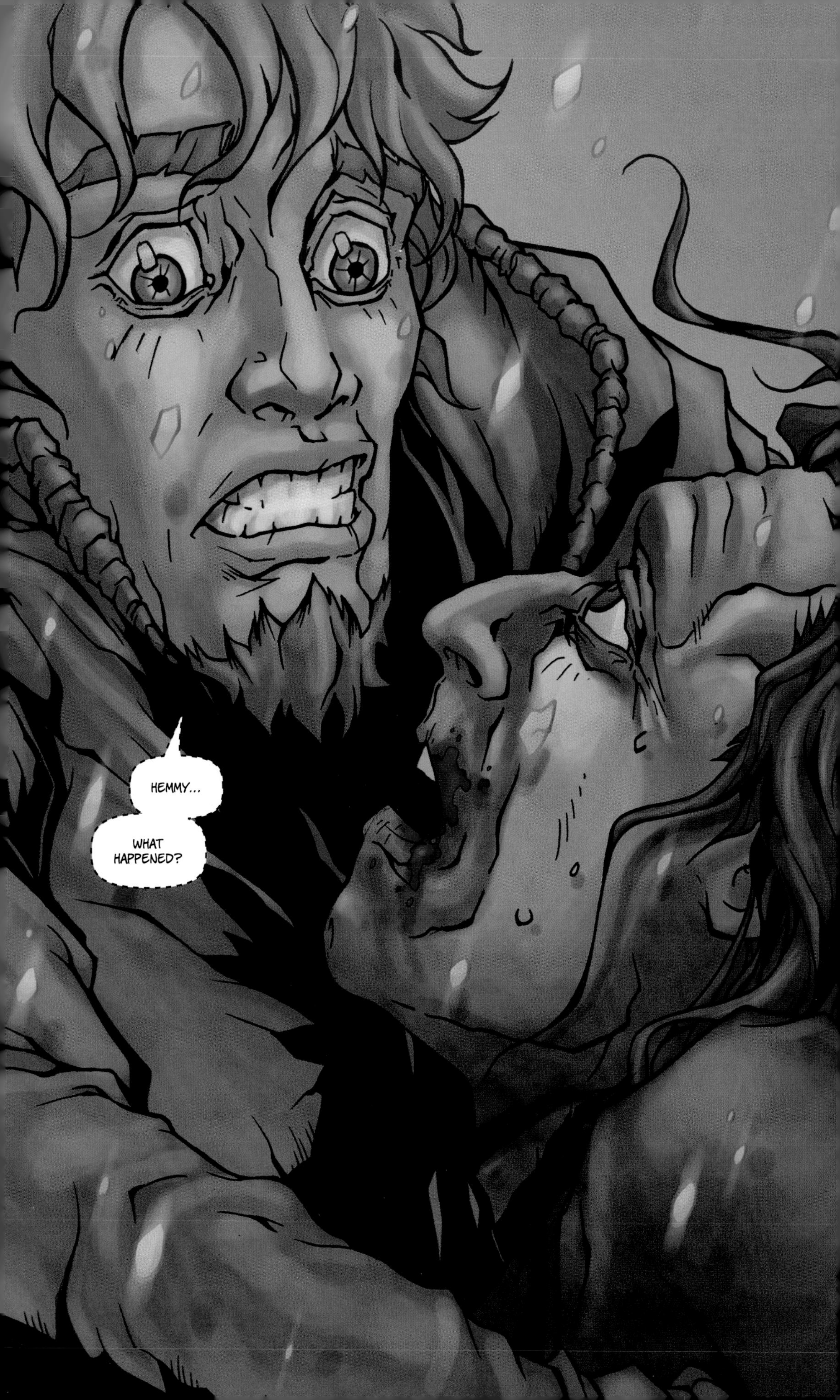
HEMMY...
WHAT HAPPENED?

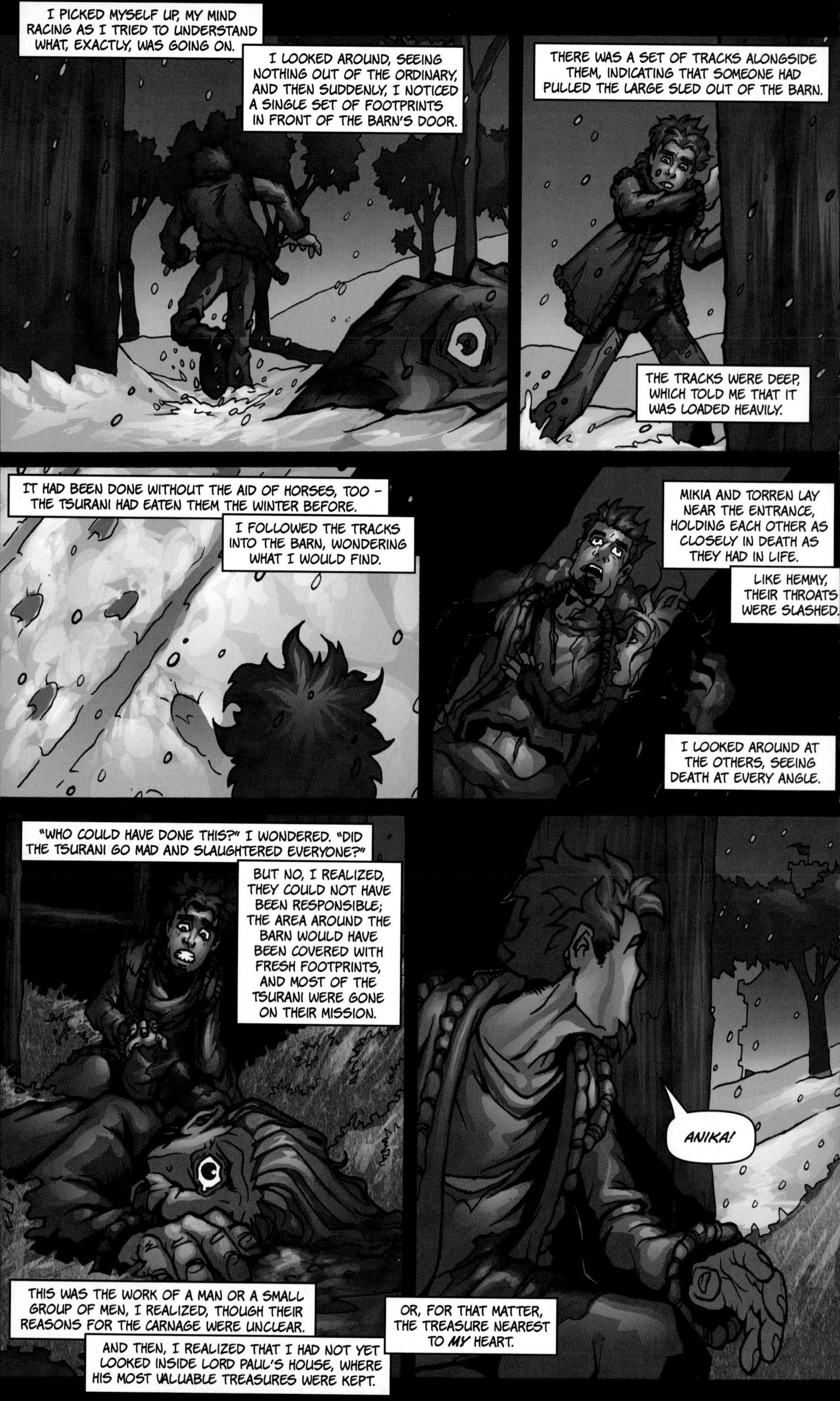

I PICKED MYSELF UP, MY MIND RACING AS I TRIED TO UNDERSTAND WHAT, EXACTLY, WAS GOING ON.
I LOOKED AROUND, SEEING NOTHING OUT OF THE ORDINARY, AND THEN SUDDENLY, I NOTICED A SINGLE SET OF FOOTPRINTS IN FRONT OF THE BARN'S DOOR.
THERE WAS A SET OF TRACKS ALONGSIDE THEM, INDICATING THAT SOMEONE HAD PULLED THE LARGE SLED OUT OF THE BARN.
THE TRACKS WERE DEEP, WHICH TOLD ME THAT IT WAS LOADED HEAVILY.
IT HAD BEEN DONE WITHOUT THE AID OF HORSES, TOO - THE TSURANI HAD EATEN THEM THE WINTER BEFORE.
I FOLLOWED THE TRACKS INTO THE BARN, WONDERING WHAT I WOULD FIND.
MIKIA AND TORREN LAY NEAR THE ENTRANCE, HOLDING EACH OTHER AS CLOSELY IN DEATH AS THEY HAD IN LIFE.
LIKE HEMMY, THEIR THROATS WERE SLASHED.
I LOOKED AROUND AT THE OTHERS, SEEING DEATH AT EVERY ANGLE.
"WHO COULD HAVE DONE THIS?" I WONDERED. "DID THE TSURANI GO MAD AND SLAUGHTERED EVERYONE?"
BUT NO, I REALIZED, THEY COULD NOT HAVE BEEN RESPONSIBLE; THE AREA AROUND THE BARN WOULD HAVE BEEN COVERED WITH FRESH FOOTPRINTS, AND MOST OF THE TSURANI WERE GONE ON THEIR MISSION.
THIS WAS THE WORK OF A MAN OR A SMALL GROUP OF MEN, I REALIZED, THOUGH THEIR REASONS FOR THE CARNAGE WERE UNCLEAR.
AND THEN, I REALIZED THAT I HAD NOT YET LOOKED INSIDE LORD PAUL'S HOUSE, WHERE HIS MOST VALUABLE TREASURES WERE KEPT.
ANIKA!
OR, FOR THAT MATTER, THE TREASURE NEAREST TO *MY* HEART.

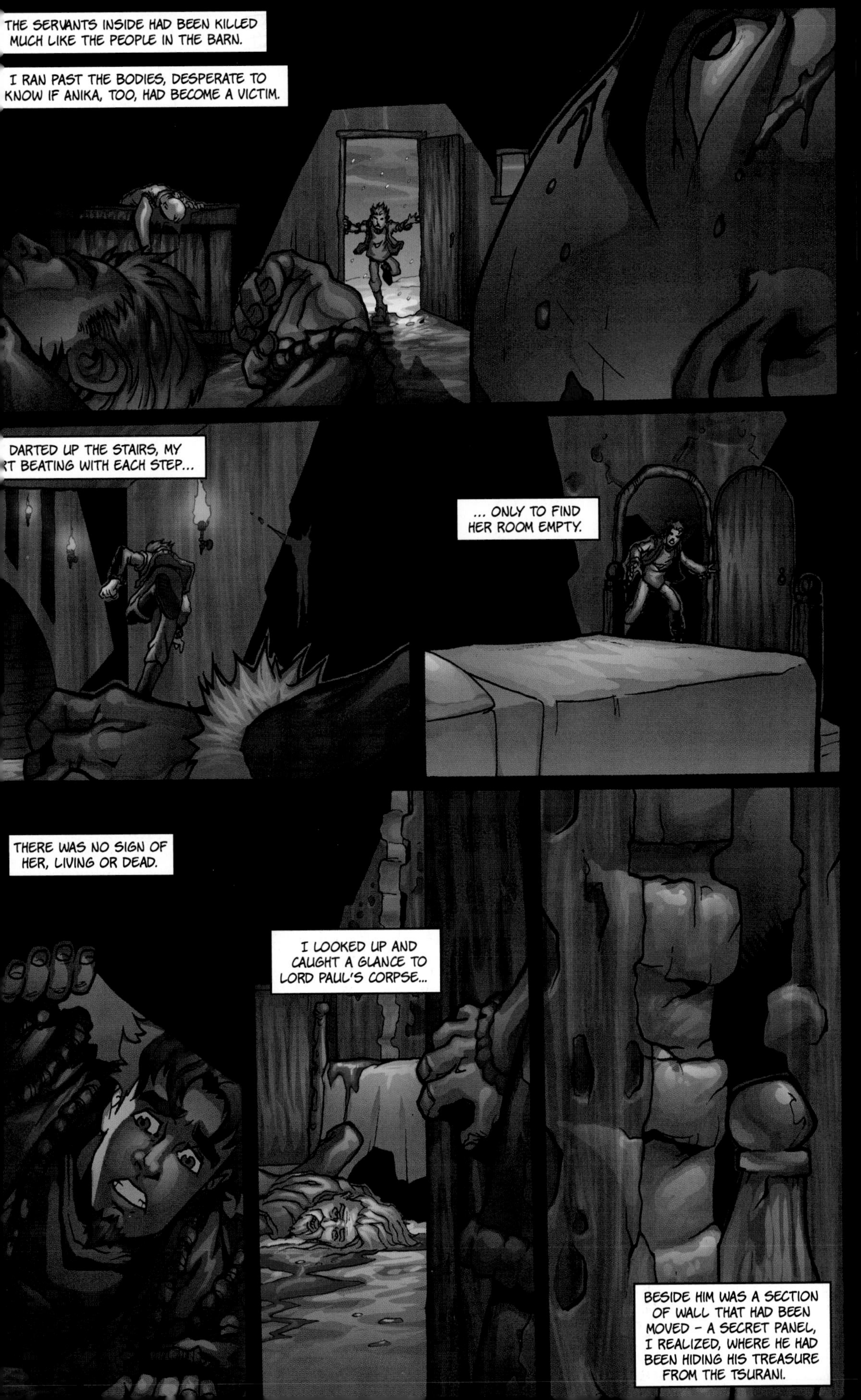
THE SERVANTS INSIDE HAD BEEN KILLED MUCH LIKE THE PEOPLE IN THE BARN.
I RAN PAST THE BODIES, DESPERATE TO KNOW IF ANIKA, TOO, HAD BECOME A VICTIM.
DARTED UP THE STAIRS, MY BEATING WITH EACH STEP...
... ONLY TO FIND HER ROOM EMPTY.
THERE WAS NO SIGN OF HER, LIVING OR DEAD.
I LOOKED UP AND CAUGHT A GLANCE TO LORD PAUL'S CORPSE...
BESIDE HIM WAS A SECTION OF WALL THAT HAD BEEN MOVED – A SECRET PANEL, I REALIZED, WHERE HE HAD BEEN HIDING HIS TREASURE FROM THE TSURANI.

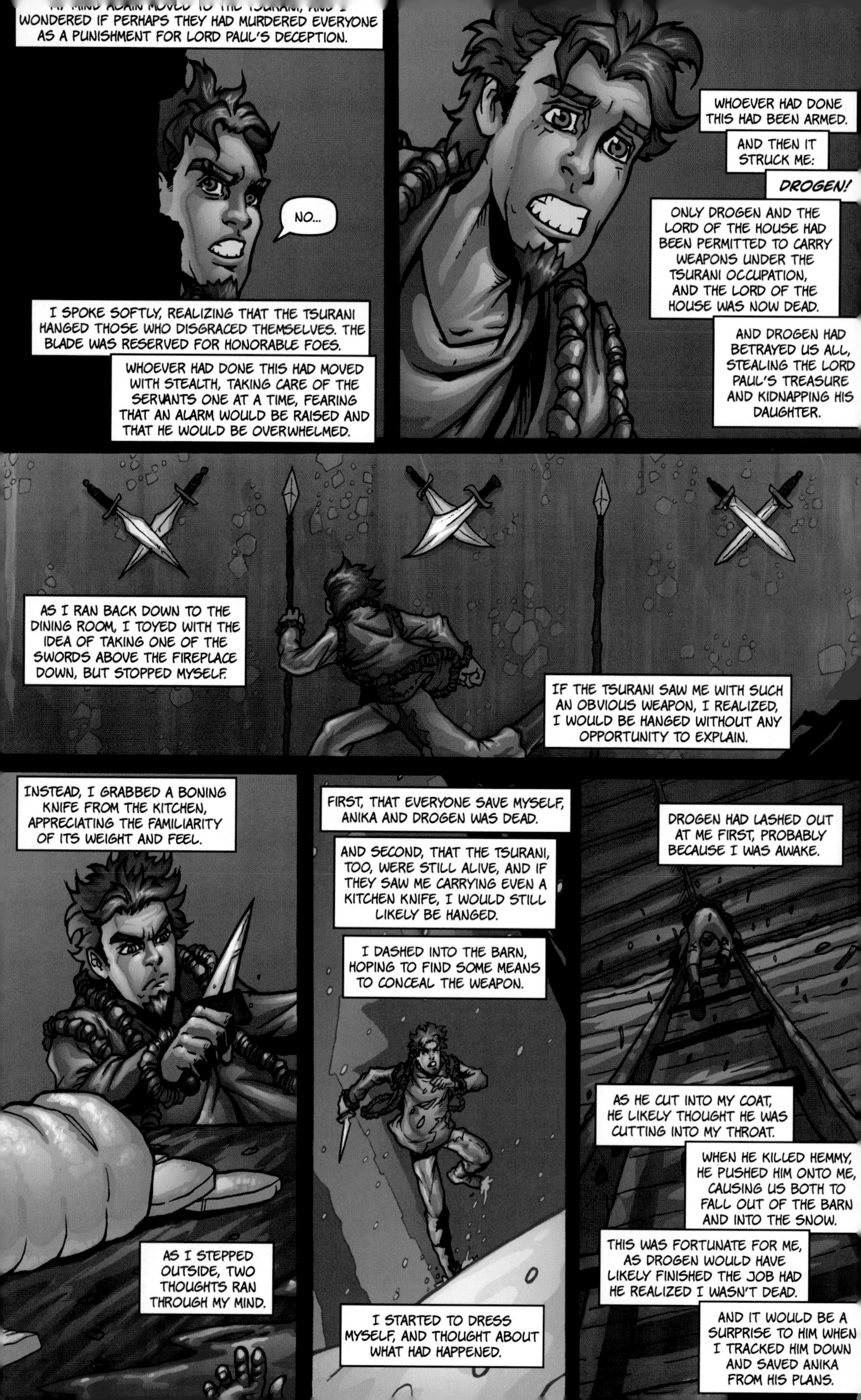
WONDERED IF PERHAPS THEY HAD MURDERED EVERYONE AS A PUNISHMENT FOR LORD PAUL'S DECEPTION.
NO...
I SPOKE SOFTLY, REALIZING THAT THE TSURANI HANGED THOSE WHO DISGRACED THEMSELVES. THE BLADE WAS RESERVED FOR HONORABLE FOES.
WHOEVER HAD DONE THIS HAD MOVED WITH STEALTH, TAKING CARE OF THE SERVANTS ONE AT A TIME, FEARING THAT AN ALARM WOULD BE RAISED AND THAT HE WOULD BE OVERWHELMED.
WHOEVER HAD DONE THIS HAD BEEN ARMED.
AND THEN IT STRUCK ME:
DROGEN!
ONLY DROGEN AND THE LORD OF THE HOUSE HAD BEEN PERMITTED TO CARRY WEAPONS UNDER THE TSURANI OCCUPATION, AND THE LORD OF THE HOUSE WAS NOW DEAD.
AND DROGEN HAD BETRAYED US ALL, STEALING THE LORD PAUL'S TREASURE AND KIDNAPPING HIS DAUGHTER.
AS I RAN BACK DOWN TO THE DINING ROOM, I TOYED WITH THE IDEA OF TAKING ONE OF THE SWORDS ABOVE THE FIREPLACE DOWN, BUT STOPPED MYSELF.
IF THE TSURANI SAW ME WITH SUCH AN OBVIOUS WEAPON, I REALIZED, I WOULD BE HANGED WITHOUT ANY OPPORTUNITY TO EXPLAIN.
INSTEAD, I GRABBED A BONING KNIFE FROM THE KITCHEN, APPRECIATING THE FAMILIARITY OF ITS WEIGHT AND FEEL.
AS I STEPPED OUTSIDE, TWO THOUGHTS RAN THROUGH MY MIND.
FIRST, THAT EVERYONE SAVE MYSELF, ANIKA AND DROGEN WAS DEAD.
AND SECOND, THAT THE TSURANI, TOO, WERE STILL ALIVE, AND IF THEY SAW ME CARRYING EVEN A KITCHEN KNIFE, I WOULD STILL LIKELY BE HANGED.
I DASHED INTO THE BARN, HOPING TO FIND SOME MEANS TO CONCEAL THE WEAPON.
I STARTED TO DRESS MYSELF, AND THOUGHT ABOUT WHAT HAD HAPPENED.
DROGEN HAD LASHED OUT AT ME FIRST, PROBABLY BECAUSE I WAS AWAKE.
AS HE CUT INTO MY COAT, HE LIKELY THOUGHT HE WAS CUTTING INTO MY THROAT.
WHEN HE KILLED HEMMY, HE PUSHED HIM ONTO ME, CAUSING US BOTH TO FALL OUT OF THE BARN AND INTO THE SNOW.
THIS WAS FORTUNATE FOR ME, AS DROGEN WOULD HAVE LIKELY FINISHED THE JOB HAD HE REALIZED I WASN'T DEAD.
AND IT WOULD BE A SURPRISE TO HIM WHEN I TRACKED HIM DOWN AND SAVED ANIKA FROM HIS PLANS.

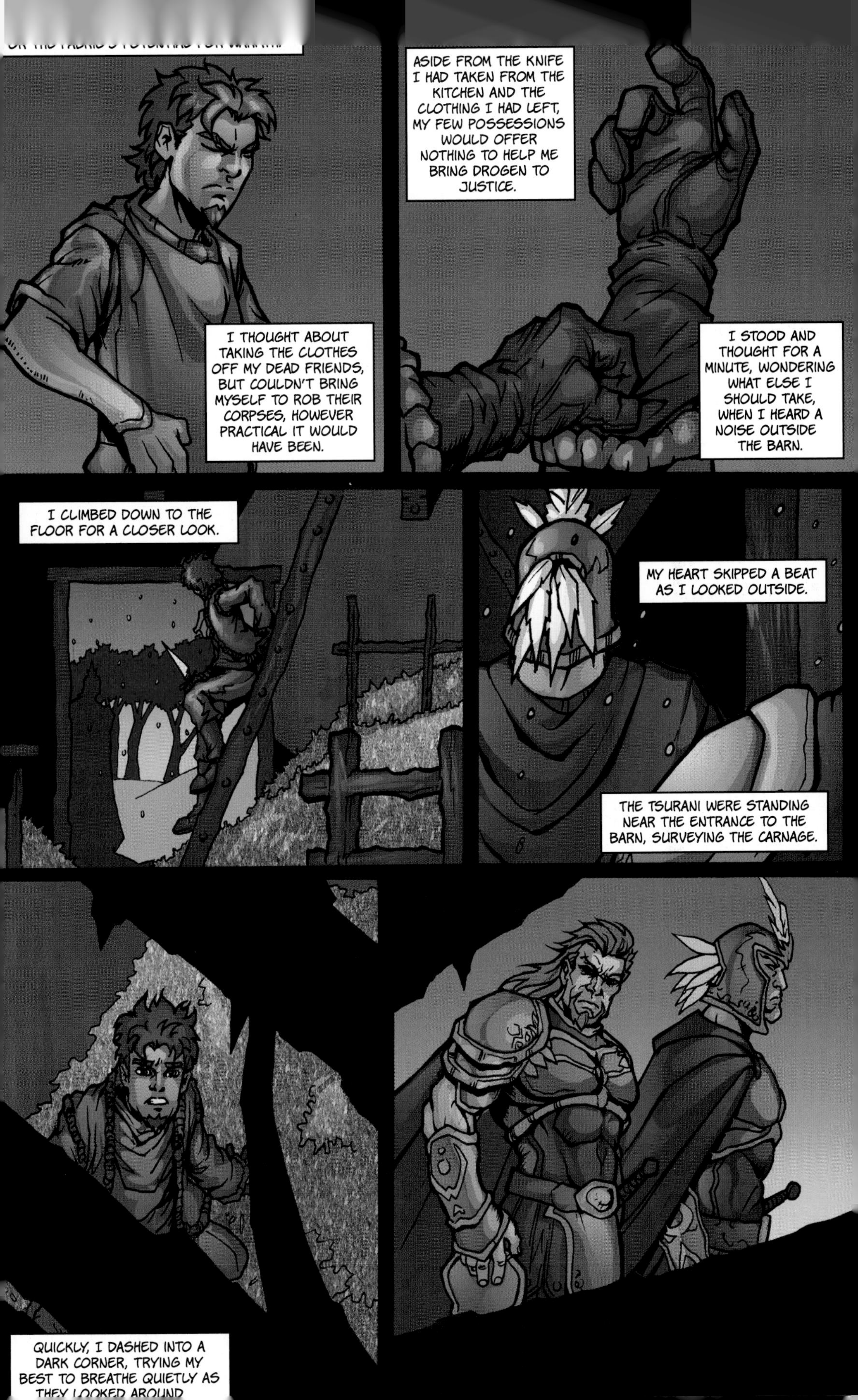

ASIDE FROM THE KNIFE I HAD TAKEN FROM THE KITCHEN AND THE CLOTHING I HAD LEFT, MY FEW POSSESSIONS WOULD OFFER NOTHING TO HELP ME BRING DROGEN TO JUSTICE.
I THOUGHT ABOUT TAKING THE CLOTHES OFF MY DEAD FRIENDS, BUT COULDN'T BRING MYSELF TO ROB THEIR CORPSES, HOWEVER PRACTICAL IT WOULD HAVE BEEN.
I STOOD AND THOUGHT FOR A MINUTE, WONDERING WHAT ELSE I SHOULD TAKE, WHEN I HEARD A NOISE OUTSIDE THE BARN.
I CLIMBED DOWN TO THE FLOOR FOR A CLOSER LOOK.
MY HEART SKIPPED A BEAT AS I LOOKED OUTSIDE.
THE TSURANI WERE STANDING NEAR THE ENTRANCE TO THE BARN, SURVEYING THE CARNAGE.
QUICKLY, I DASHED INTO A DARK CORNER, TRYING MY BEST TO BREATHE QUIETLY AS THEY LOOKED AROUND

ONCE THEY HAD SEEN THE EXTENT OF THE SLAUGHTER, THE TSURANI NOTICED THE TRACKS IN THE SNOW.

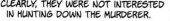

THEY DISCUSSED THEM FOR A MOMENT, AND THEN LEFT, UNCONCERNED.

CLEARLY, THEY WERE NOT INTERESTED IN HUNTING DOWN THE MURDERER.

I WAITED FOR A MOMENT, ENSURING THAT THEY WERE GONE.

AS I LEFT MY HIDING SPOT, I KNEW THAT THIS WOULD LIKELY BE THE LAST TIME I WOULD EVER SEE THE MANOR.

BUT MY MIND WAS CROWDED WITH THOUGHTS OF ANIKA SUFFERING IN THE CLUTCHES OF DROGEN, AND I FOLLOWED

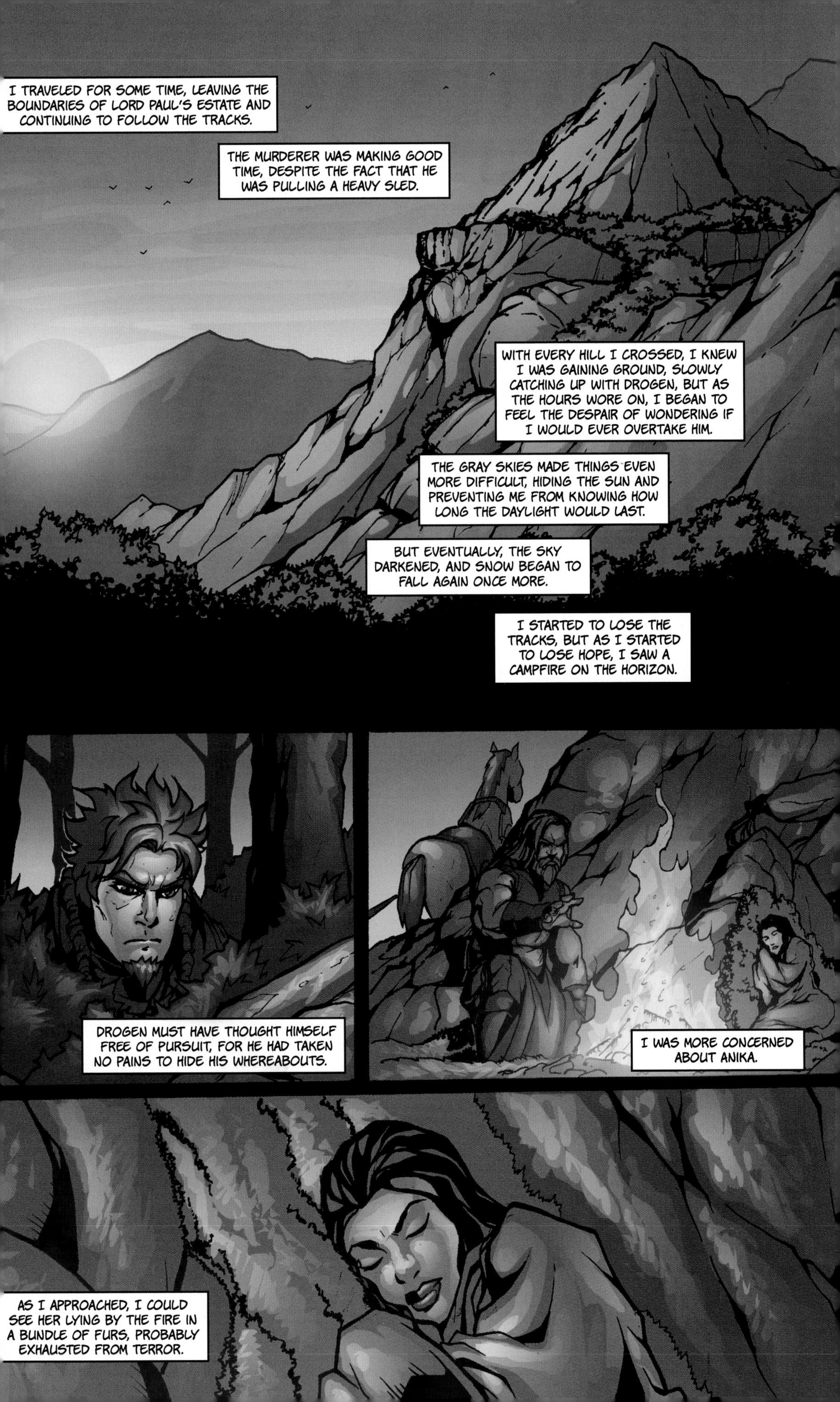
I TRAVELED FOR SOME TIME, LEAVING THE BOUNDARIES OF LORD PAUL'S ESTATE AND CONTINUING TO FOLLOW THE TRACKS.
THE MURDERER WAS MAKING GOOD TIME, DESPITE THE FACT THAT HE WAS PULLING A HEAVY SLED.
WITH EVERY HILL I CROSSED, I KNEW I WAS GAINING GROUND, SLOWLY CATCHING UP WITH DROGEN, BUT AS THE HOURS WORE ON, I BEGAN TO FEEL THE DESPAIR OF WONDERING IF I WOULD EVER OVERTAKE HIM.
THE GRAY SKIES MADE THINGS EVEN MORE DIFFICULT, HIDING THE SUN AND PREVENTING ME FROM KNOWING HOW LONG THE DAYLIGHT WOULD LAST.
BUT EVENTUALLY, THE SKY DARKENED, AND SNOW BEGAN TO FALL AGAIN ONCE MORE.
I STARTED TO LOSE THE TRACKS, BUT AS I STARTED TO LOSE HOPE, I SAW A CAMPFIRE ON THE HORIZON.
DROGEN MUST HAVE THOUGHT HIMSELF FREE OF PURSUIT, FOR HE HAD TAKEN NO PAINS TO HIDE HIS WHEREABOUTS.
I WAS MORE CONCERNED ABOUT ANIKA.
AS I APPROACHED, I COULD SEE HER LYING BY THE FIRE IN A BUNDLE OF FURS, PROBABLY EXHAUSTED FROM TERROR.

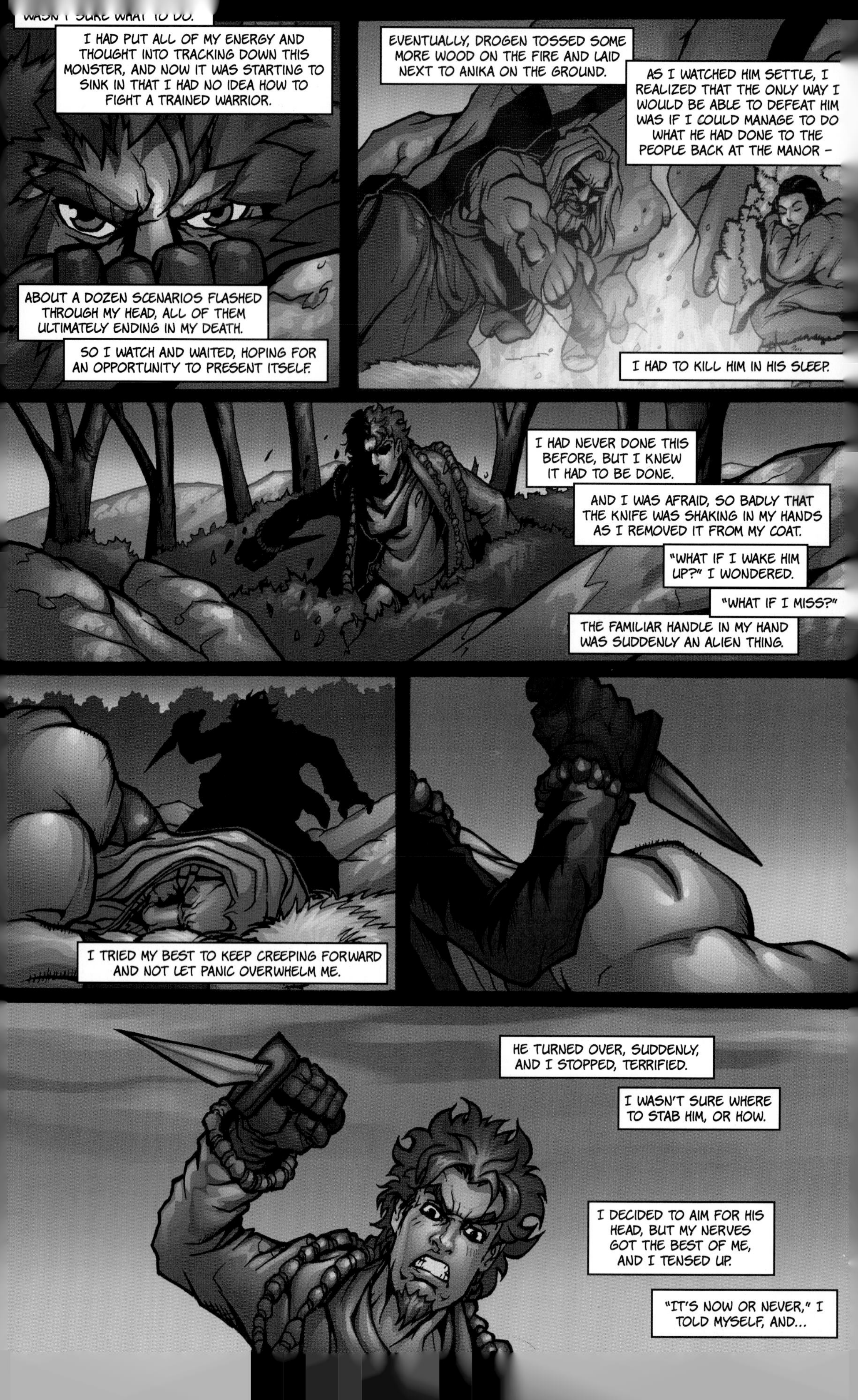
I HAD PUT ALL OF MY ENERGY AND THOUGHT INTO TRACKING DOWN THIS MONSTER, AND NOW IT WAS STARTING TO SINK IN THAT I HAD NO IDEA HOW TO FIGHT A TRAINED WARRIOR.
ABOUT A DOZEN SCENARIOS FLASHED THROUGH MY HEAD, ALL OF THEM ULTIMATELY ENDING IN MY DEATH.
SO I WATCH AND WAITED, HOPING FOR AN OPPORTUNITY TO PRESENT ITSELF.
EVENTUALLY, DROGEN TOSSED SOME MORE WOOD ON THE FIRE AND LAID NEXT TO ANIKA ON THE GROUND.
AS I WATCHED HIM SETTLE, I REALIZED THAT THE ONLY WAY I WOULD BE ABLE TO DEFEAT HIM WAS IF I COULD MANAGE TO DO WHAT HE HAD DONE TO THE PEOPLE BACK AT THE MANOR –
I HAD TO KILL HIM IN HIS SLEEP.
I HAD NEVER DONE THIS BEFORE, BUT I KNEW IT HAD TO BE DONE.
AND I WAS AFRAID, SO BADLY THAT THE KNIFE WAS SHAKING IN MY HANDS AS I REMOVED IT FROM MY COAT.
"WHAT IF I WAKE HIM UP?" I WONDERED.
"WHAT IF I MISS?"
THE FAMILIAR HANDLE IN MY HAND WAS SUDDENLY AN ALIEN THING.
I TRIED MY BEST TO KEEP CREEPING FORWARD AND NOT LET PANIC OVERWHELM ME.
HE TURNED OVER, SUDDENLY, AND I STOPPED, TERRIFIED.
I WASN'T SURE WHERE TO STAB HIM, OR HOW.
I DECIDED TO AIM FOR HIS HEAD, BUT MY NERVES GOT THE BEST OF ME, AND I TENSED UP.
"IT'S NOW OR NEVER," I TOLD MYSELF, AND...

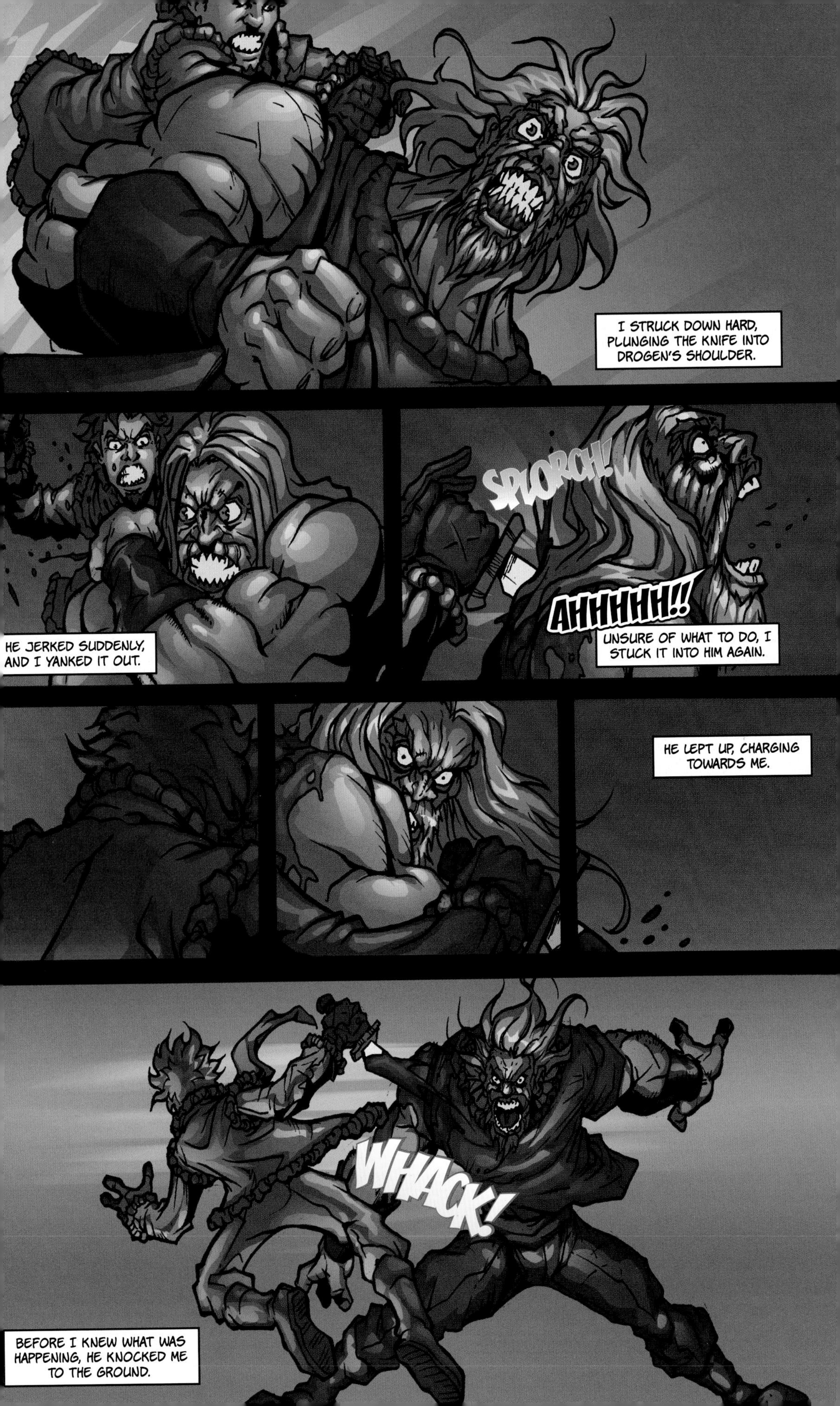
I STRUCK DOWN HARD, PLUNGING THE KNIFE INTO DROGEN'S SHOULDER.
HE JERKED SUDDENLY, AND I YANKED IT OUT.
SPLORCH!
AHHHHH!!
UNSURE OF WHAT TO DO, I STUCK IT INTO HIM AGAIN.
HE LEPT UP, CHARGING TOWARDS ME.
WHACK!
BEFORE I KNEW WHAT WAS HAPPENING, HE KNOCKED ME TO THE GROUND.

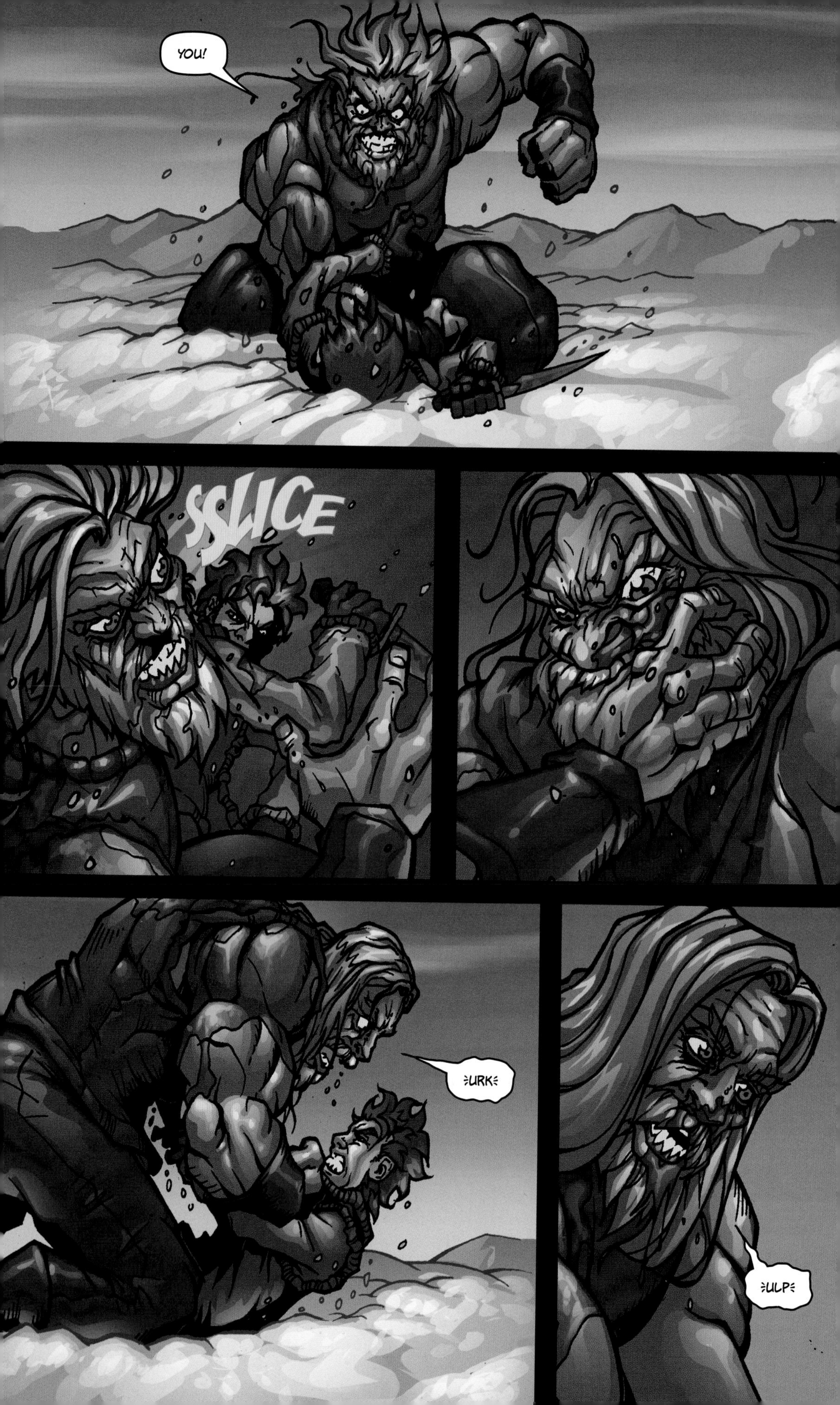
YOU!
SSLICE
URK
ULP

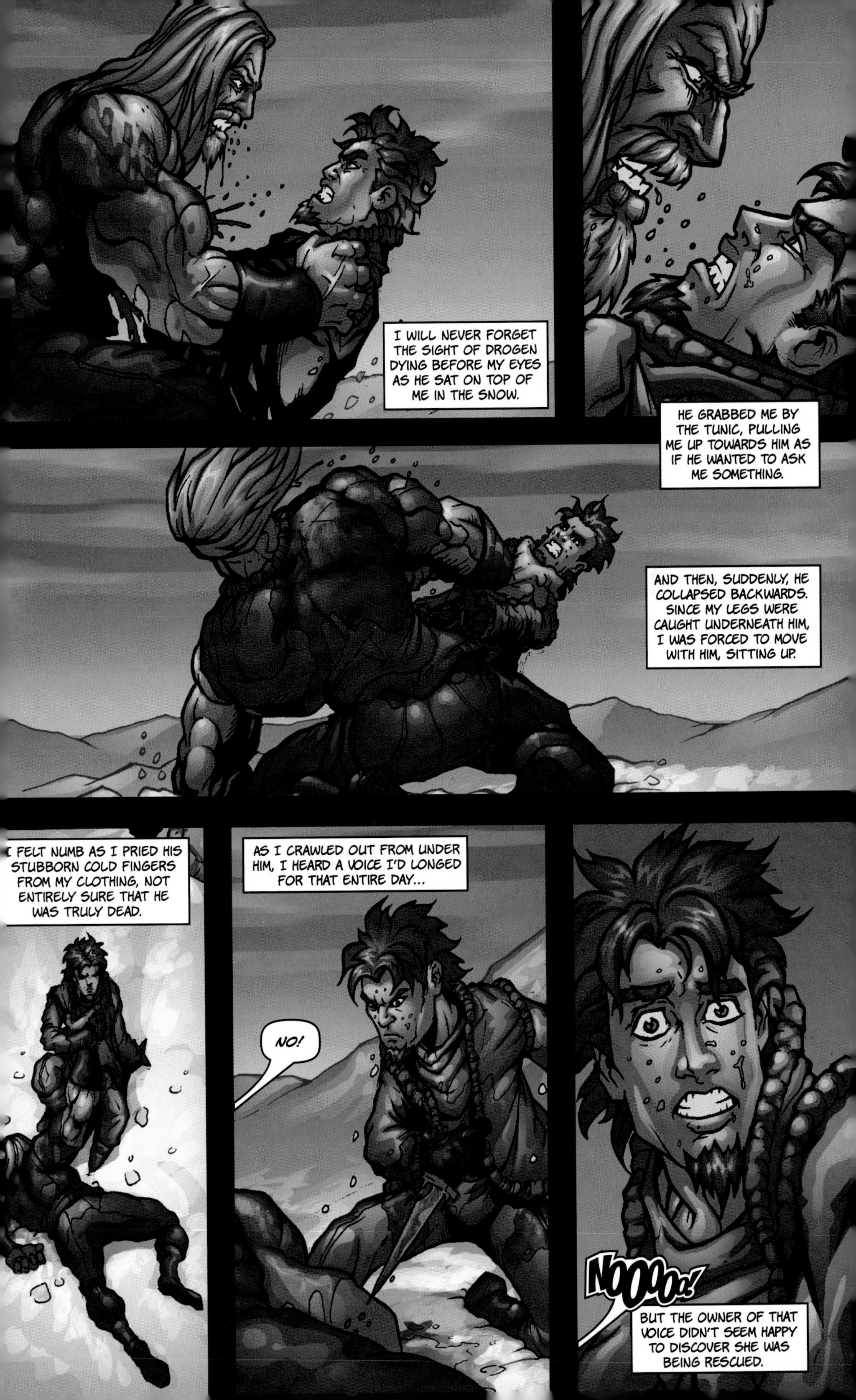
I WILL NEVER FORGET THE SIGHT OF DROGEN DYING BEFORE MY EYES AS HE SAT ON TOP OF ME IN THE SNOW.
HE GRABBED ME BY THE TUNIC, PULLING ME UP TOWARDS HIM AS IF HE WANTED TO ASK ME SOMETHING.
AND THEN, SUDDENLY, HE COLLAPSED BACKWARDS. SINCE MY LEGS WERE CAUGHT UNDERNEATH HIM, I WAS FORCED TO MOVE WITH HIM, SITTING UP.
I FELT NUMB AS I PRIED HIS STUBBORN COLD FINGERS FROM MY CLOTHING, NOT ENTIRELY SURE THAT HE WAS TRULY DEAD.
AS I CRAWLED OUT FROM UNDER HIM, I HEARD A VOICE I'D LONGED FOR THAT ENTIRE DAY...
NO!
NOOOOo!
BUT THE OWNER OF THAT VOICE DIDN'T SEEM HAPPY TO DISCOVER SHE WAS BEING RESCUED.

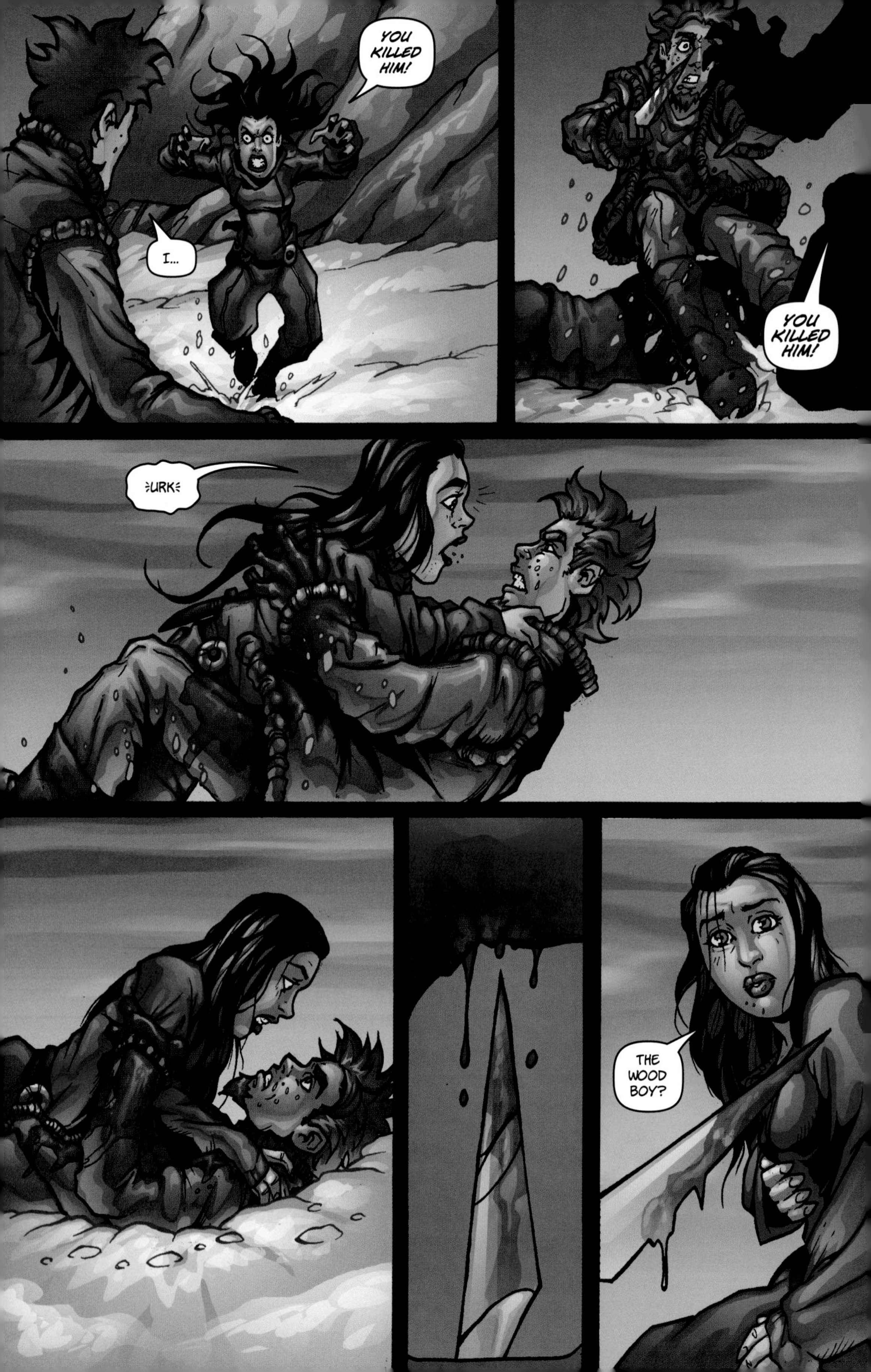
YOU KILLED HIM!
I...
YOU KILLED HIM!
URK
THE WOOD BOY?

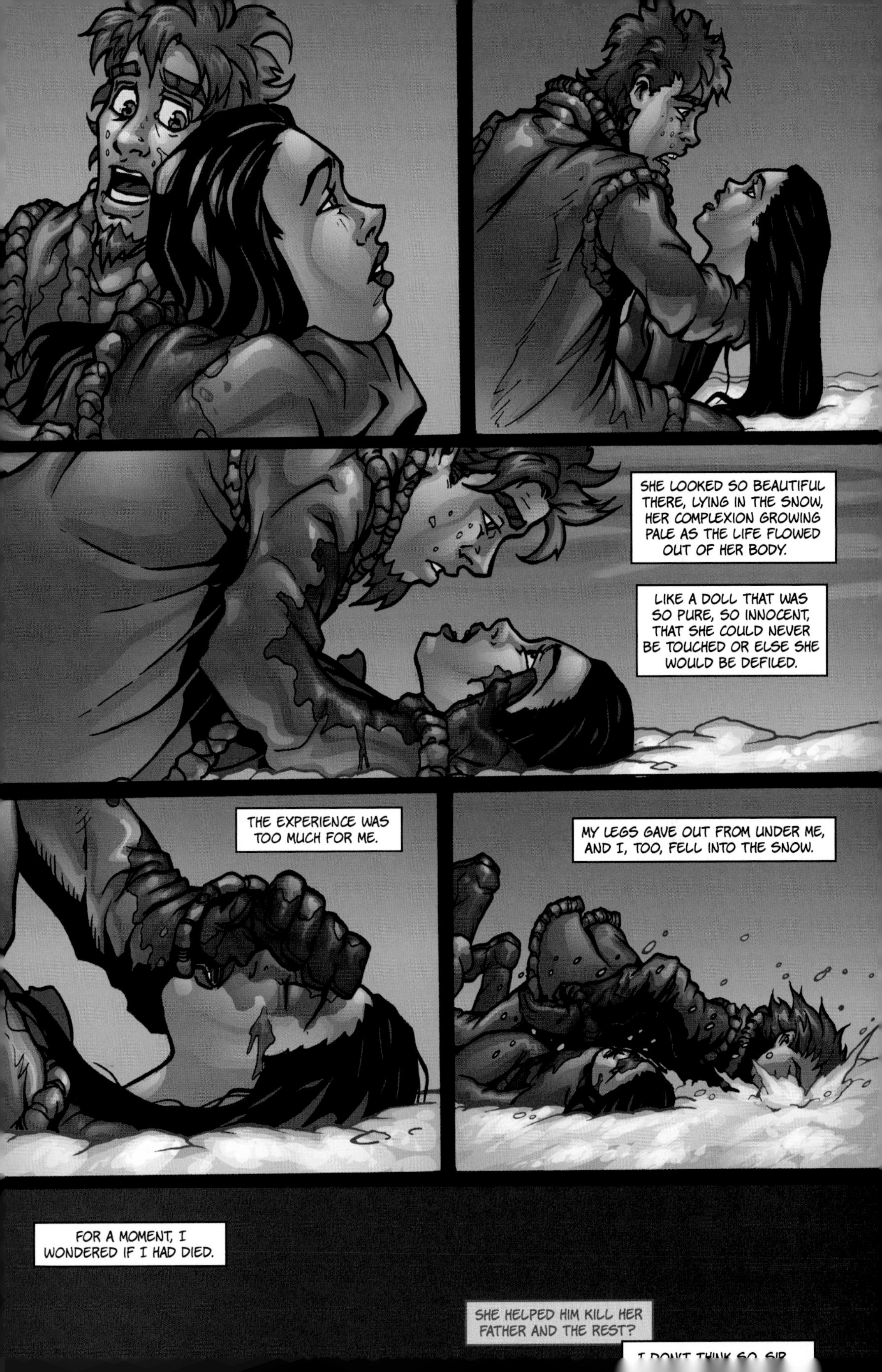
SHE LOOKED SO BEAUTIFUL THERE, LYING IN THE SNOW, HER COMPLEXION GROWING PALE AS THE LIFE FLOWED OUT OF HER BODY.
LIKE A DOLL THAT WAS SO PURE, SO INNOCENT, THAT SHE COULD NEVER BE TOUCHED OR ELSE SHE WOULD BE DEFILED.
THE EXPERIENCE WAS TOO MUCH FOR ME.
MY LEGS GAVE OUT FROM UNDER ME, AND I, TOO, FELL INTO THE SNOW.
FOR A MOMENT, I WONDERED IF I HAD DIED.
SHE HELPED HIM KILL HER FATHER AND THE REST?

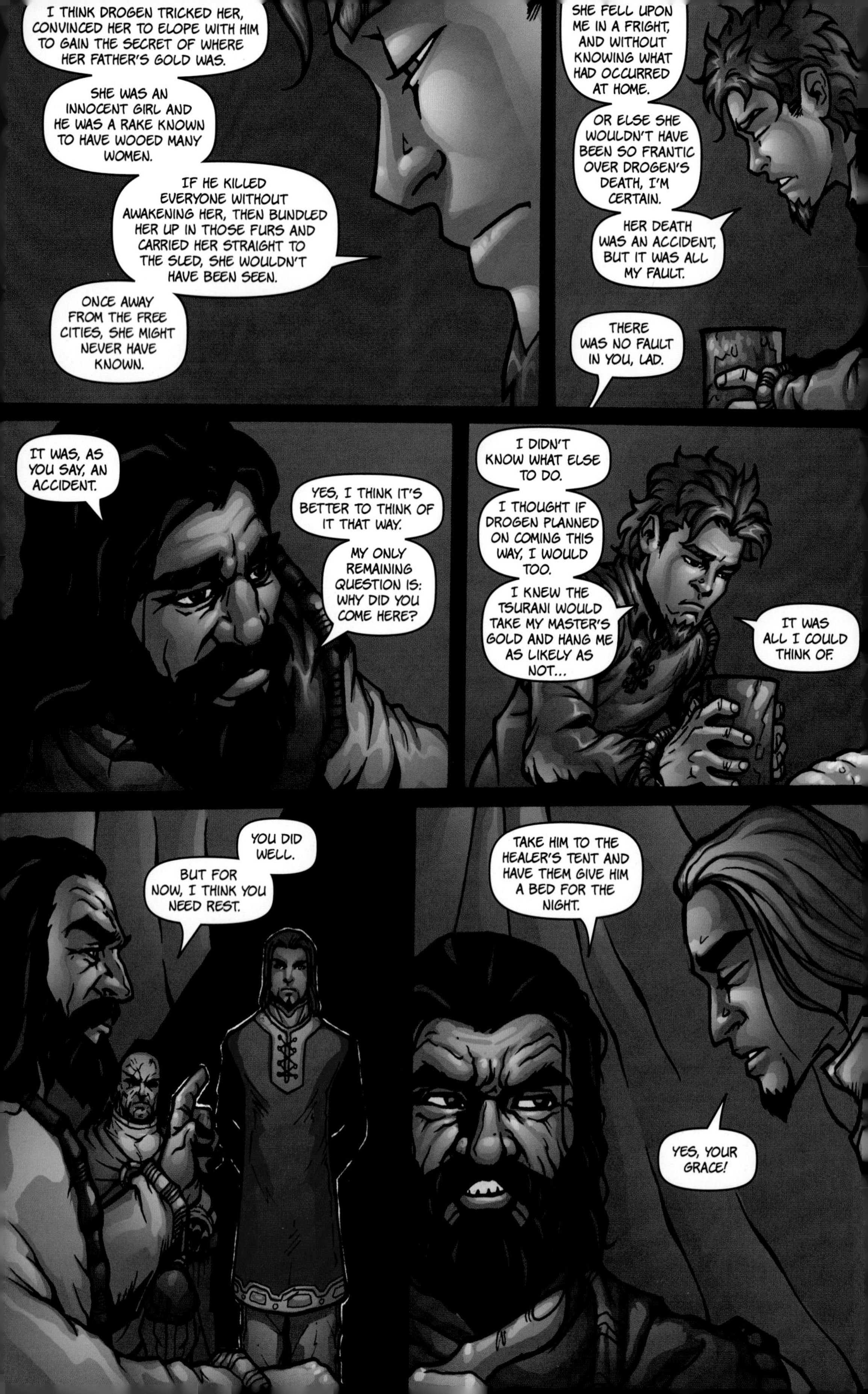
I THINK DROGEN TRICKED HER, CONVINCED HER TO ELOPE WITH HIM TO GAIN THE SECRET OF WHERE HER FATHER'S GOLD WAS.
SHE WAS AN INNOCENT GIRL AND HE WAS A RAKE KNOWN TO HAVE WOOED MANY WOMEN.
IF HE KILLED EVERYONE WITHOUT AWAKENING HER, THEN BUNDLED HER UP IN THOSE FURS AND CARRIED HER STRAIGHT TO THE SLED, SHE WOULDN'T HAVE BEEN SEEN.
ONCE AWAY FROM THE FREE CITIES, SHE MIGHT NEVER HAVE KNOWN.
SHE FELL UPON ME IN A FRIGHT, AND WITHOUT KNOWING WHAT HAD OCCURRED AT HOME.
OR ELSE SHE WOULDN'T HAVE BEEN SO FRANTIC OVER DROGEN'S DEATH, I'M CERTAIN.
HER DEATH WAS AN ACCIDENT, BUT IT WAS ALL MY FAULT.
THERE WAS NO FAULT IN YOU, LAD.
IT WAS, AS YOU SAY, AN ACCIDENT.
YES, I THINK IT'S BETTER TO THINK OF IT THAT WAY.
MY ONLY REMAINING QUESTION IS: WHY DID YOU COME HERE?
I DIDN'T KNOW WHAT ELSE TO DO.
I THOUGHT IF DROGEN PLANNED ON COMING THIS WAY, I WOULD TOO.
I KNEW THE TSURANI WOULD TAKE MY MASTER'S GOLD AND HANG ME AS LIKELY AS NOT...
IT WAS ALL I COULD THINK OF.
YOU DID WELL.
BUT FOR NOW, I THINK YOU NEED REST.
TAKE HIM TO THE HEALER'S TENT AND HAVE THEM GIVE HIM A BED FOR THE NIGHT.
YES, YOUR GRACE!

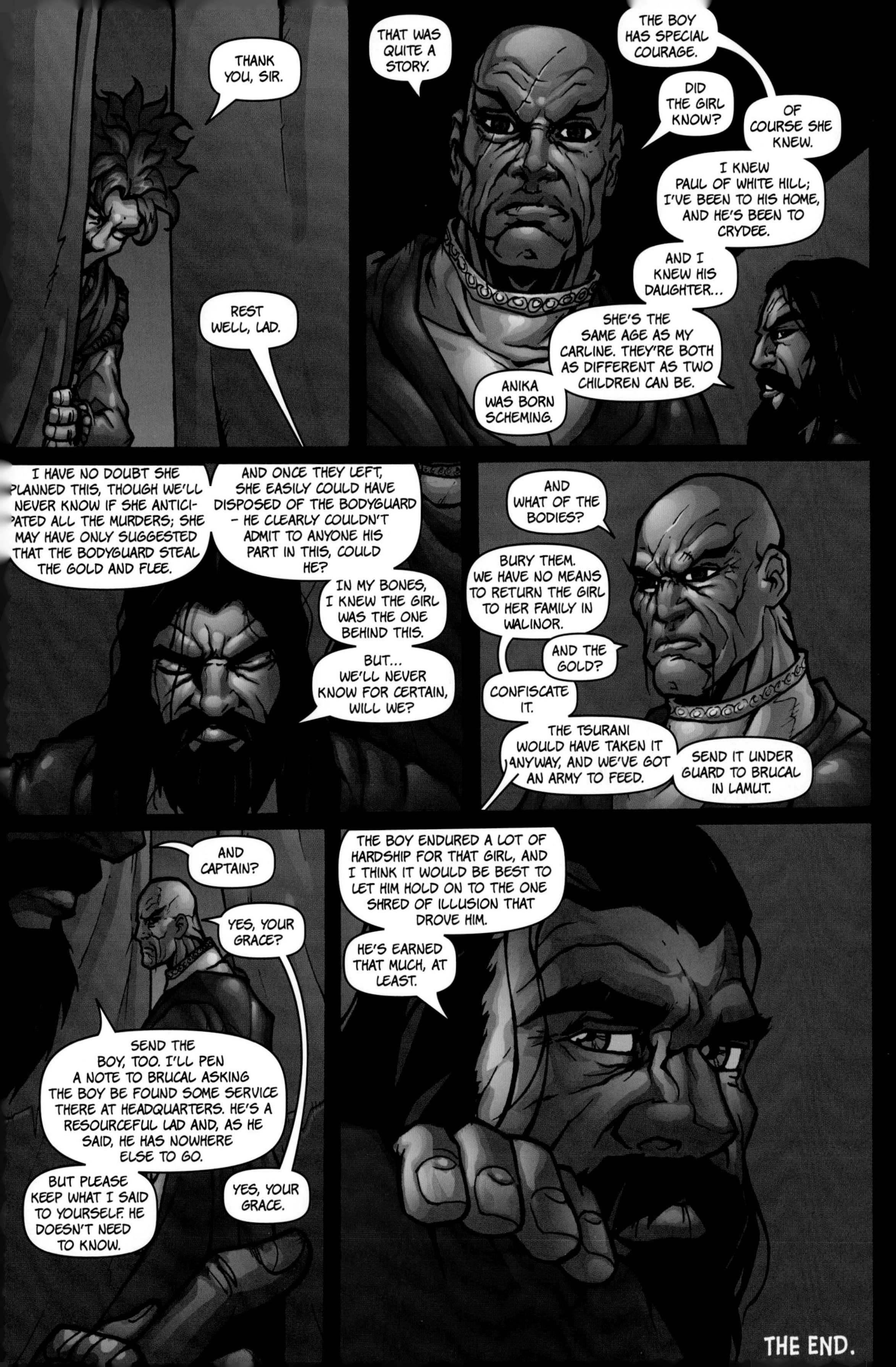
THANK YOU, SIR.
REST WELL, LAD.
THAT WAS QUITE A STORY.
THE BOY HAS SPECIAL COURAGE.
DID THE GIRL KNOW?
OF COURSE SHE KNEW.
I KNEW PAUL OF WHITE HILL; I'VE BEEN TO HIS HOME, AND HE'S BEEN TO CRYDEE.
AND I KNEW HIS DAUGHTER...
SHE'S THE SAME AGE AS MY CARLINE. THEY'RE BOTH AS DIFFERENT AS TWO CHILDREN CAN BE.
ANIKA WAS BORN SCHEMING.
I HAVE NO DOUBT SHE PLANNED THIS, THOUGH WE'LL NEVER KNOW IF SHE ANTICIPATED ALL THE MURDERS; SHE MAY HAVE ONLY SUGGESTED THAT THE BODYGUARD STEAL THE GOLD AND FLEE.
AND ONCE THEY LEFT, SHE EASILY COULD HAVE DISPOSED OF THE BODYGUARD - HE CLEARLY COULDN'T ADMIT TO ANYONE HIS PART IN THIS, COULD HE?
IN MY BONES, I KNEW THE GIRL WAS THE ONE BEHIND THIS.
BUT... WE'LL NEVER KNOW FOR CERTAIN, WILL WE?
AND WHAT OF THE BODIES?
BURY THEM. WE HAVE NO MEANS TO RETURN THE GIRL TO HER FAMILY IN WALINOR.
AND THE GOLD?
CONFISCATE IT.
THE TSURANI WOULD HAVE TAKEN IT ANYWAY, AND WE'VE GOT AN ARMY TO FEED.
SEND IT UNDER GUARD TO BRUCAL IN LAMUT.
AND CAPTAIN?
YES, YOUR GRACE?
SEND THE BOY, TOO. I'LL PEN A NOTE TO BRUCAL ASKING THE BOY BE FOUND SOME SERVICE THERE AT HEADQUARTERS. HE'S A RESOURCEFUL LAD AND, AS HE SAID, HE HAS NOWHERE ELSE TO GO.
BUT PLEASE KEEP WHAT I SAID TO YOURSELF. HE DOESN'T NEED TO KNOW.
YES, YOUR GRACE.
THE BOY ENDURED A LOT OF HARDSHIP FOR THAT GIRL, AND I THINK IT WOULD BE BEST TO LET HIM HOLD ON TO THE ONE SHRED OF ILLUSION THAT DROVE HIM.
HE'S EARNED THAT MUCH, AT LEAST.
THE END.

The Hall of Worlds
A Raymonde. Feist Experience

The Hall of Worlds is the premier fansite dedicated to Raymond E. Feist and his works. The site features news, fan-art, an encyclopedia on various topics and above all, an enthusiastic community. Although the works of Feist are central, we'll keep track of all things related to the world of Midkemia, such as games and the comics.

At the heart of the Hall of Worlds is Honest John's, the discussion forums of this community-driven site. Over here you'll find people all over the world talking about Feist and his works, fantasy in general and other topics, all in a friendly atmosphere ensured by volunteering staff-members.

Visit the Hall of Worlds at:
http://hallofworlds.net

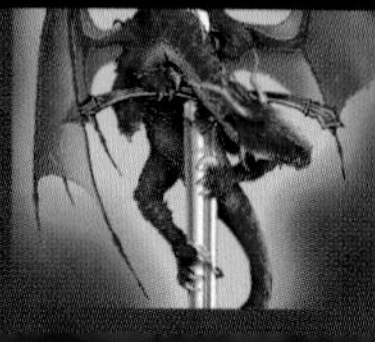

And visit Honest John's at
http://forum.hallofworlds.net

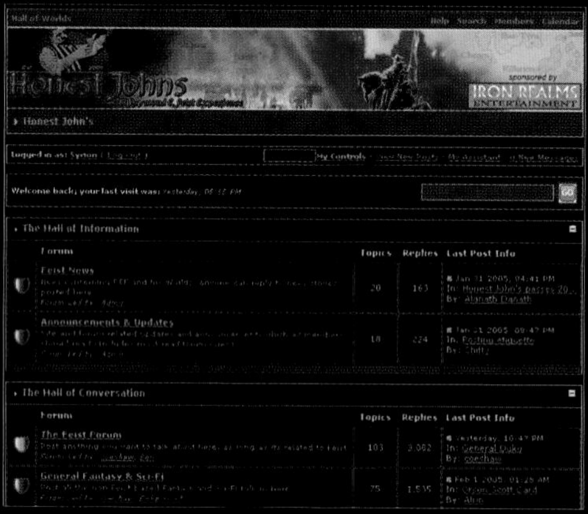

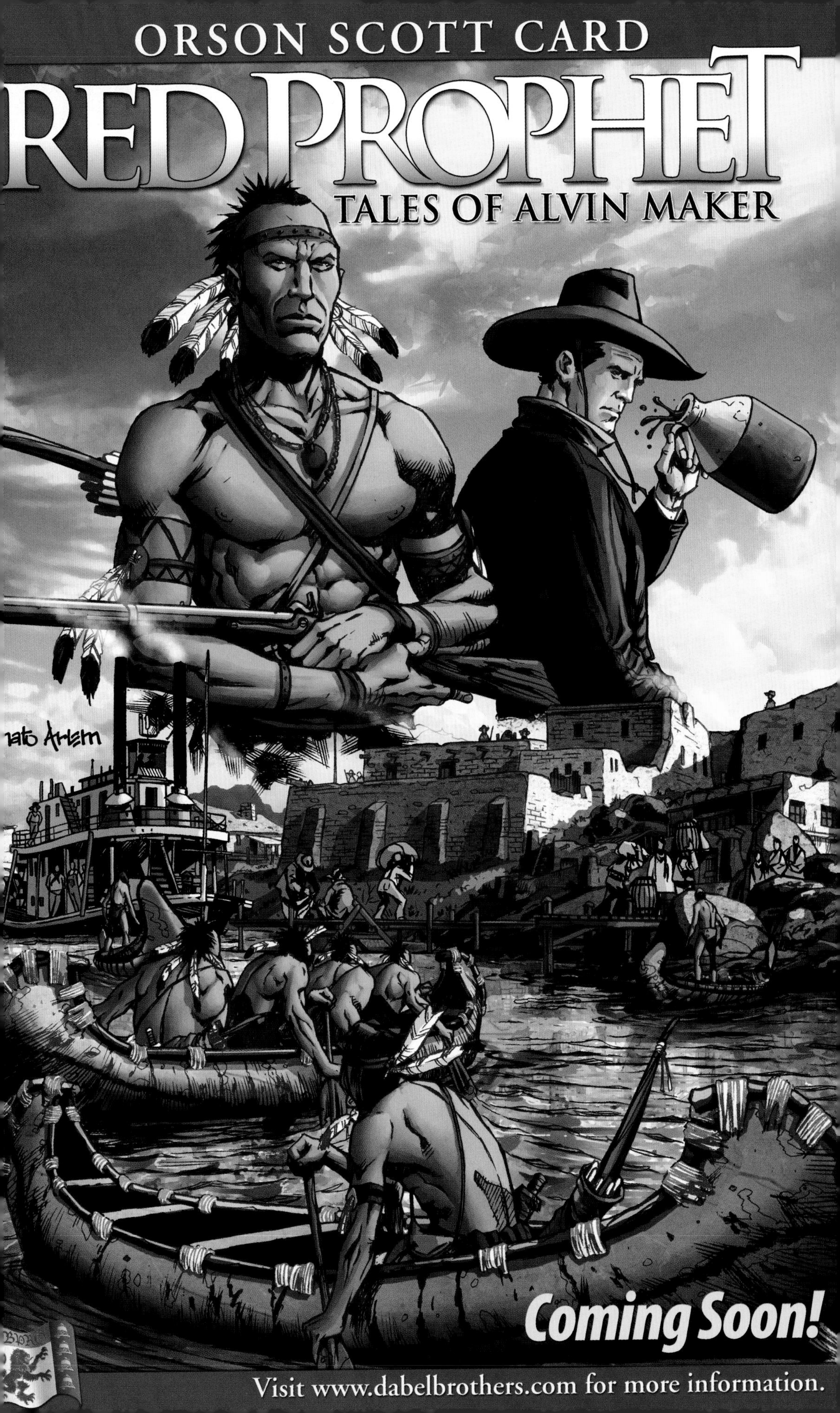
ORSON SCOTT CARD
RED PROPHET
TALES OF ALVIN MAKER
Coming Soon!
Visit www.dabelbrothers.com for more information.

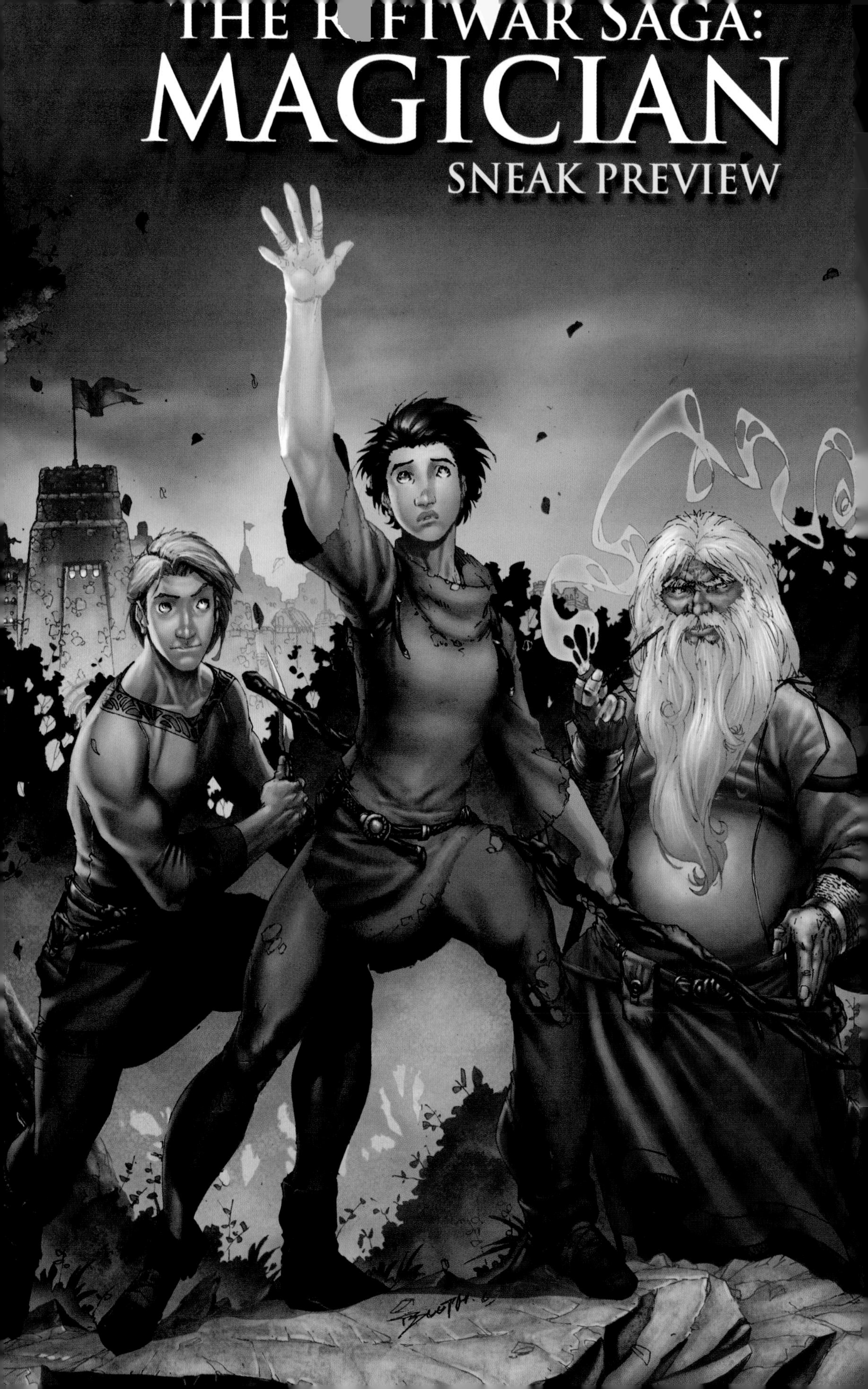
THE RIFTWAR SAGA:
MAGICIAN
SNEAK PREVIEW

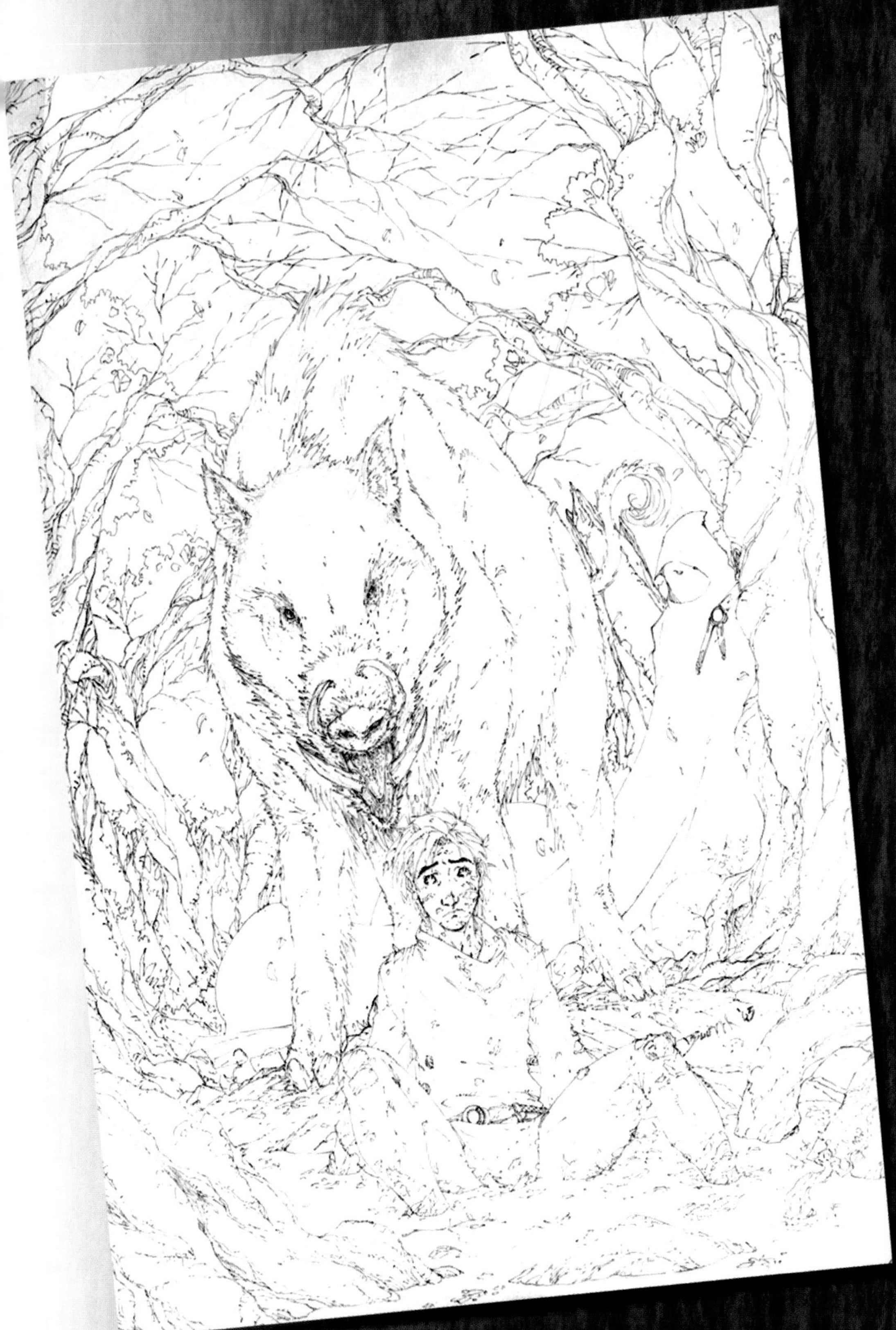

Artwork **Brett Booth**

Colors **Jess Ruffner-Booth**

Design **Bill Tortolini**

Panel 1
Swordmaster Fannon looks to the off-panel boys with a stern but pleasant grin, as if
he's just heard the voice of someone he's been thinking about.

FANNON
Tomas! A moment's word, if you please...

Panel 2
Full-figure LS. Swordmaster Fannon with one hand on his hip, gestures enquiringly
with the other toward Tomas, who stands respectfully, hands clasped before him.
Pug does not look as if he belongs in the discussion, as he awkwardly steps in the
opposite direction, in a dawdling pose, head cocked, looking sideways at the small
puff of dirt kicked up by his feet.

TOMAS
Swordmaster Fannon! Yes, sir!

FANNON
In private, please...
I've a few questions for you.

Panel 3
CU Pug glances up in the opposite direction, even as his head is still cocked down
and to the side, as if something just caught his eye.

TOMAS V.O.
Of course, sir!

Panel 4

Pug's POV. Within the keep, a tower that rises above the living quarters of the Duke
and his royal family. We see few details, but the distant feminine form is Princess
Carline standing at the edge of the parapet looking at the distant horizon (not
looking down at Pug). We don't get a clear look at her yet.

Panel 5
Med. Pug looks up longingly, as Tomas re-appears at his side with a grin.

TOMAS
You've no chance, my friend...

Panel 6
High angle looking down at Princess Carline from above, and from slightly behind as
she looks down into the courtyard of the castle. We still don't have a clear look at
her. The distant small figures of Tomas & Pug look up at her. Swordmaster Fannon
strides away. There is other miscellaneous activity within the courtyard amongst
guards, carts and horses, but nothing to distract from the two boys. Squire Roland
enters the parapet scene from the bottom of the page to enquire after the Princess.

TOMAS
She's far, far out of your league.

Panel 7
Tomas gives Pug a reassuring pat on the back as the two start to go their separate
ways, both grinning.

TOMAS
I need to run an errand for Fannon...

And you had better fill that sack with sandcrawlers or you just might find yourself
boiled in oil and served to her Highness for supper.

PUG
All right, I'm going already!

TOMAS
Do that.
And remember, Pug, whatever you do…

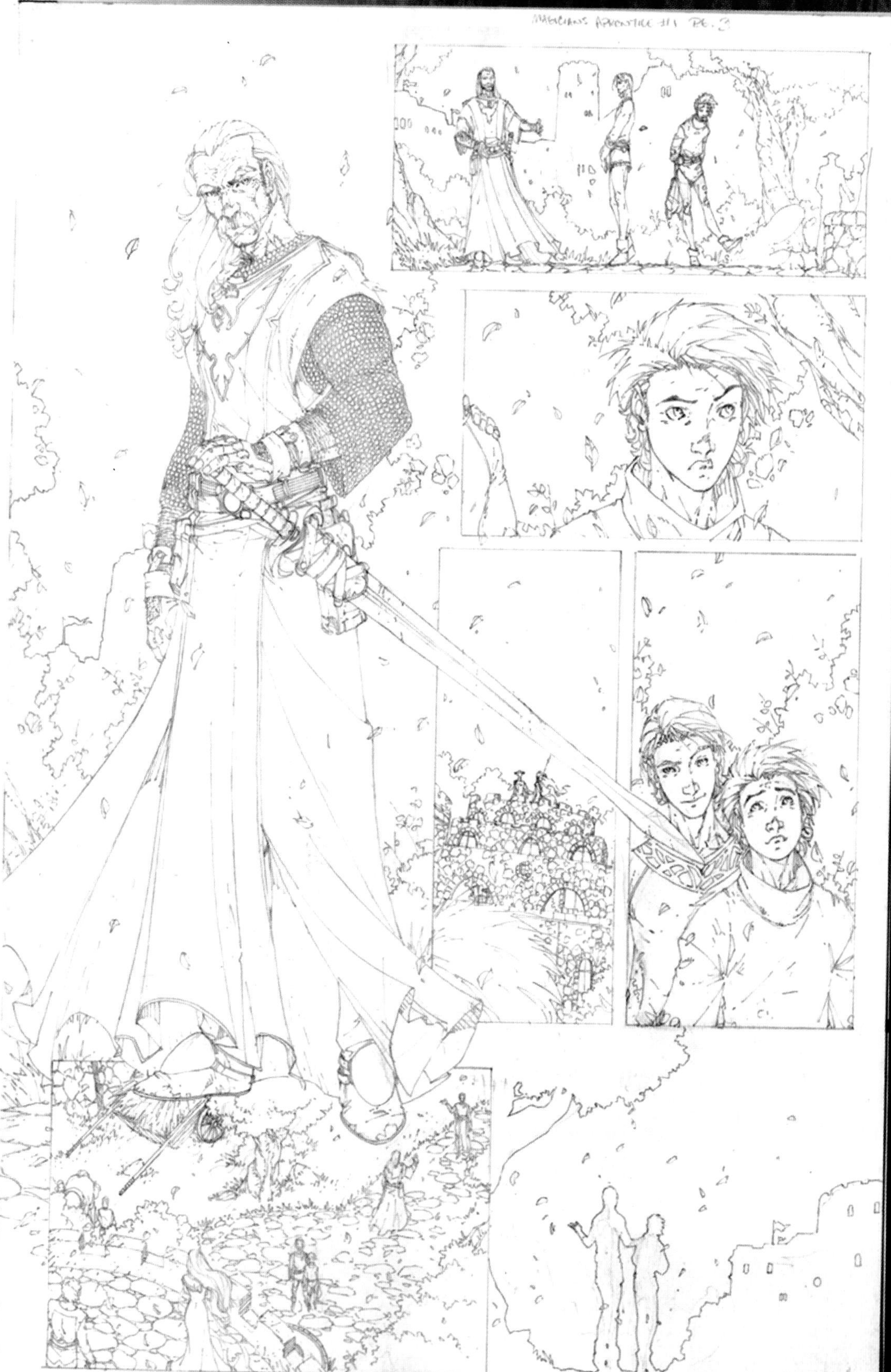
MAGICIANS APPRENTICE #1 PG. 3

Page 4

Panel 1
Widescreen panel of the rocks on the edge of the sea. Unlike
the opening scene, the sun has gone out, blocked by dark, low
rolling storm clouds. No rain yet. Wind has picked up the
waves.

Colors grey and monochrome in contrast to the bright day
scenes we've had so far.

Close in on the rocks and we see PUG sleeping against the
rocks, unaware of the sea picking up nearby. His sack of
sandcrawlers next to him near pool of sea water.
Brett, give the rock he's under some distinctive carving-
maybe a face carved into the stone a few hundred years back-
we'll need this as a landmark for a few pages later.

CAPTION
"…don't fall asleep on the job this time!"

Panel 2
Close on Pug sleeping.

Panel 3
Same, but now a wave splashes over him, startling him awake!

PUG
UGH! What?!?

Panel 4
From behind Pug in his half sitting/squatting position as he
quickly wakes and tries to stand- he looks on a sea ready to
burst with storm! The sea is suddenly rough and the sky is
grey- the hint of raindrops here and there.
Far away, Pug sees Sailor's Grief, a small island bluff is
being pounded by white capped waves.

PUG
Oh no, I can't believe what a fool I am!
Megar's going to kill me!

Panel 6

Pug leaps over one of the many small ponds of water in the
rocks teaming with shell life- bag in hand.
He looks worried, as a small wave crashes on the rocks behind
him, sending white mist into the air.

PUG
Storm's coming. I'd better hurry.

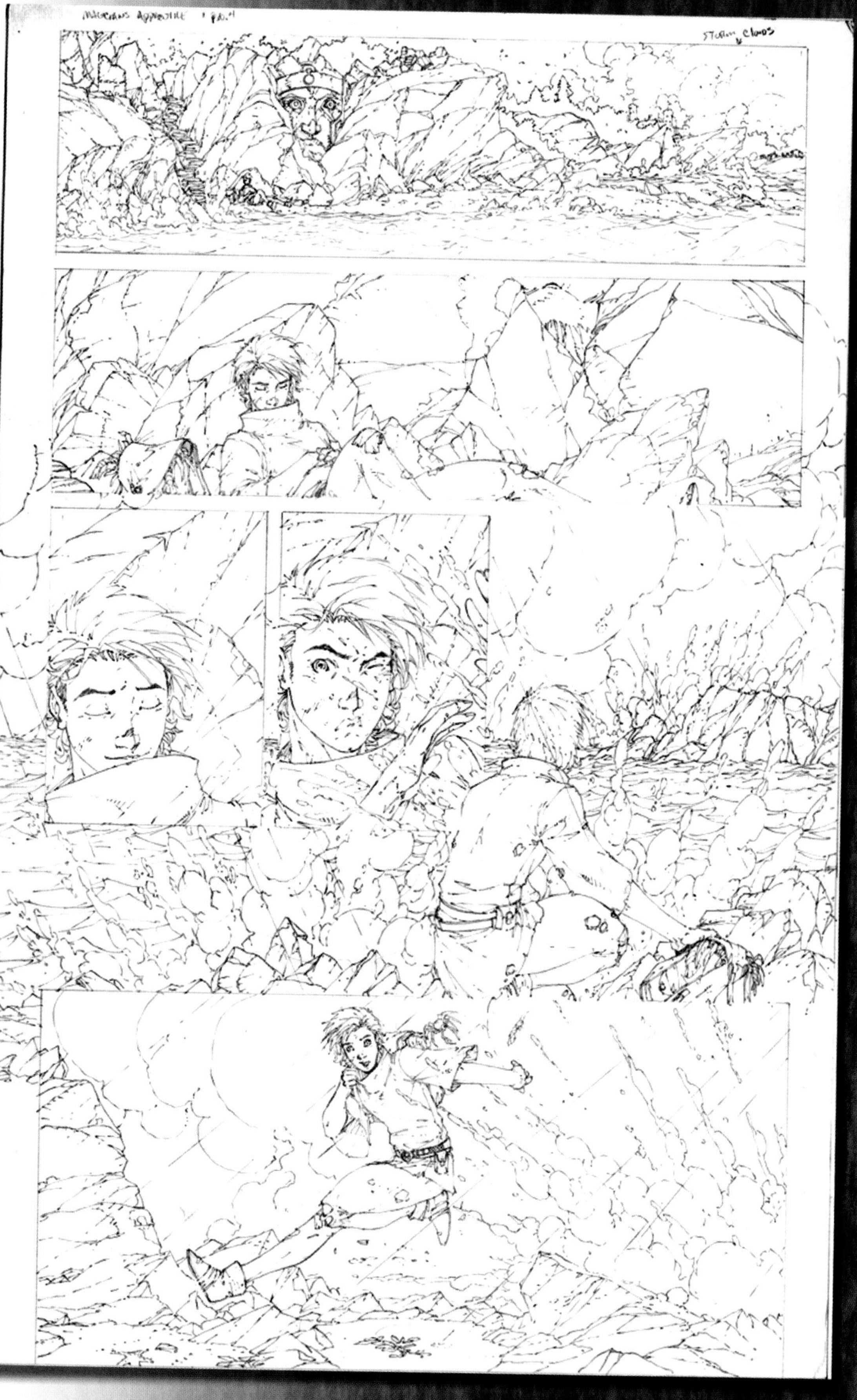
Storm clouds

Page 5

Panel 1

Pug leaps off the low rocks onto some actual sand- it is peppered with small islands of rocks that leads to the cliff bluffs further ahead.

Thunder rumbles in the sky- no lightning yet.

More rain now, but not a downpour yet. A crab falls out of Pug's bag

SFX
Brakkakroom!

PUG
Okay, thunder, but no lightning, that means the storm's not that-

Panel 2

Lightning shoots across the sky overhead. Pug stumbles as a small wave hits his calves and rushes over the rocks and sand around him.

Pug covers his head with the bag as the sound scares the crap out of him.

SFX
KKRAKKTHOOM!

PUG
AGH!

Panel 3
Pug falls in the water. The rain picks up now.

Panel 4
Pug stands up, bag in both arms, the contents ready to fall- he's panicking a bit- he dares a look down, the thought that he can look as he moves.

Panel 5

Pug gets his foot trapped in a rock- cutting his ankle.

PUG
AH!

Panel 6

Pug is hit by a big wave- it pours over his body- and takes away his bag even as he reaches for it.

SFX

Sploosshh!

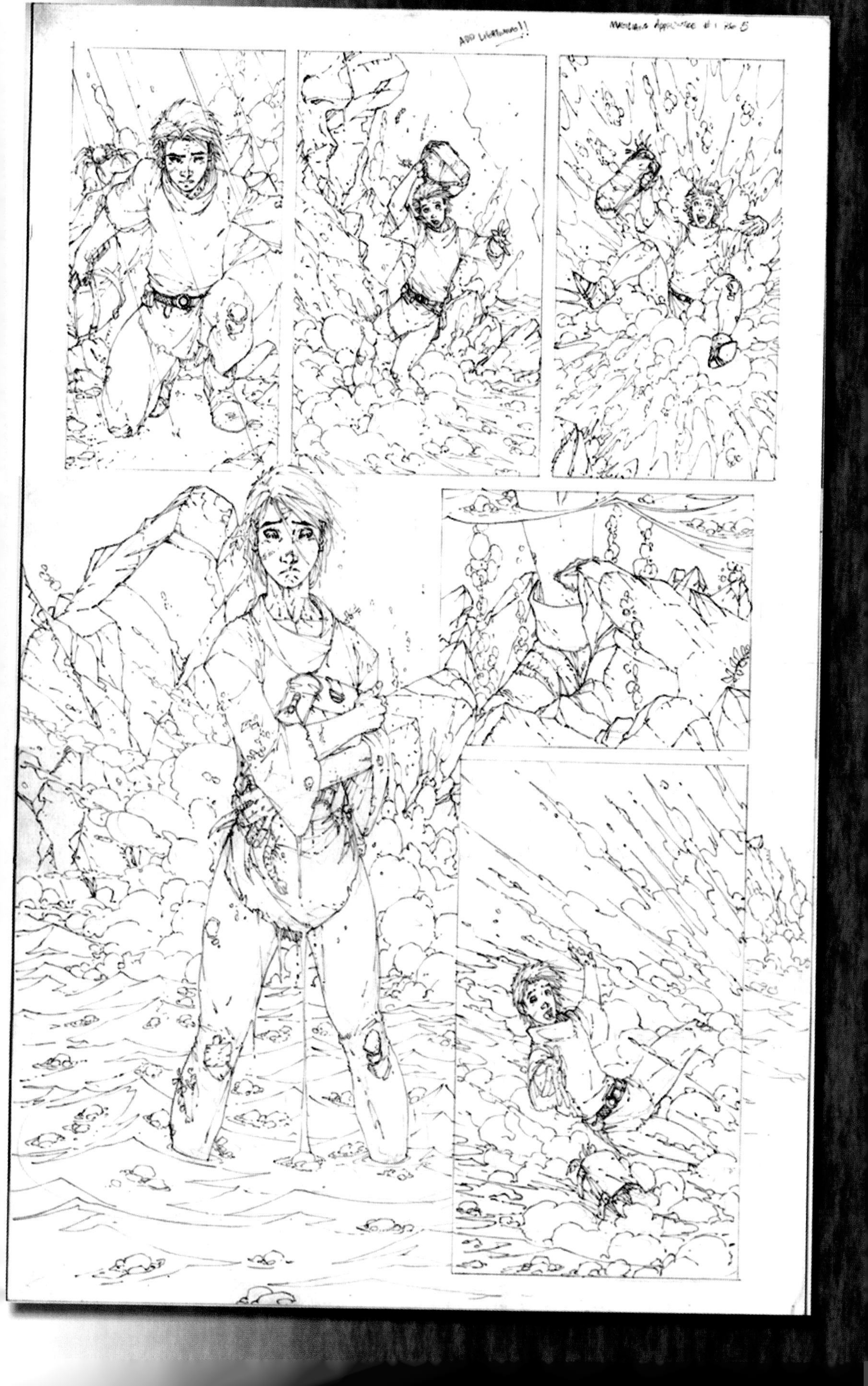
ADD LIGHTNING!!

Page 6

Panel 1

From low in the water we look past Crabs and Shellfish and
the empty bag as Pug half stands in the water, mouth open in
shock from the cold water.

Panel 2

Pug reaches for the bag.

PUG
Argh!

Panel 3

But another wave hits him, not flowing over him, but knocking
him down.
SFX
Foosh!

Panel 4

Pug hops on his one foot in the calf- high water- we see his
other foot- his ankle bleeds.
Lightning strikes, and now we see the sea really raging
behind him- big ass waves- the rock he was on in the opening
with the distinctive carving is half under water!

SFX

KkkkkAABABOOOM!

Panel 5

Pug hugs the lower rocks of the cliff face- rough steps have
been cut out there- Pug looks back at the water realizing he
could have died there.

Panel 6

Pug half sits on the steps to catch his breath and examine
his ankle.

PUG

Yikes. That doesn't look good…

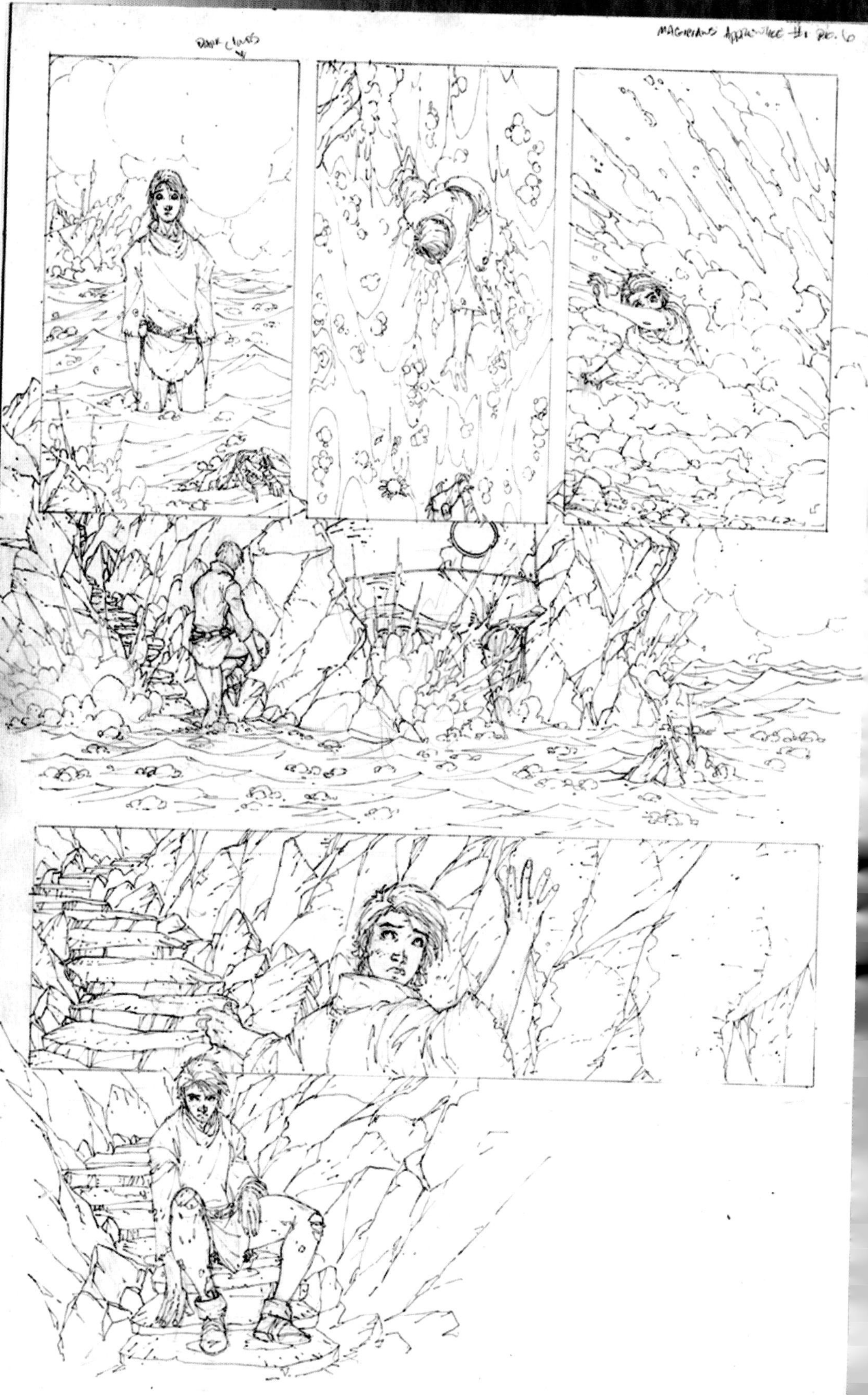

MAGICIANS APPRENTICE #1 PG. 6
DARK CLOUDS

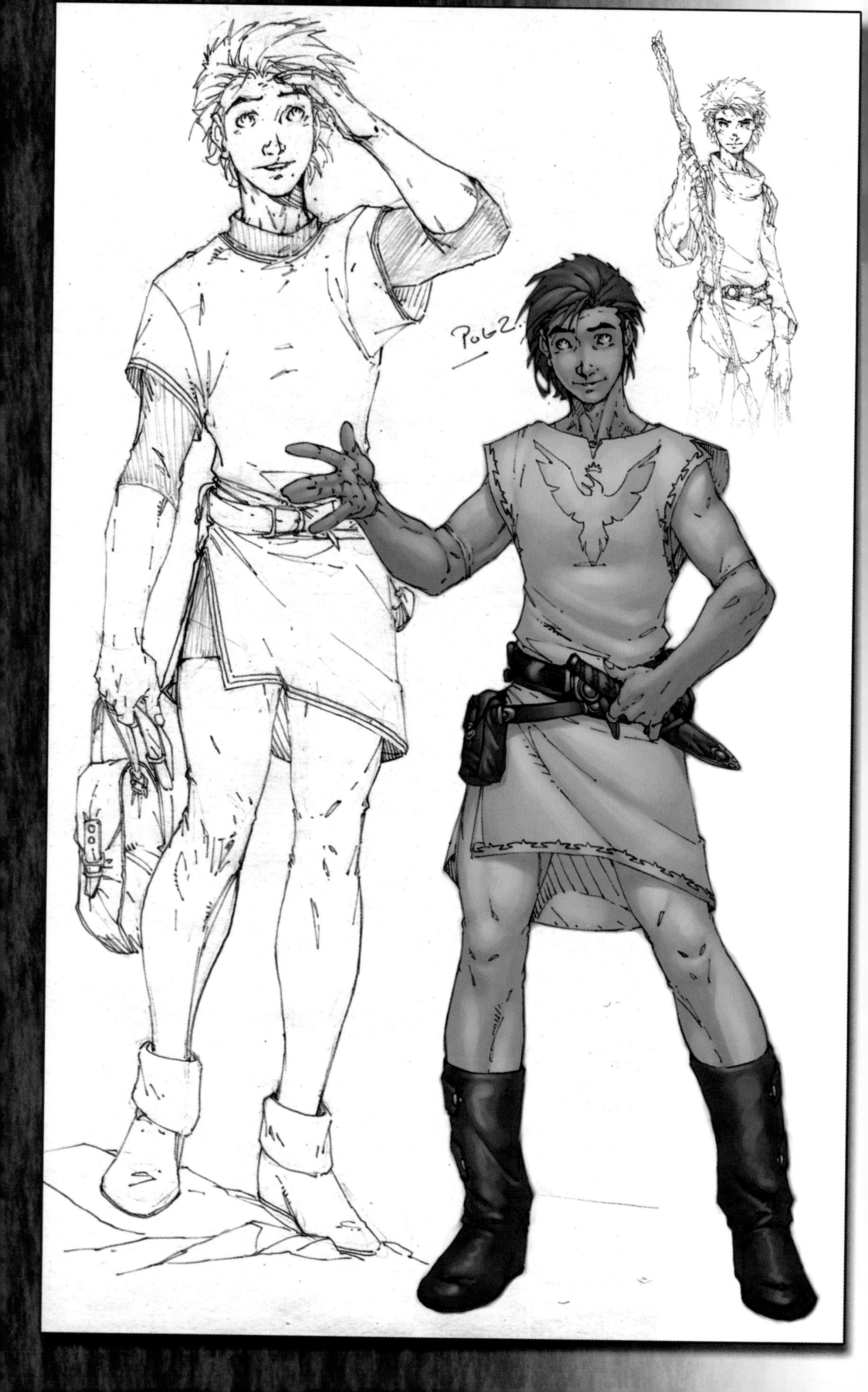
Pogz.

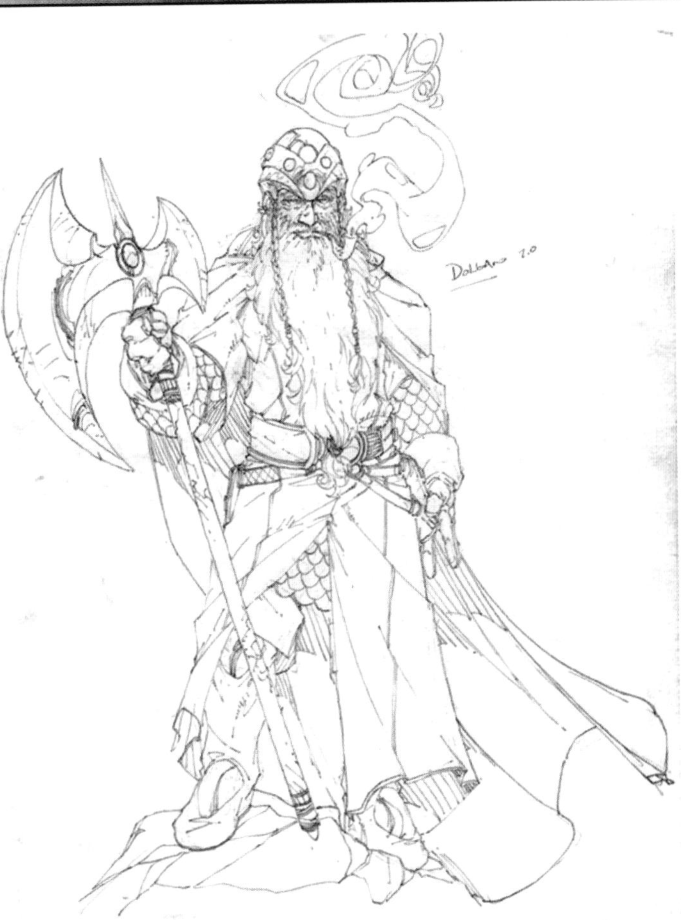

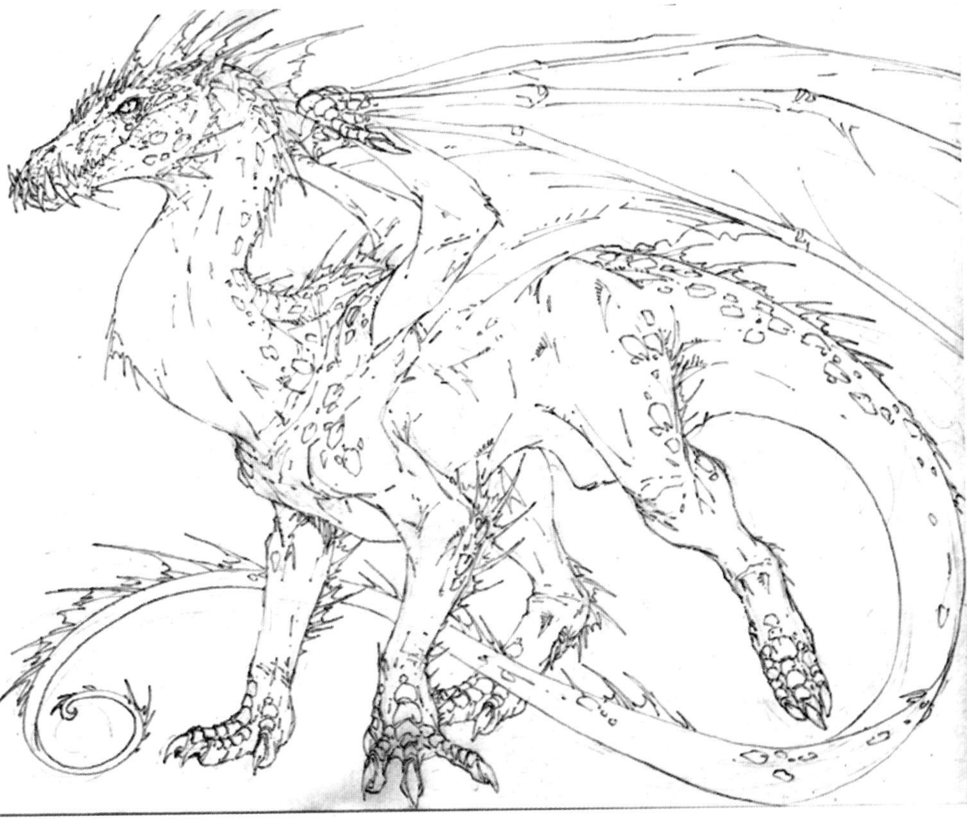

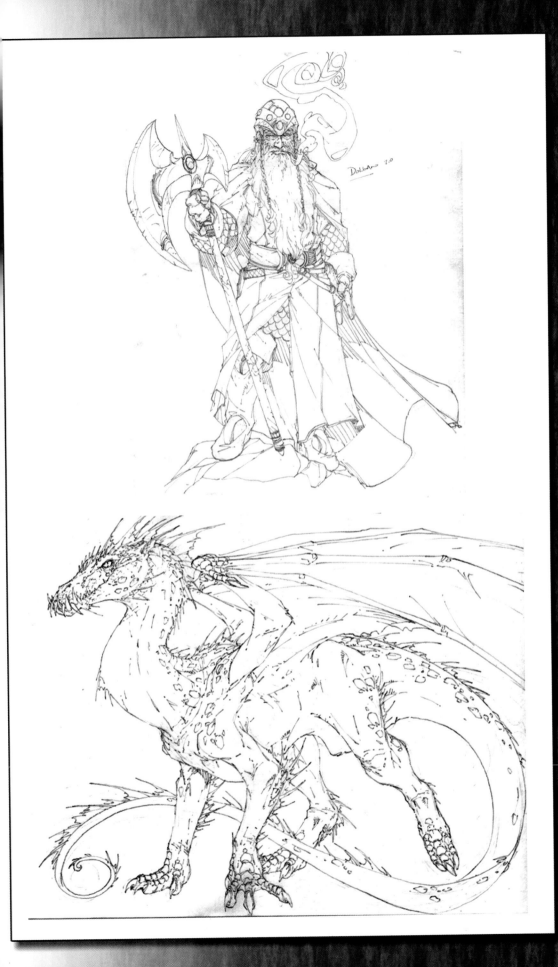

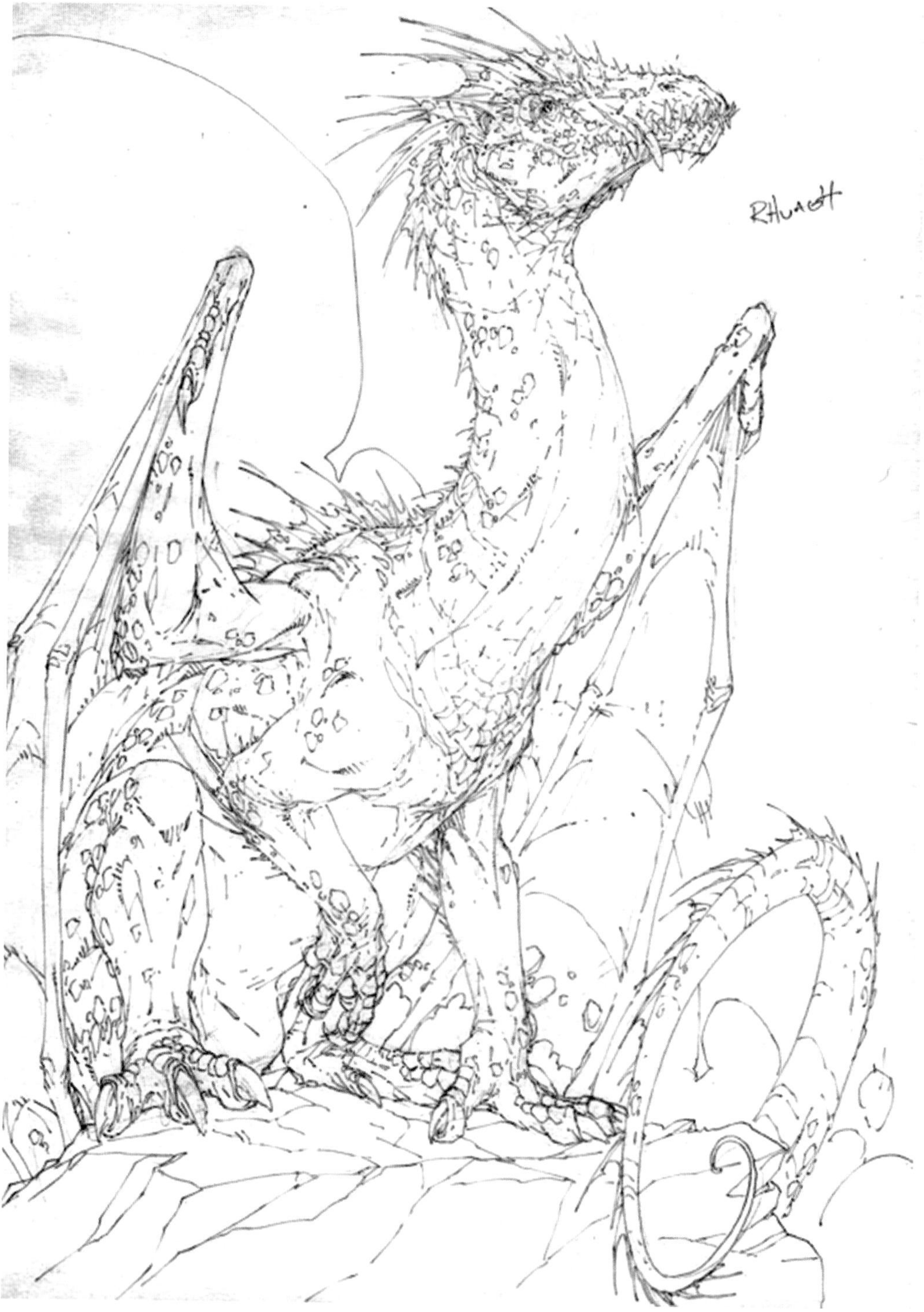
RHUANG

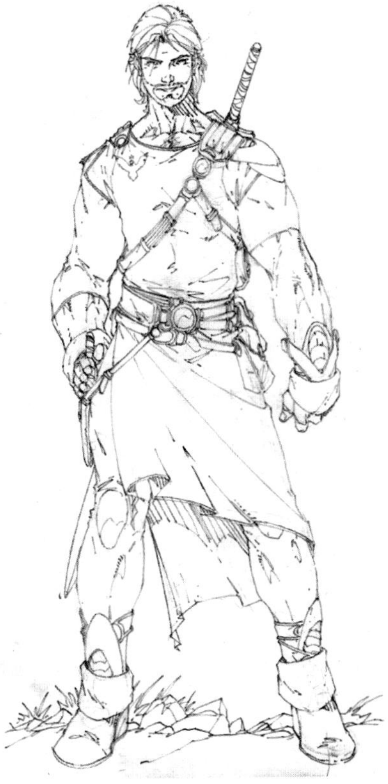

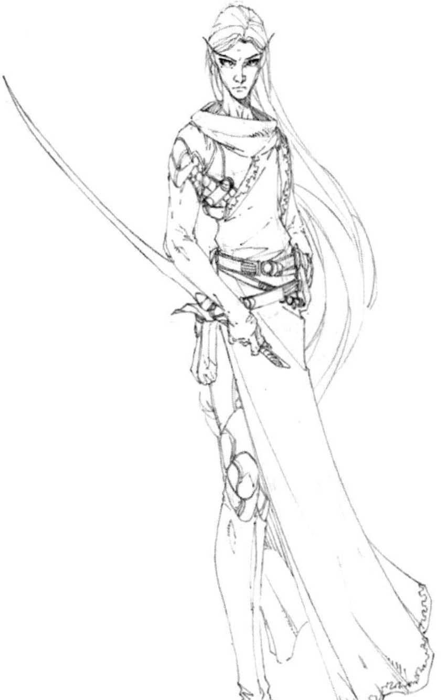

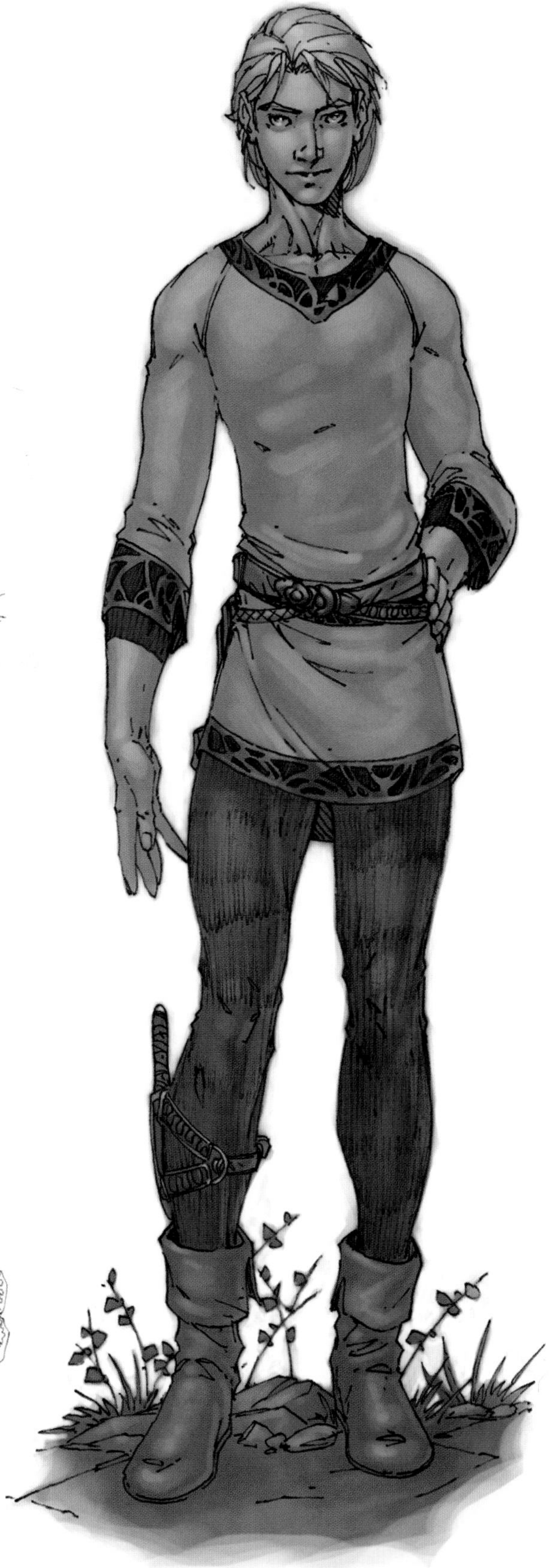

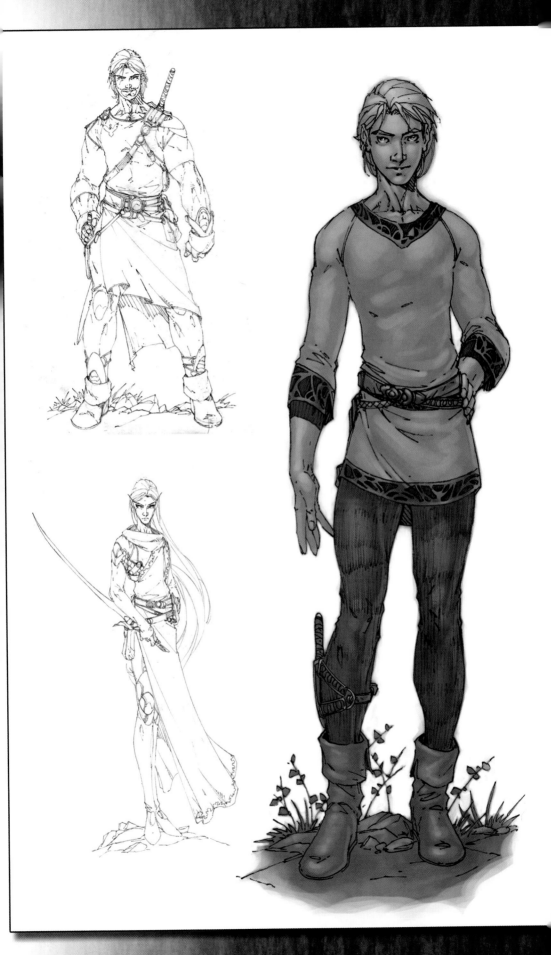

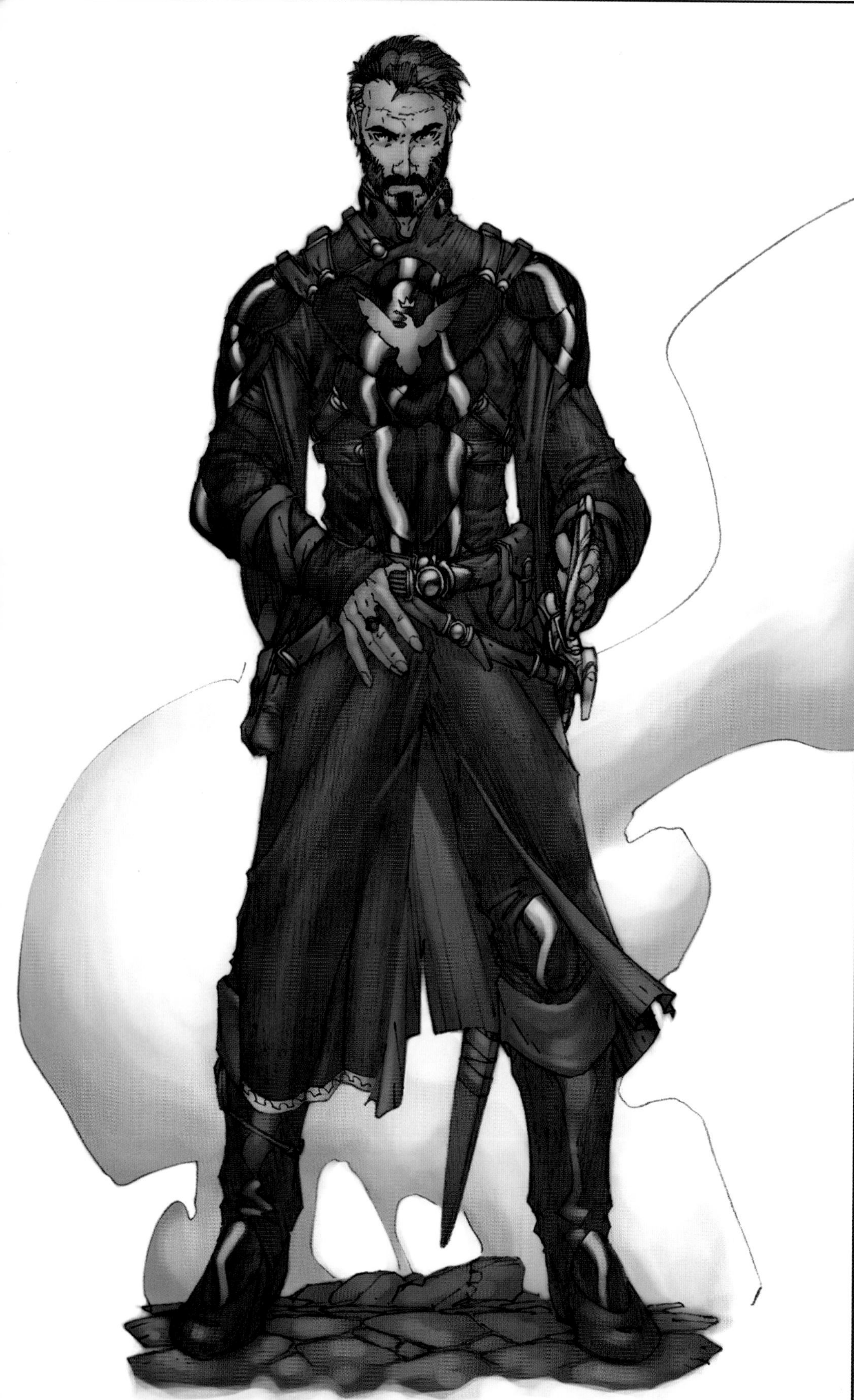

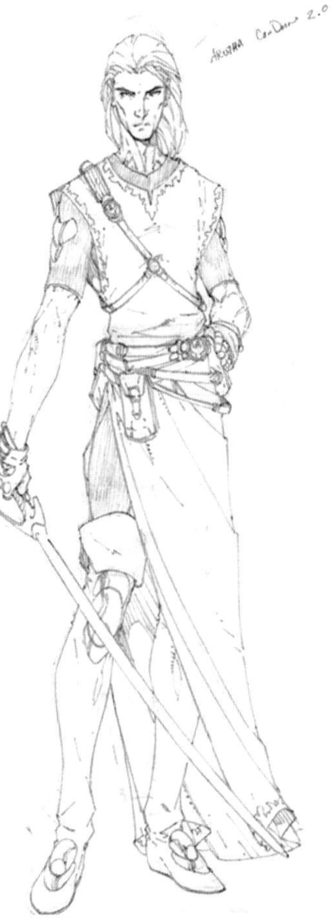

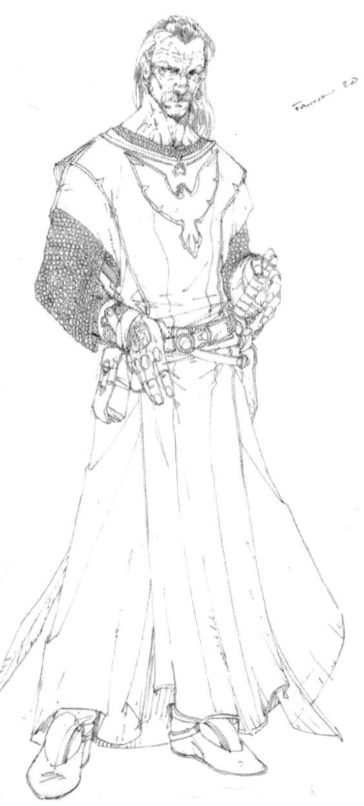

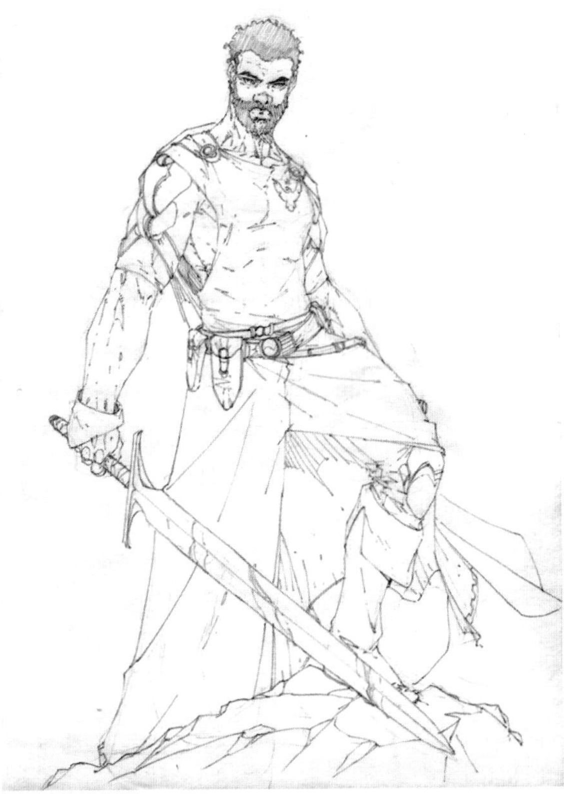

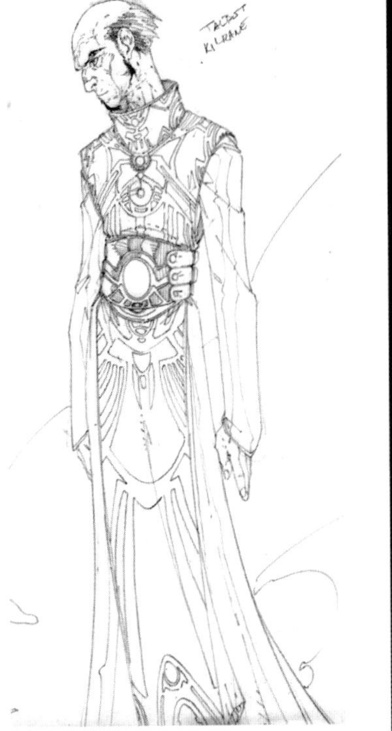
TALBOT KILRANE

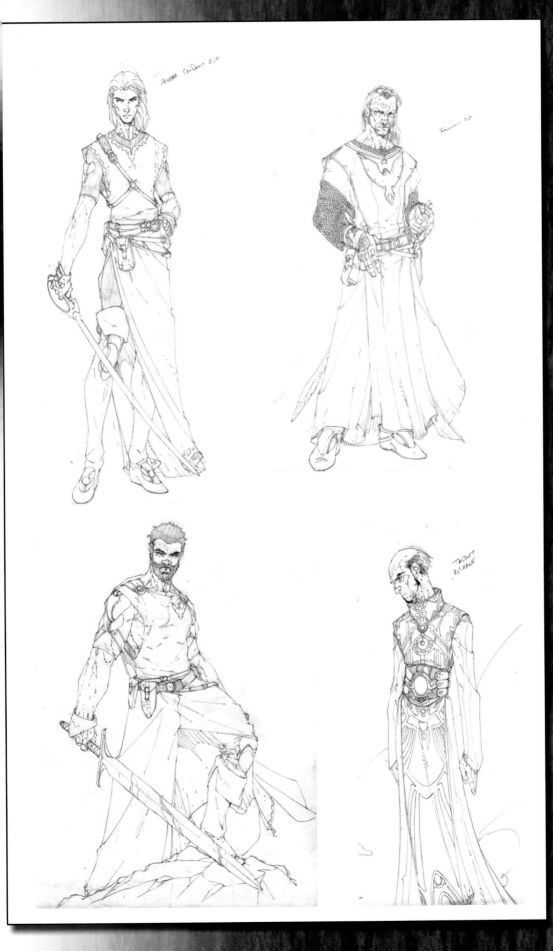

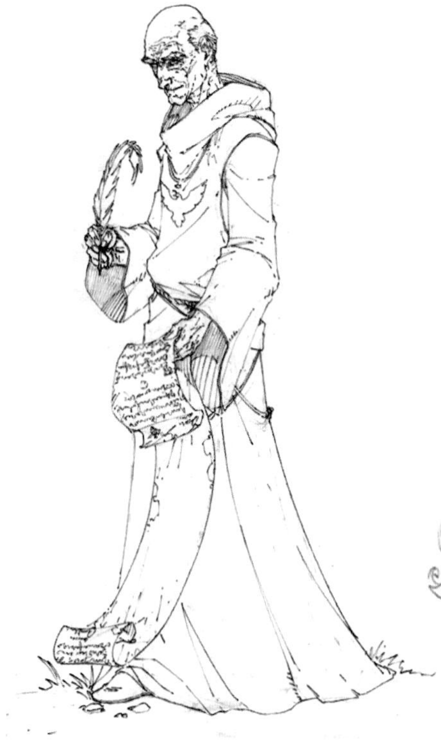

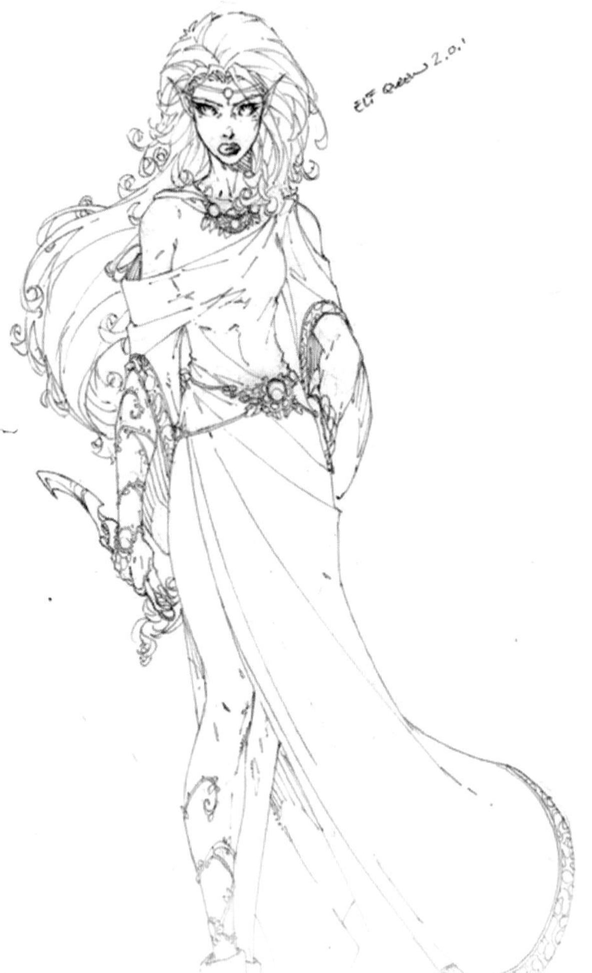
Elf Queen 2.0.1

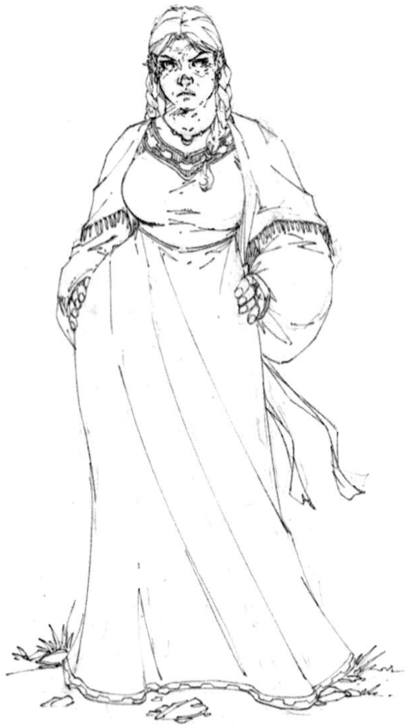

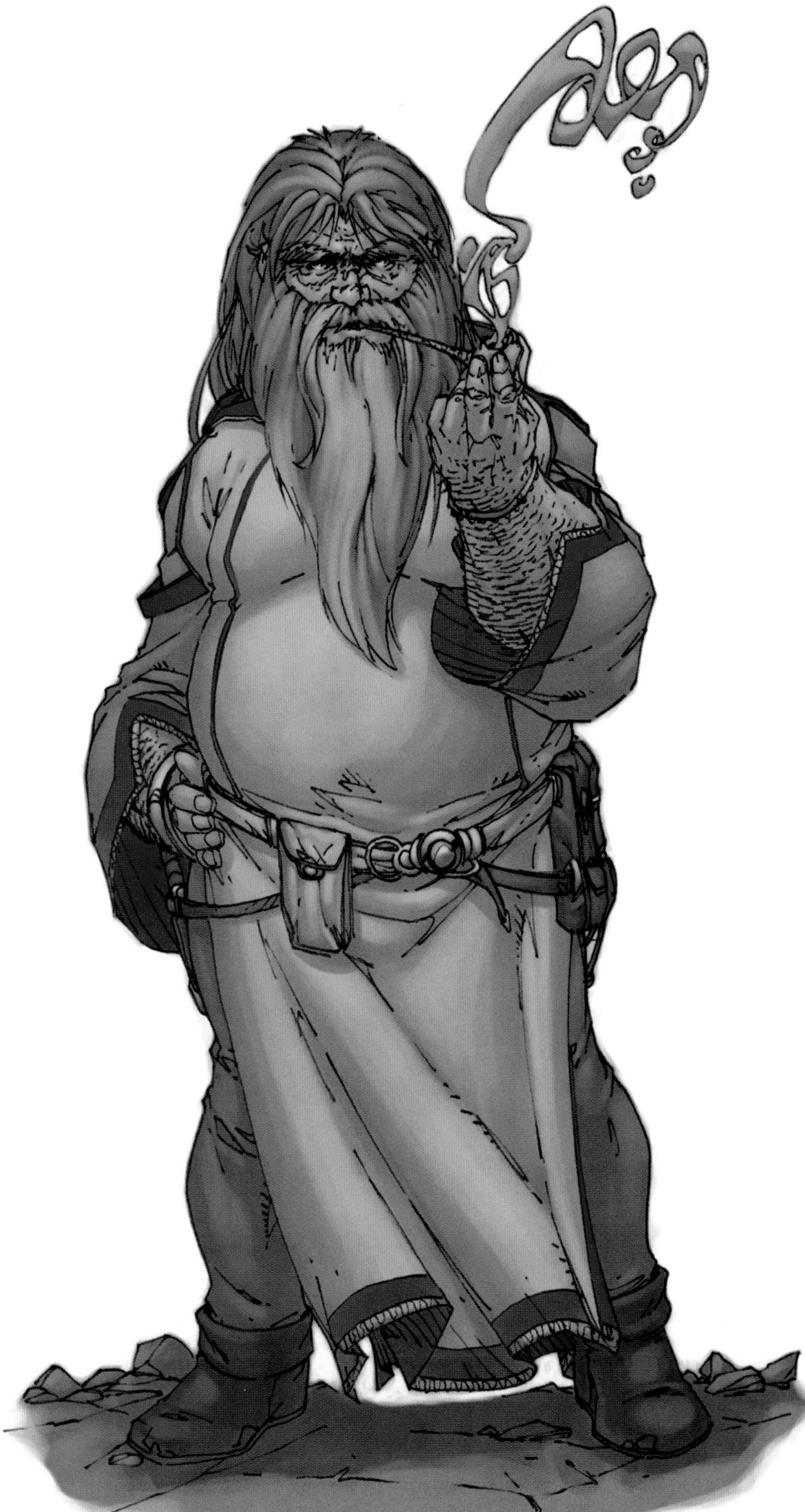

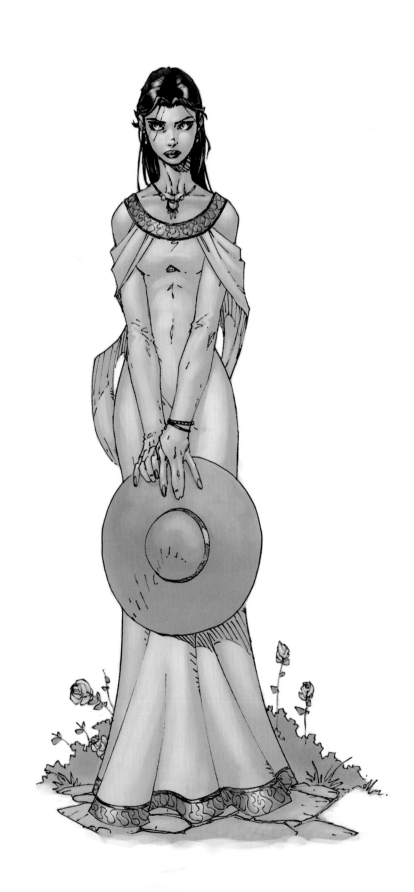

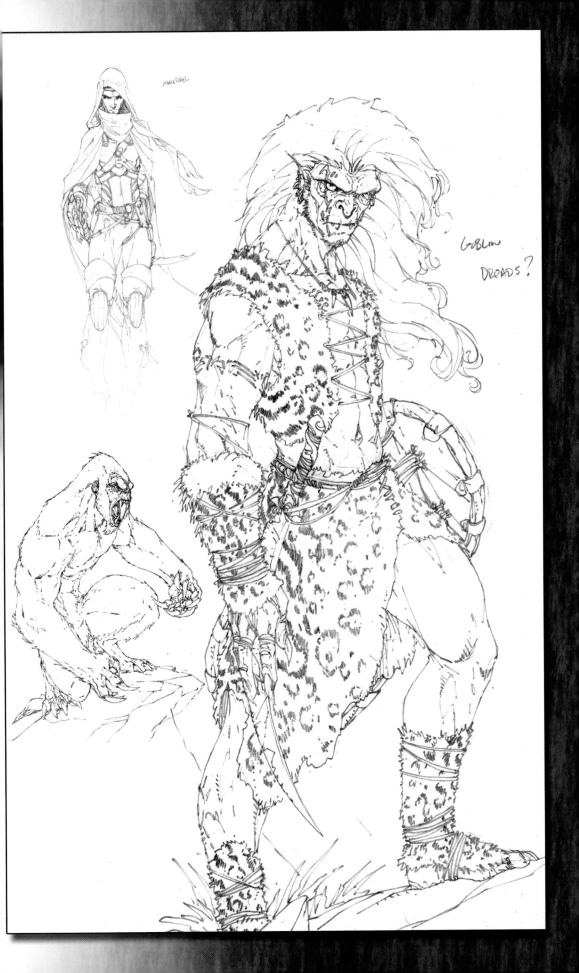

MARCSILVESTRI

GOBLIN
DROADS?

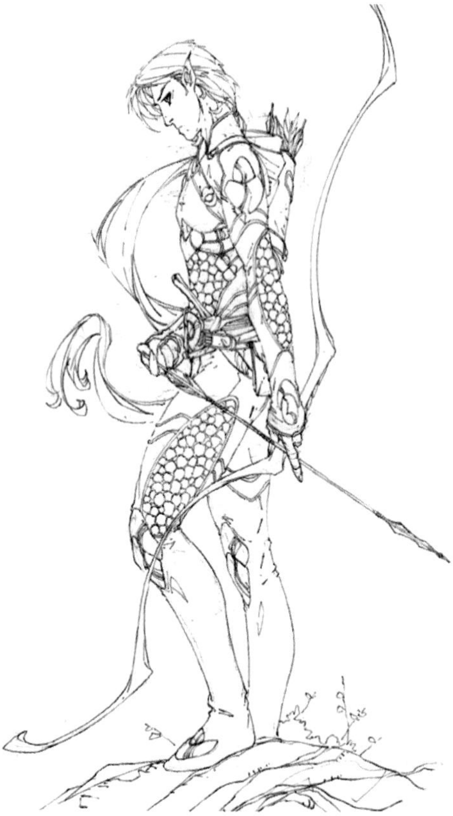

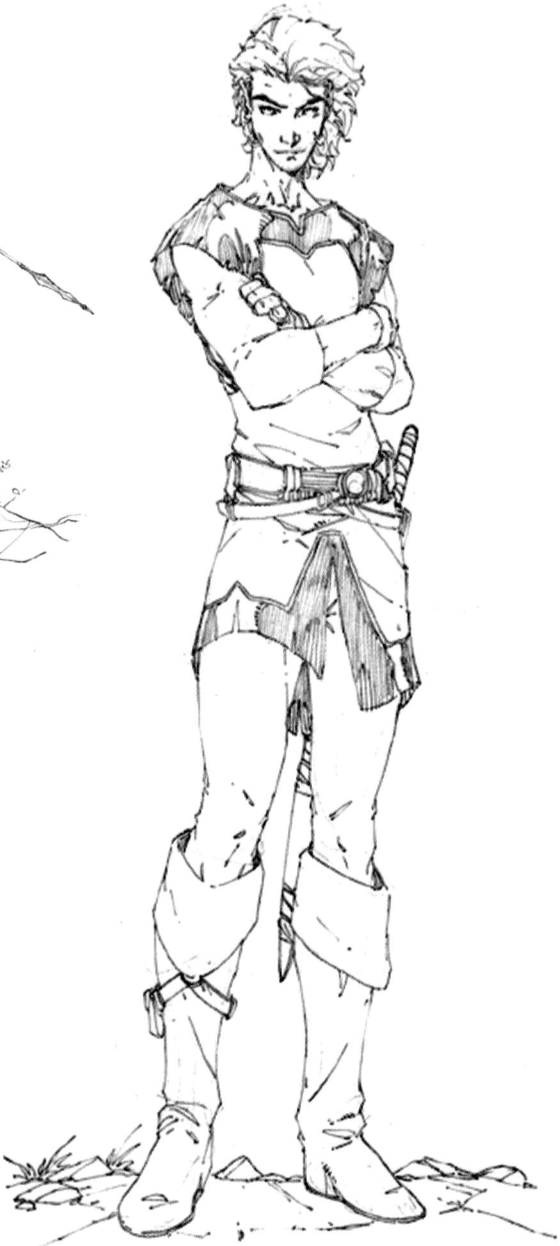

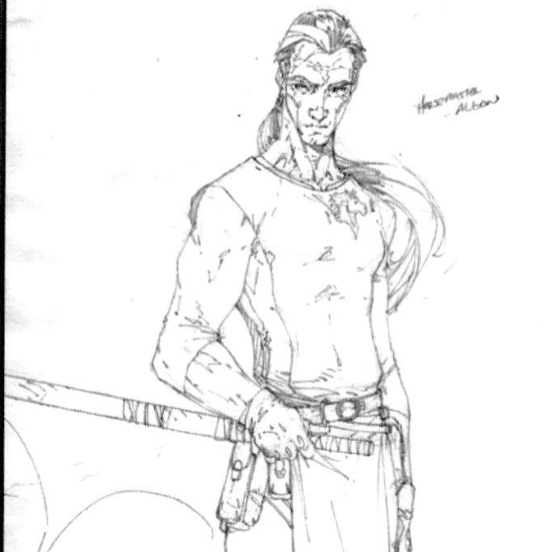

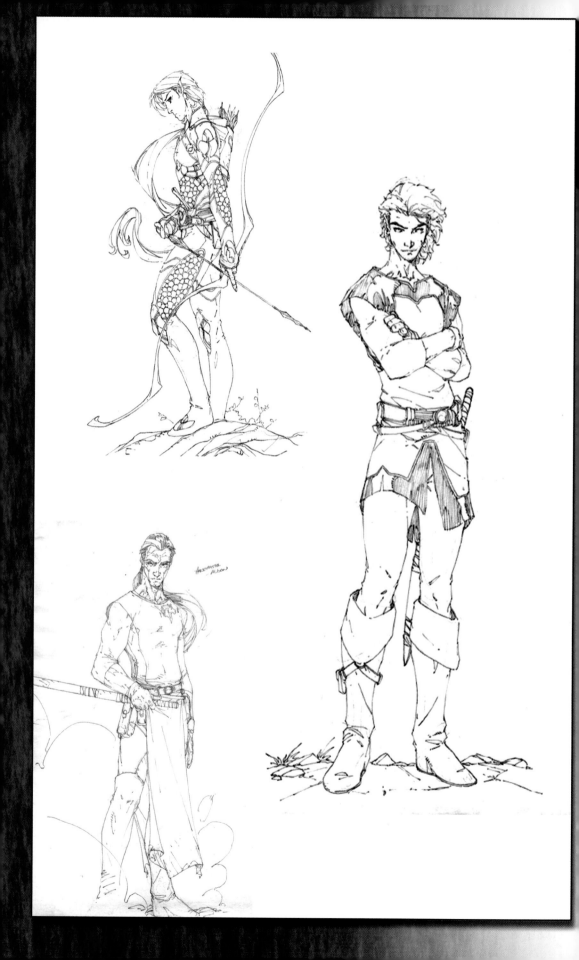

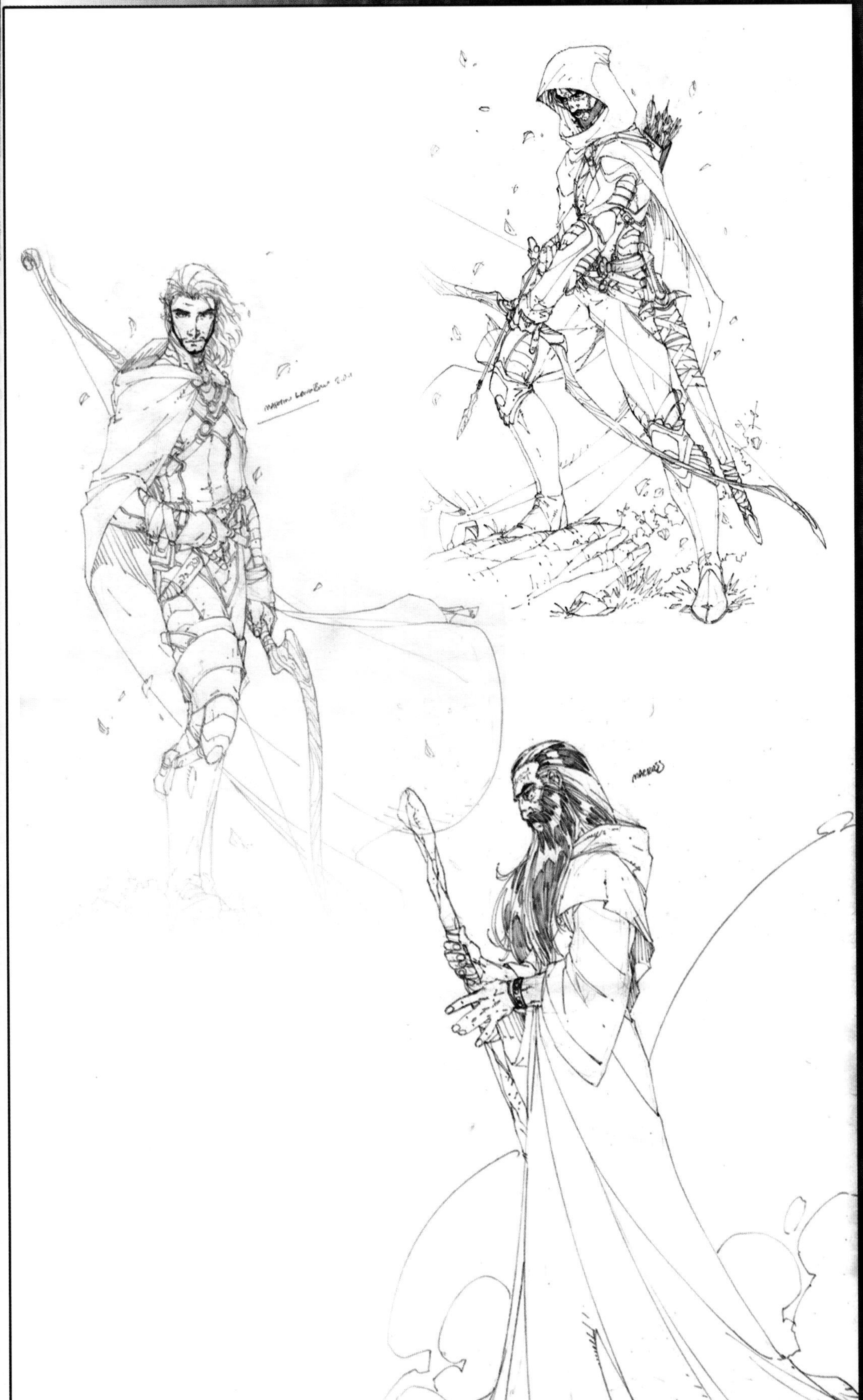

Dear Fans,

"This book represents so many things to me.
On a professional level, it is
my first collaboration with penciler extrodinaire,
Brett Booth. I was honored to have been
approached to work with Brett, and as you will see on
the following pages, he presents a daunting task for
any inker. One that feverently hope I passed.

On a personal level, my work on this project
came at a time of great pain, loss, and heartache in
my life. Many times, it was all I could do to continue
to press ahead, despite what was occurring in
my life. Working on this title also reaffirmed
something of great value to me: never allow anyone
or anything to cause you to give up your dreams. Ever.

So, with that, I would like to dedicate this book to
La Detrick Danielle Smith: thank you for reminding
me that, although some things fail despite your best efforts
others remain everlasting."

" To my son, Cameron Xavier Underwood: Love is eternal
and forgiving. My love for art is only exceeded by my
undying love for you."

Le Beau L. Underwood, Inker

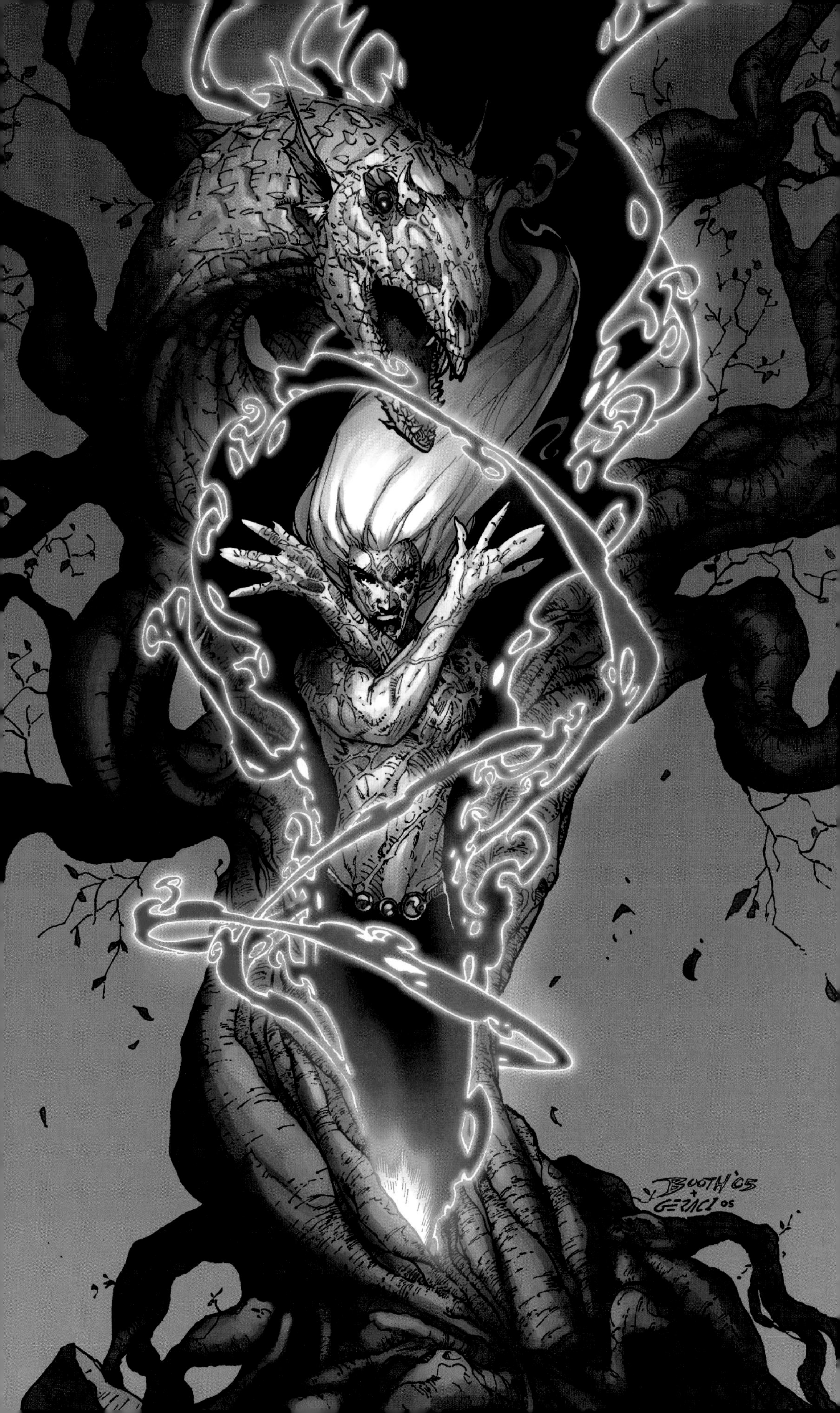
BOOTH '05
+
GERACI 05

The
Burning Man

Tad Williams
WRITER

Sean J Jordan
ADAPTATION

Brett Booth
ARTWORK

Bobby Souza and Manny Clark
ARTWORK (Pages 127-137)

Arif Priyanto
& Sakti
COLORS (Imaginary Friends Studios)

Simon Bowland
LETTERING (LithiumPro Design)

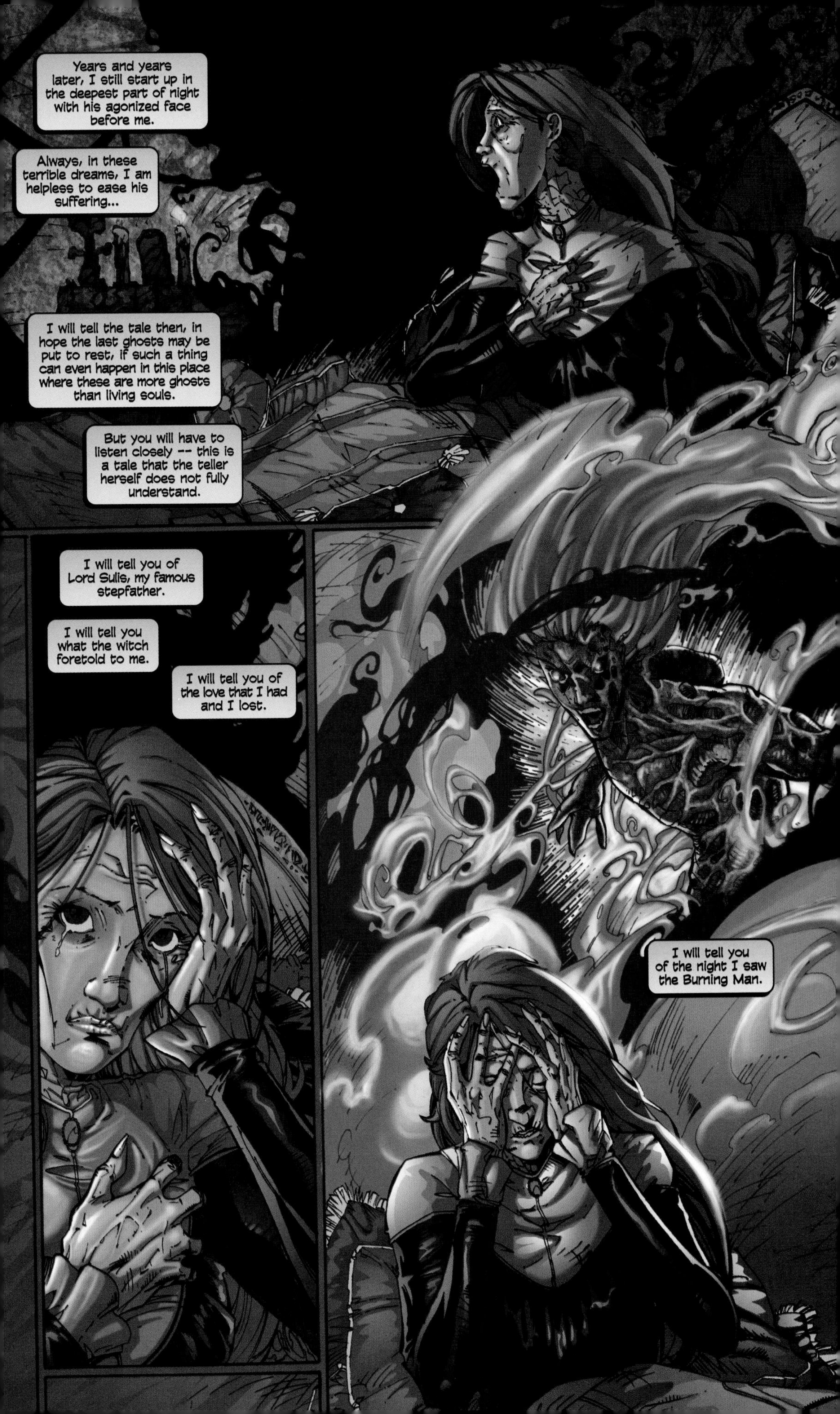
Years and years later, I still start up in the deepest part of night with his agonized face before me.
Always, in these terrible dreams, I am helpless to ease his suffering...
I will tell the tale then, in hope the last ghosts may be put to rest, if such a thing can even happen in this place where these are more ghosts than living souls.
But you will have to listen closely -- this is a tale that the teller herself does not fully understand.
I will tell you of Lord Sulis, my famous stepfather.
I will tell you what the witch foretold to me.
I will tell you of the love that I had and I lost.
I will tell you of the night I saw the Burning Man.

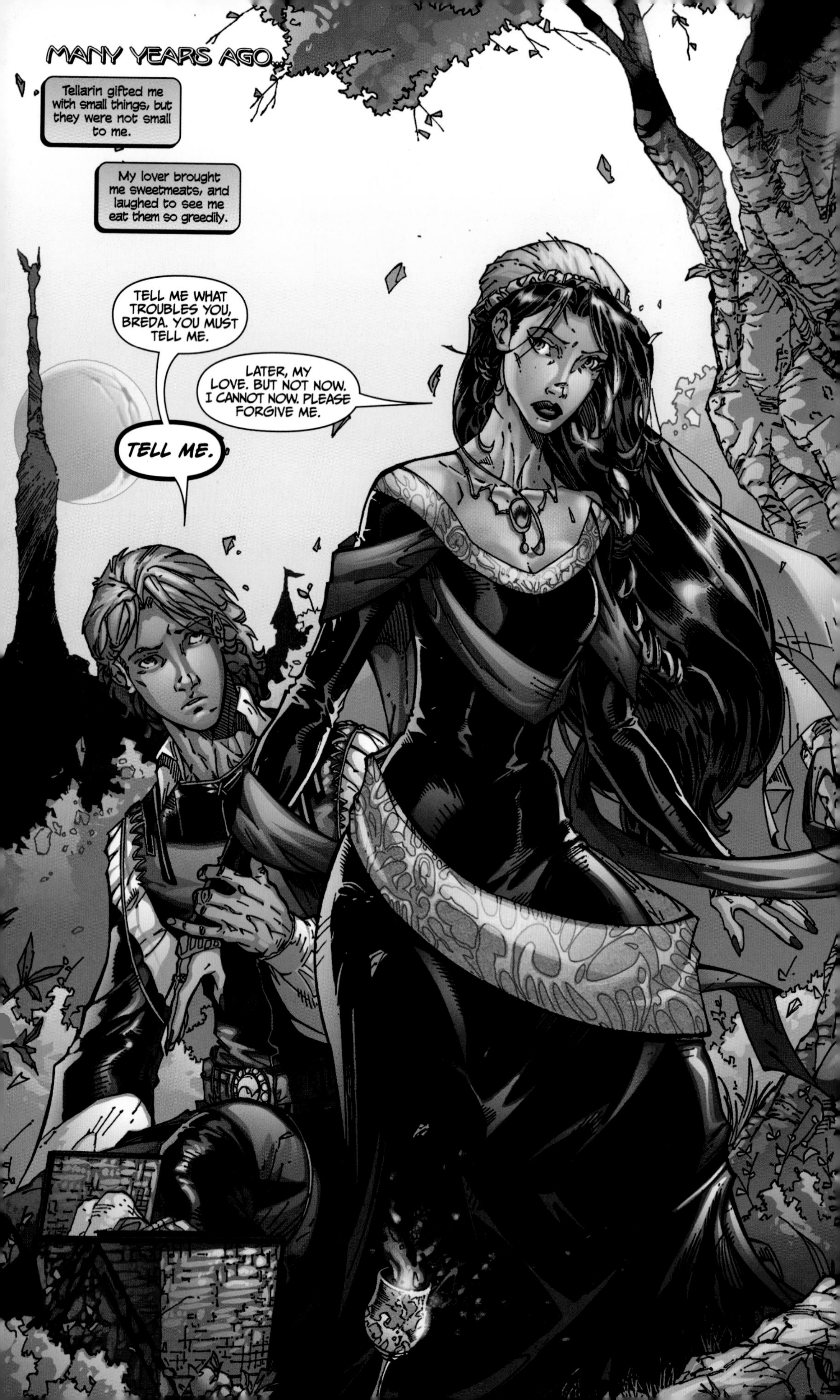
MANY YEARS AGO...
Tellarin gifted me with small things, but they were not small to me.
My lover brought me sweetmeats, and laughed to see me eat them so greedily.
TELL ME WHAT TROUBLES YOU, BREDA. YOU MUST TELL ME.
LATER, MY LOVE. BUT NOT NOW. I CANNOT NOW. PLEASE FORGIVE ME.
TELL ME.

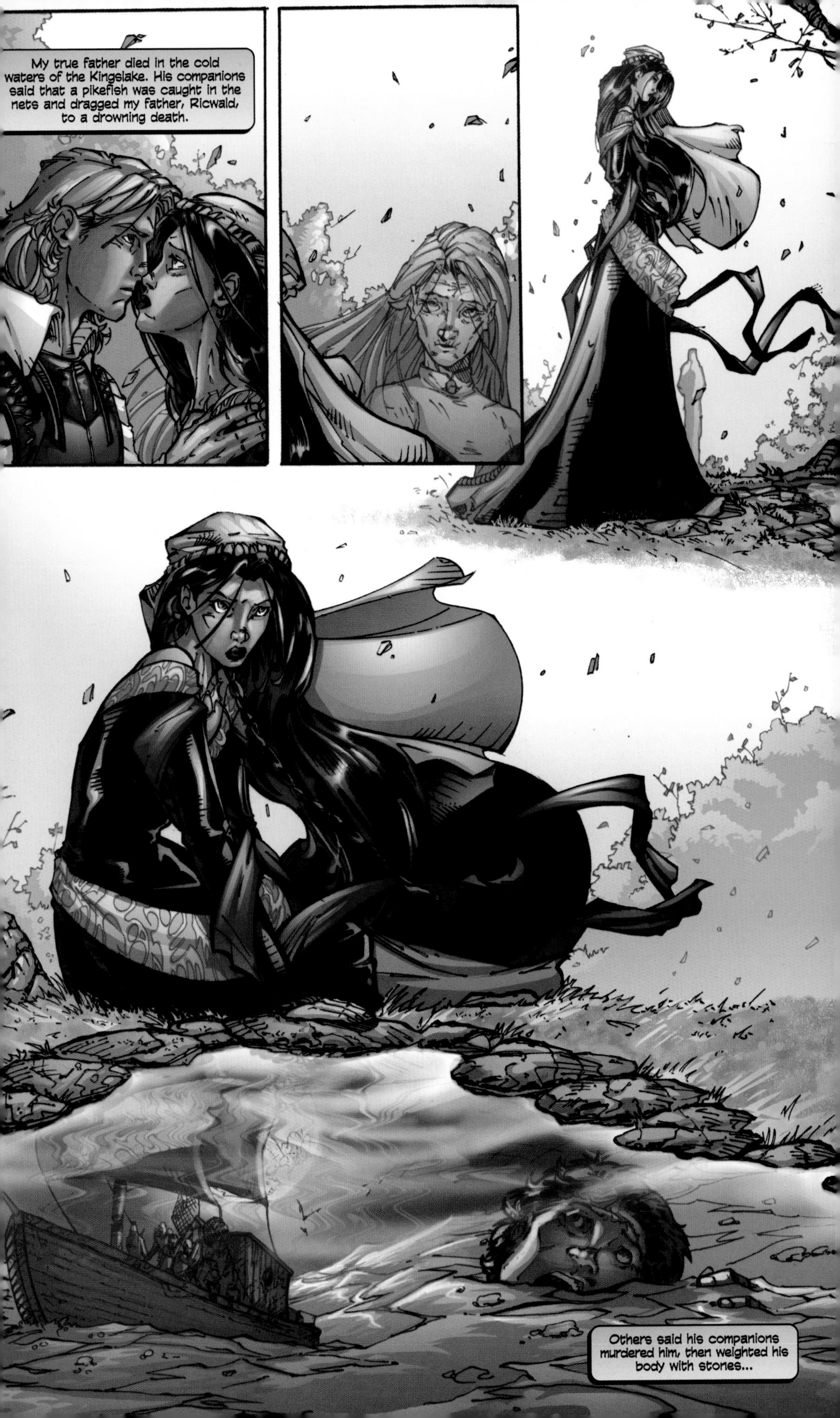
My true father died in the cold waters of the Kingslake. His companions said that a pikefish was caught in the nets and dragged my father, Ricwald, to a drowning death.
Others said his companions murdered him, then weighted his body with stones...

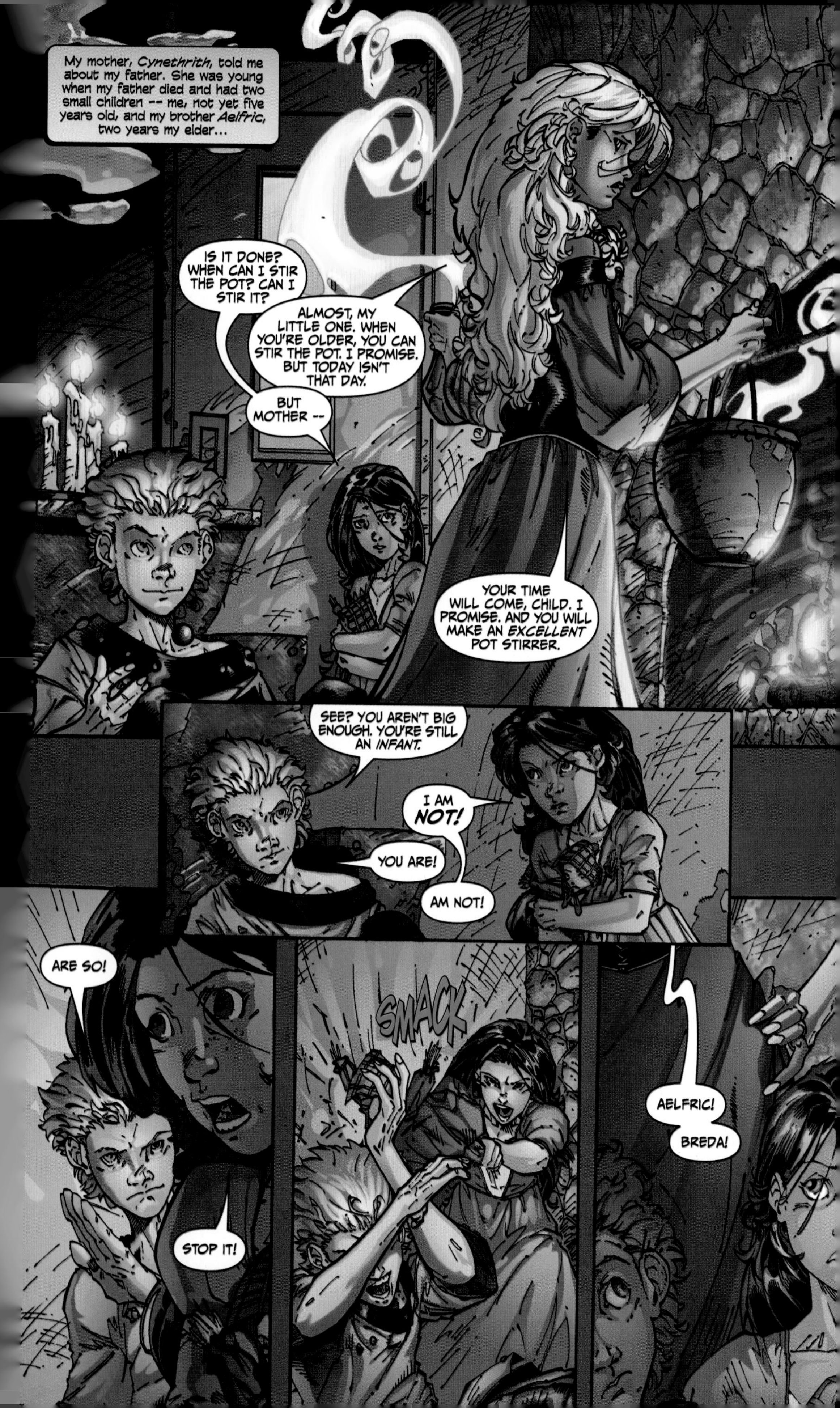

My mother, *Cynethrith*, told me about my father. She was young when my father died and had two small children -- me, not yet five years old, and my brother *Aelfric*, two years my elder...
IS IT DONE? WHEN CAN I STIR THE POT? CAN I STIR IT?
ALMOST, MY LITTLE ONE. WHEN YOU'RE OLDER, YOU CAN STIR THE POT. I PROMISE. BUT TODAY ISN'T THAT DAY.
BUT MOTHER --
YOUR TIME WILL COME, CHILD. I PROMISE. AND YOU WILL MAKE AN *EXCELLENT* POT STIRRER.
SEE? YOU AREN'T BIG ENOUGH. YOU'RE STILL AN *INFANT.*
I AM **NOT!**
YOU ARE!
AM NOT!
ARE SO!
STOP IT!
SMACK
AELFRIC!
BREDA!

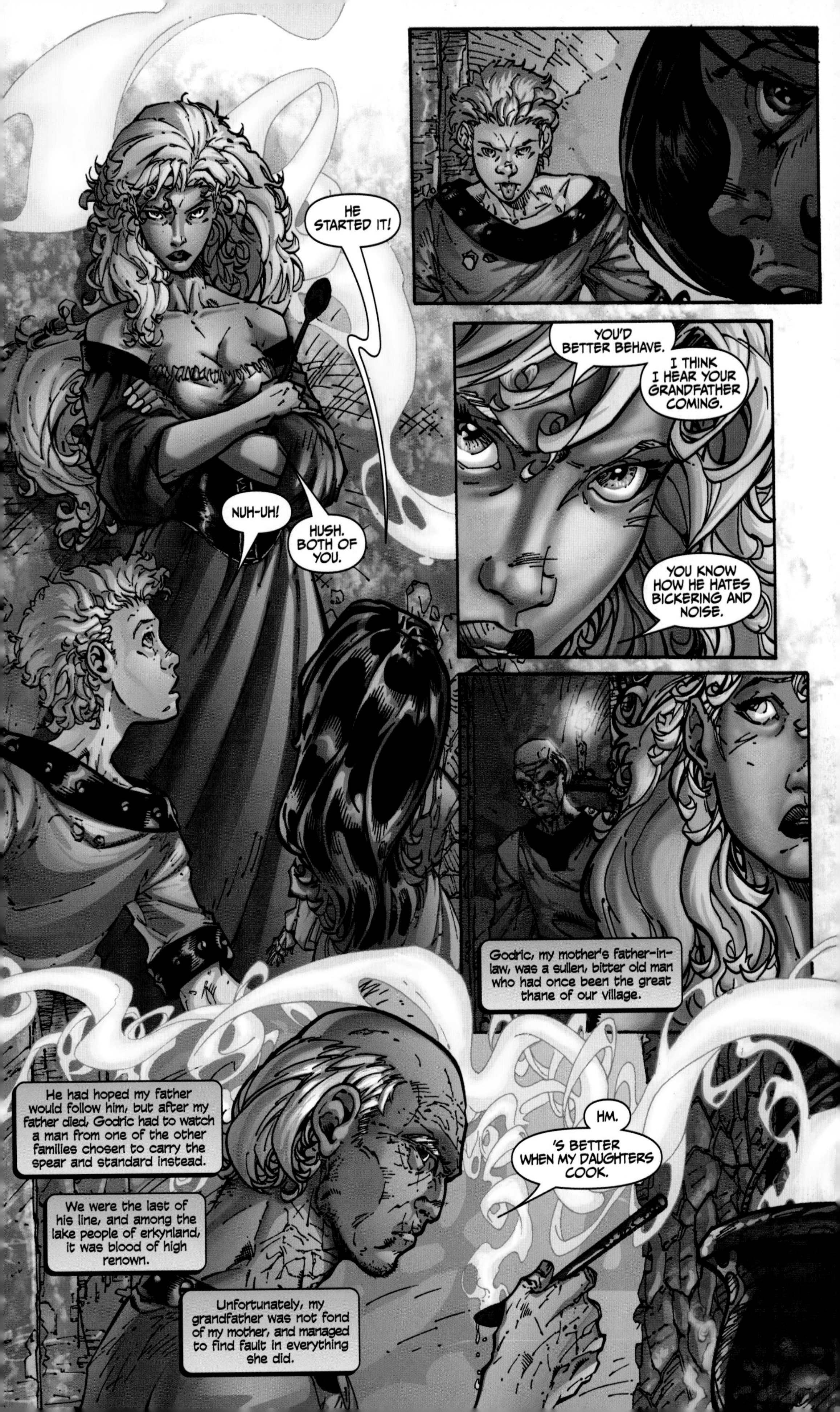
HE STARTED IT!
NUH-UH!
HUSH. BOTH OF YOU.
YOU'D BETTER BEHAVE.
I THINK I HEAR YOUR GRANDFATHER COMING.
YOU KNOW HOW HE HATES BICKERING AND NOISE.
Godric, my mother's father-in-law, was a sullen, bitter old man who had once been the great thane of our village.
He had hoped my father would follow him, but after my father died, Godric had to watch a man from one of the other families chosen to carry the spear and standard instead.
We were the last of his line, and among the lake people of erkynland, it was blood of high renown.
Unfortunately, my grandfather was not fond of my mother, and managed to find fault in everything she did.
HM.
'S BETTER WHEN MY DAUGHTERS COOK.

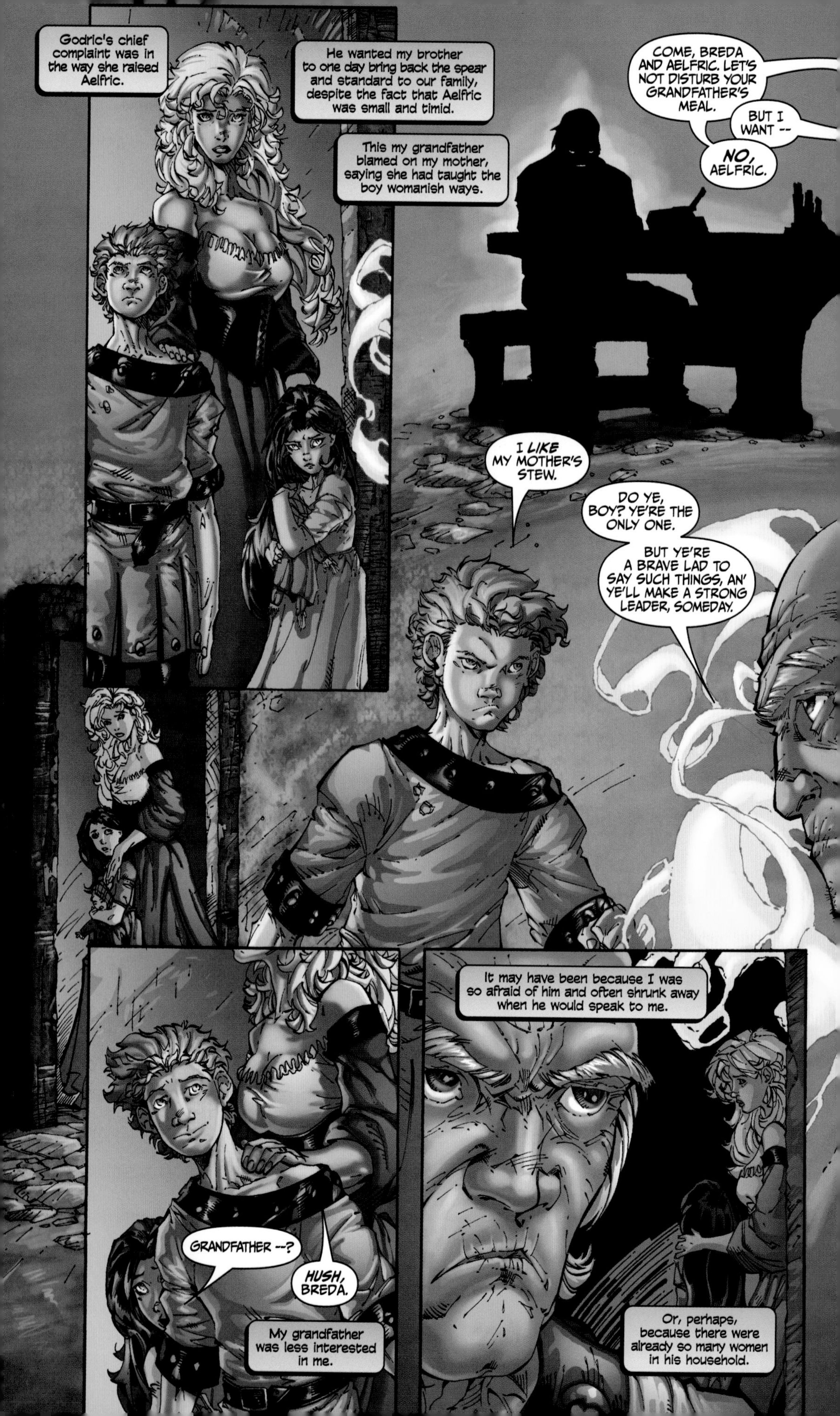
Godric's chief complaint was in the way she raised Aelfric.
He wanted my brother to one day bring back the spear and standard to our family, despite the fact that Aelfric was small and timid.
This my grandfather blamed on my mother, saying she had taught the boy womanish ways.
COME, BREDA AND AELFRIC. LET'S NOT DISTURB YOUR GRANDFATHER'S MEAL.
BUT I WANT --
NO, AELFRIC.
I LIKE MY MOTHER'S STEW.
DO YE, BOY? YE'RE THE ONLY ONE.
BUT YE'RE A BRAVE LAD TO SAY SUCH THINGS, AN' YE'LL MAKE A STRONG LEADER, SOMEDAY.
GRANDFATHER --?
HUSH, BREDA.
My grandfather was less interested in me.
It may have been because I was so afraid of him and often shrunk away when he would speak to me.
Or, perhaps, because there were already so many women in his household.

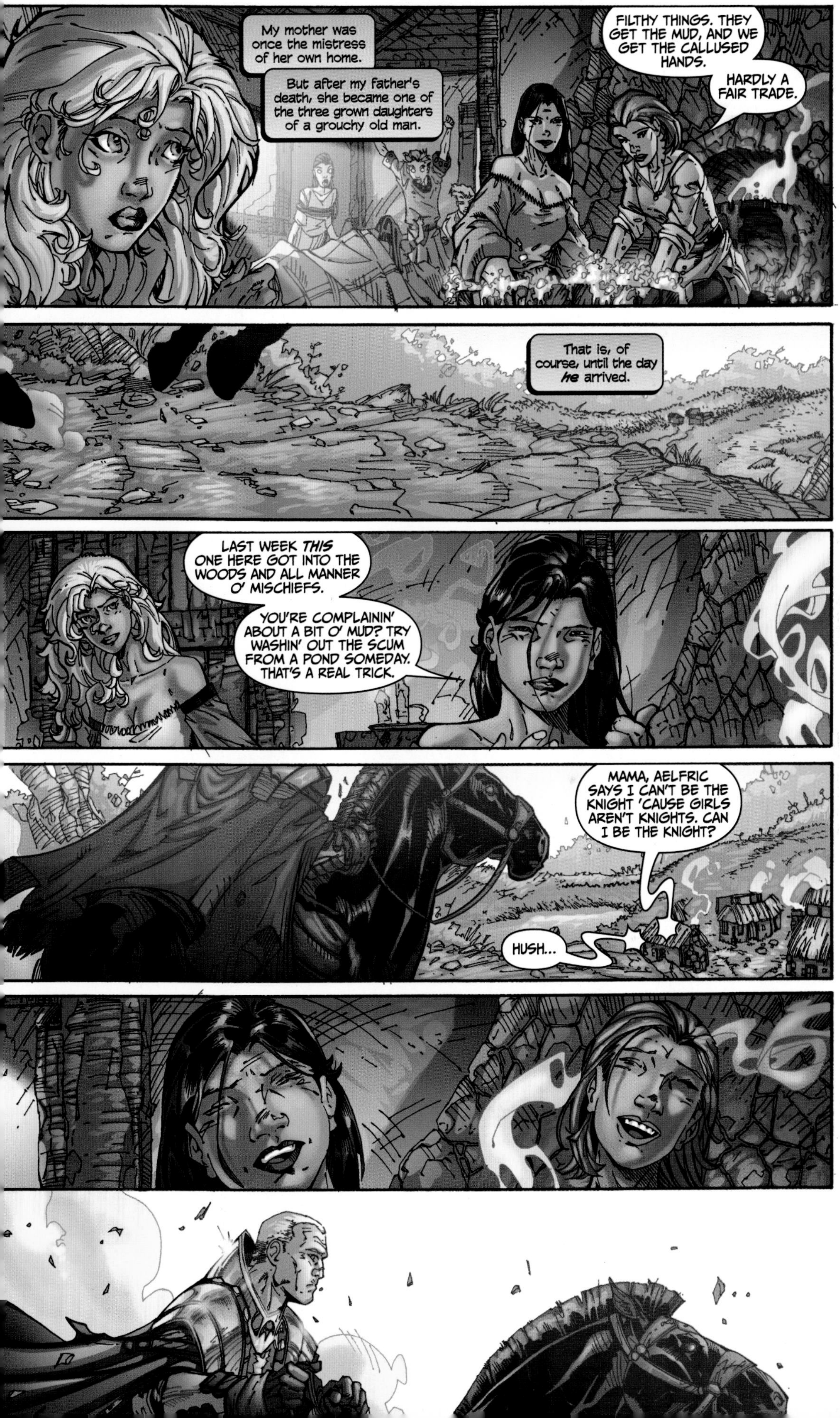

My mother was once the mistress of her own home.
But after my father's death, she became one of the three grown daughters of a grouchy old man.
FILTHY THINGS. THEY GET THE MUD, AND WE GET THE CALLUSED HANDS.
HARDLY A FAIR TRADE.
That is, of course, until the day *he* arrived.
LAST WEEK *THIS* ONE HERE GOT INTO THE WOODS AND ALL MANNER O' MISCHIEFS.
YOU'RE COMPLAININ' ABOUT A BIT O' MUD? TRY WASHIN' OUT THE SCUM FROM A POND SOMEDAY. THAT'S A REAL TRICK.
MAMA, AELFRIC SAYS I CAN'T BE THE KNIGHT 'CAUSE GIRLS AREN'T KNIGHTS. CAN I BE THE KNIGHT?
HUSH...

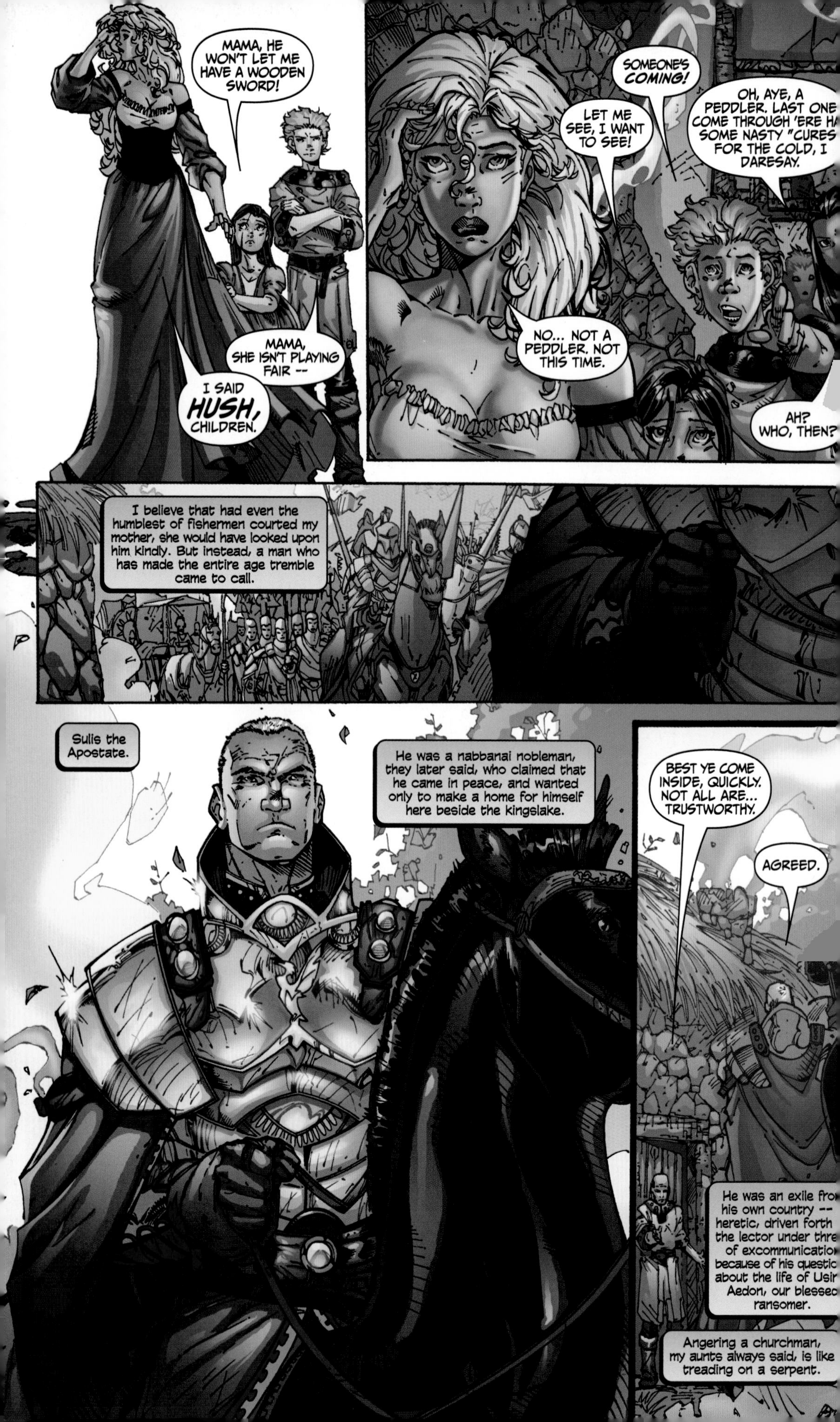
MAMA, HE WON'T LET ME HAVE A WOODEN SWORD!
MAMA, SHE ISN'T PLAYING FAIR --
I SAID HUSH, CHILDREN.
LET ME SEE, I WANT TO SEE!
SOMEONE'S COMING!
OH, AYE, A PEDDLER. LAST ONE COME THROUGH 'ERE HA SOME NASTY "CURES FOR THE COLD, I DARESAY.
NO... NOT A PEDDLER. NOT THIS TIME.
AH? WHO, THEN?
I believe that had even the humblest of fishermen courted my mother, she would have looked upon him kindly. But instead, a man who has made the entire age tremble came to call.
Sulis the Apostate.
He was a nabbanai nobleman, they later said, who claimed that he came in peace, and wanted only to make a home for himself here beside the kingslake.
BEST YE COME INSIDE, QUICKLY. NOT ALL ARE... TRUSTWORTHY.
AGREED.
He was an exile fro his own country -- heretic, driven forth the lector under thre of excommunicatio because of his questic about the life of Usir Aedon, our blessec ransomer.
Angering a churchman, my aunts always said, is like treading on a serpent.

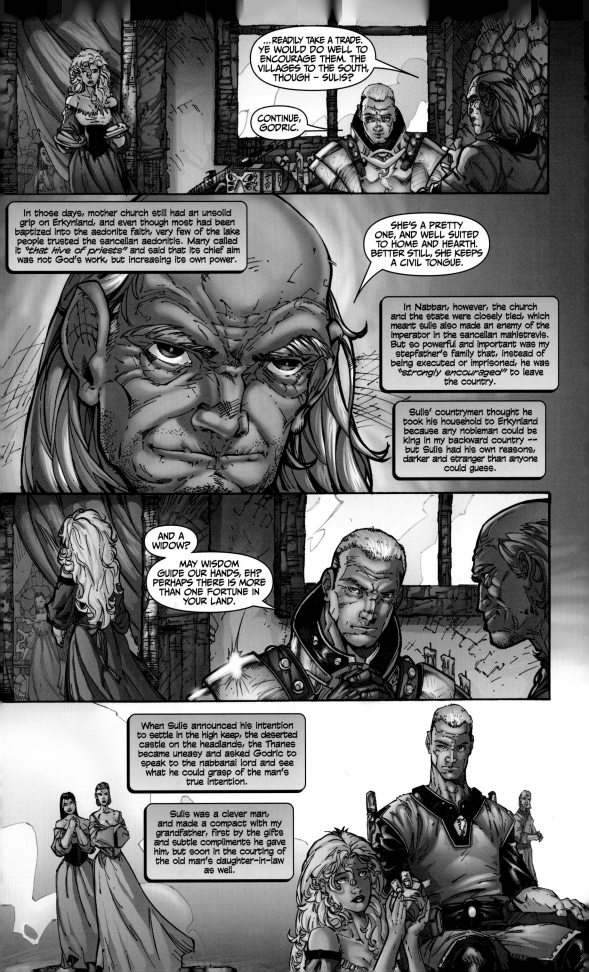

...READILY TAKE A TRADE. YE WOULD DO WELL TO ENCOURAGE THEM. THE VILLAGES TO THE SOUTH, THOUGH – SULIS?

CONTINUE, GODRIC.

In those days, mother church still had an unsolid grip on Erkynland, and even though most had been baptized into the aedonite faith, very few of the lake people trusted the sancellan aedonitis. Many called it *"that hive of priests"* and said that its chief aim was not God's work, but increasing its own power.

SHE'S A PRETTY ONE, AND WELL SUITED TO HOME AND HEARTH. BETTER STILL, SHE KEEPS A CIVIL TONGUE.

In Nabban, however, the church and the state were closely tied, which meant sulis also made an enemy of the imperator in the sancellan mahistrevis. But so powerful and important was my stepfather's family that, instead of being executed or imprisoned, he was *"strongly encouraged"* to leave the country.

Sulis' countrymen thought he took his household to Erkynland because any nobleman could be king in my backward country -- but Sulis had his own reasons, darker and stranger than anyone could guess.

AND A WIDOW?

MAY WISDOM GUIDE OUR HANDS, EH? PERHAPS THERE IS MORE THAN ONE FORTUNE IN YOUR LAND.

When Sulis announced his intention to settle in the high keep, the deserted castle on the headlands, the Thanes became uneasy and asked Godric to speak to the nabbanai lord and see what he could grasp of the man's true intention.

Sulis was a clever man, and made a compact with my grandfather, first by the gifts and subtle compliments he gave him, but soon in the courting of the old man's daughter-in-law as well.

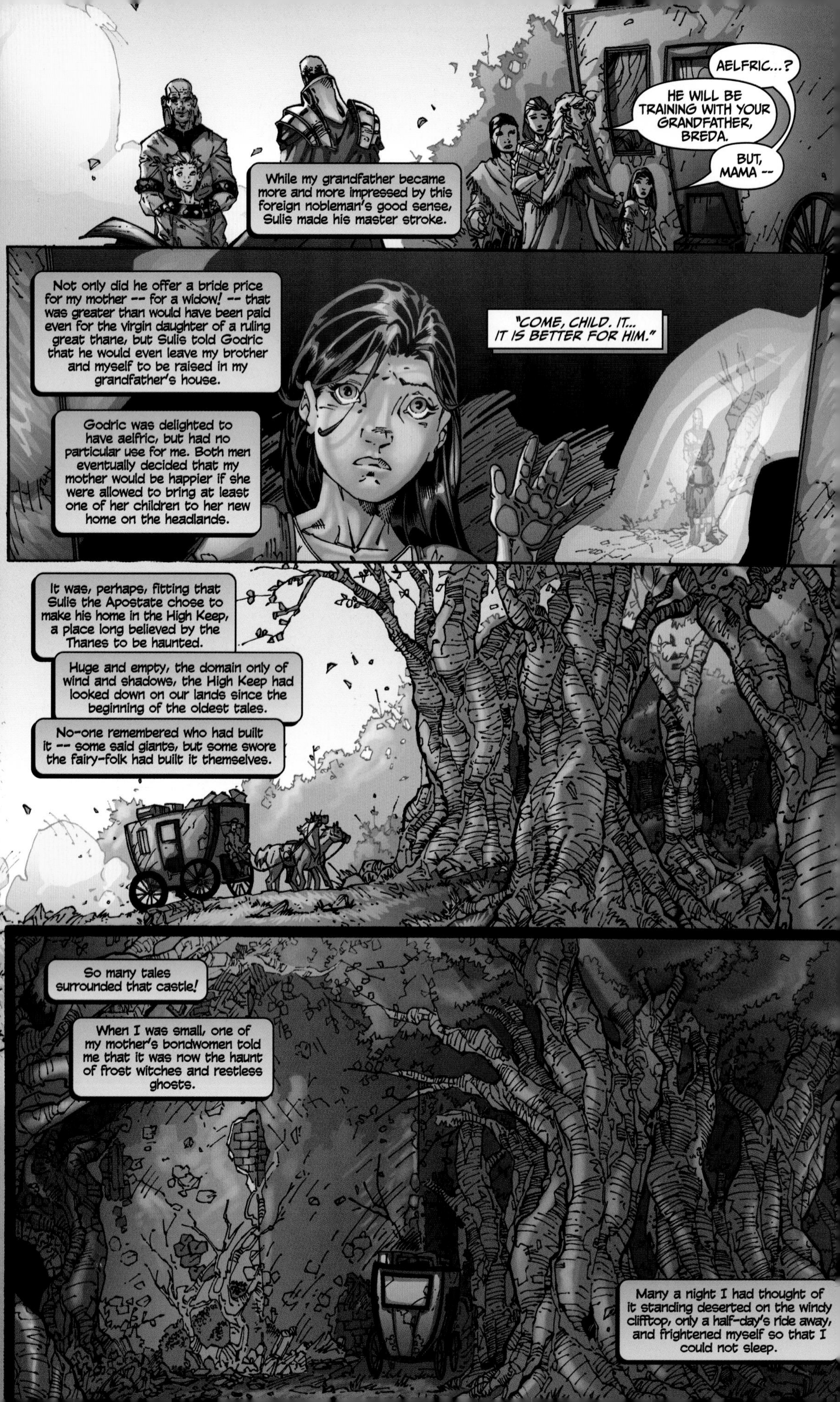
While my grandfather became more and more impressed by this foreign nobleman's good sense, Sulis made his master stroke.
AELFRIC...?
HE WILL BE TRAINING WITH YOUR GRANDFATHER, BREDA.
BUT, MAMA --
Not only did he offer a bride price for my mother -- for a widow! -- that was greater than would have been paid even for the virgin daughter of a ruling great thane, but Sulis told Godric that he would even leave my brother and myself to be raised in my grandfather's house.
"COME, CHILD. IT... IT IS BETTER FOR HIM."
Godric was delighted to have aelfric, but had no particular use for me. Both men eventually decided that my mother would be happier if she were allowed to bring at least one of her children to her new home on the headlands.
It was, perhaps, fitting that Sulis the Apostate chose to make his home in the High Keep, a place long believed by the Thanes to be haunted.
Huge and empty, the domain only of wind and shadows, the High Keep had looked down on our lands since the beginning of the oldest tales.
No-one remembered who had built it -- some said giants, but some swore the fairy-folk had built it themselves.
So many tales surrounded that castle!
When I was small, one of my mother's bondwomen told me that it was now the haunt of frost witches and restless ghosts.
Many a night I had thought of it standing deserted on the windy clifftop, only a half-day's ride away, and frightened myself so that I could not sleep.

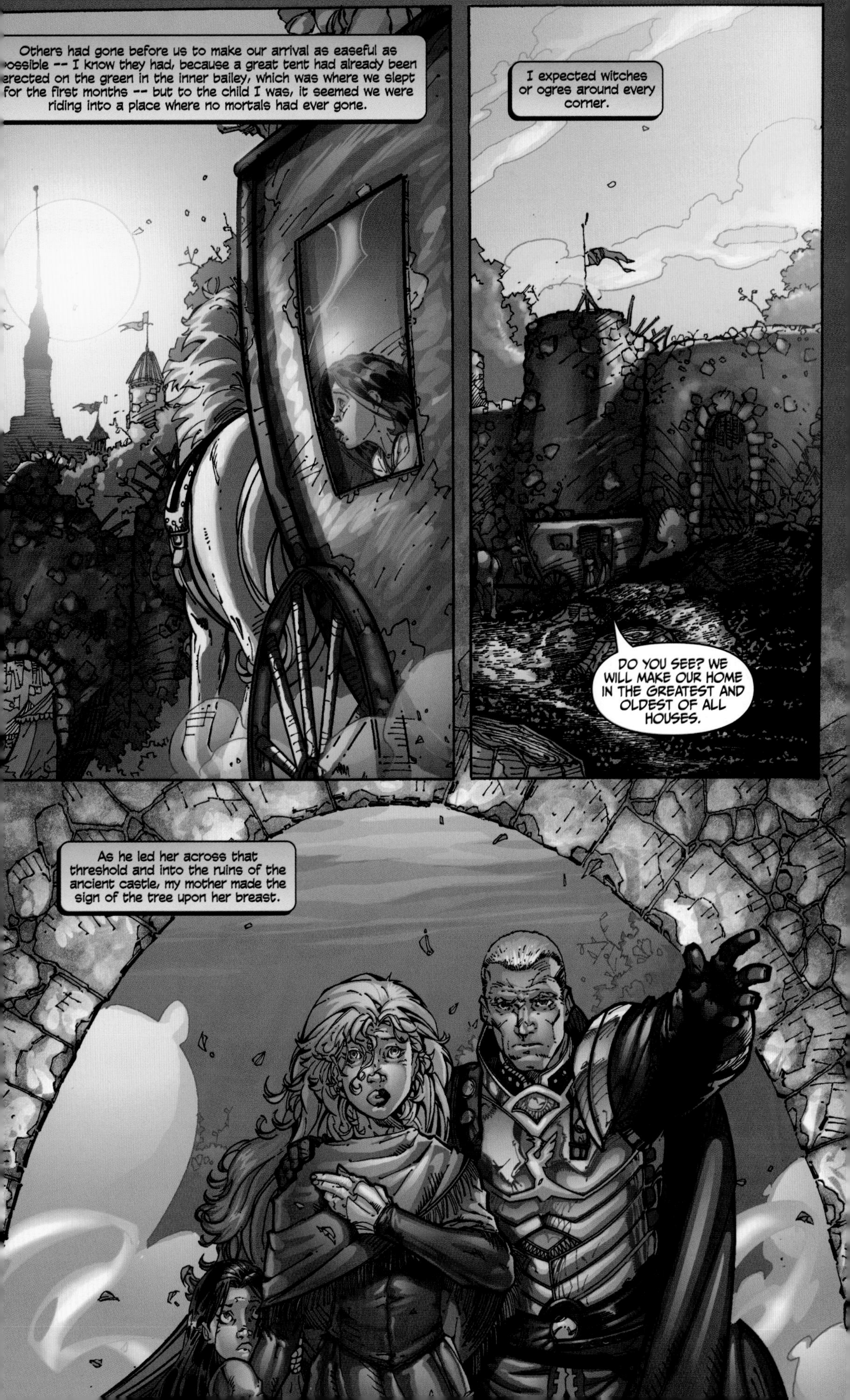

Others had gone before us to make our arrival as easeful as possible -- I know they had, because a great tent had already been erected on the green in the inner bailey, which was where we slept for the first months -- but to the child I was, it seemed we were riding into a place where no mortals had ever gone.
I expected witches or ogres around every corner.
DO YOU SEE? WE WILL MAKE OUR HOME IN THE GREATEST AND OLDEST OF ALL HOUSES.
As he led her across that threshold and into the ruins of the ancient castle, my mother made the sign of the tree upon her breast.

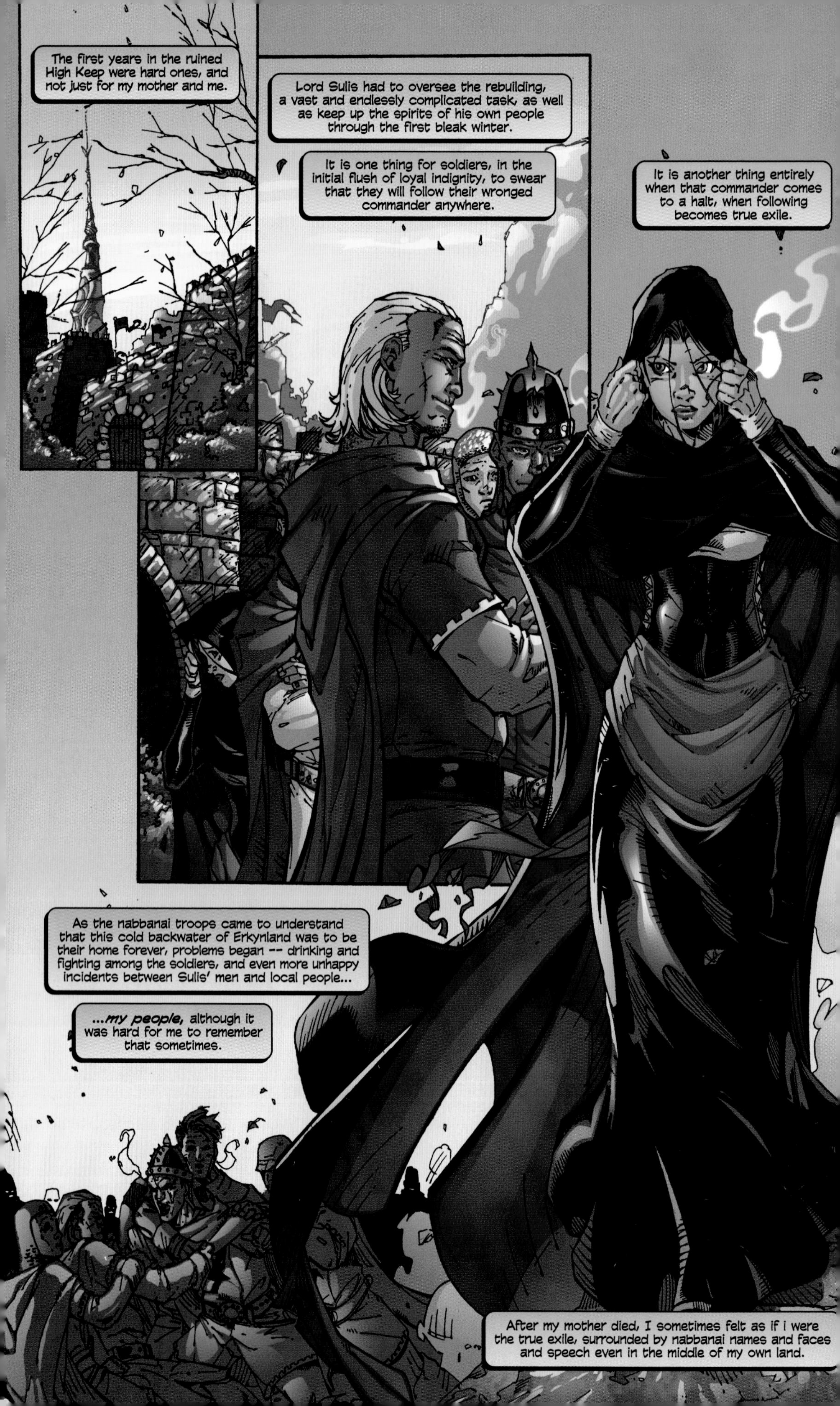

The first years in the ruined High Keep were hard ones, and not just for my mother and me.
Lord Sulis had to oversee the rebuilding, a vast and endlessly complicated task, as well as keep up the spirits of his own people through the first bleak winter.
It is one thing for soldiers, in the initial flush of loyal indignity, to swear that they will follow their wronged commander anywhere.
It is another thing entirely when that commander comes to a halt, when following becomes true exile.
As the nabbanai troops came to understand that this cold backwater of Erkynland was to be their home forever, problems began -- drinking and fighting among the soldiers, and even more unhappy incidents between Sulis' men and local people...
...*my people,* although it was hard for me to remember that sometimes.
After my mother died, I sometimes felt as if i were the true exile, surrounded by nabbanai names and faces and speech even in the middle of my own land.

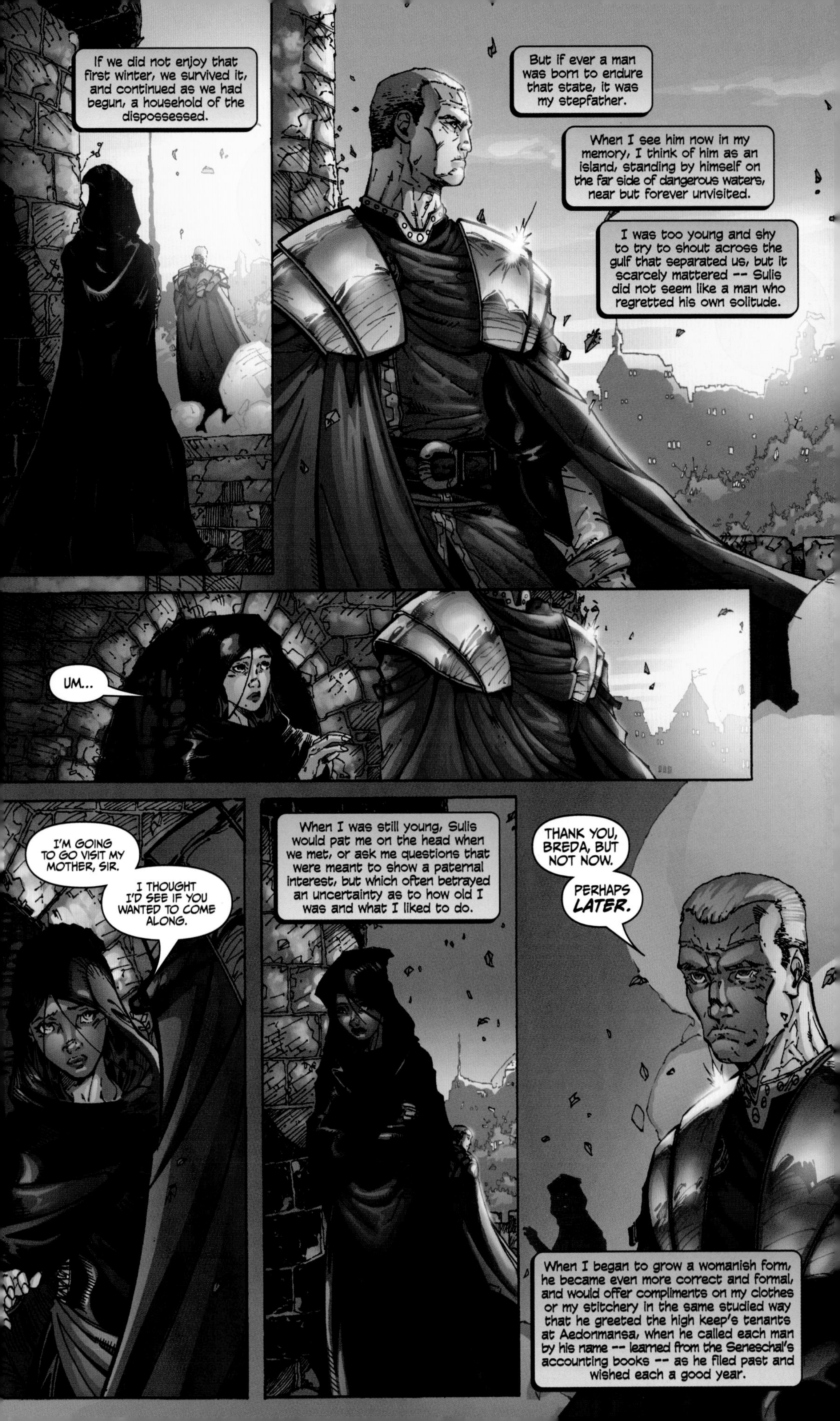

If we did not enjoy that first winter, we survived it, and continued as we had begun, a household of the dispossessed.
But if ever a man was born to endure that state, it was my stepfather.
When I see him now in my memory, I think of him as an island, standing by himself on the far side of dangerous waters, near but forever unvisited.
I was too young and shy to try to shout across the gulf that separated us, but it scarcely mattered -- Sulis did not seem like a man who regretted his own solitude.
UM...
I'M GOING TO GO VISIT MY MOTHER, SIR.
I THOUGHT I'D SEE IF YOU WANTED TO COME ALONG.
When I was still young, Sulis would pat me on the head when we met, or ask me questions that were meant to show a paternal interest, but which often betrayed an uncertainty as to how old I was and what I liked to do.
THANK YOU, BREDA, BUT NOT NOW.
PERHAPS *LATER.*
When I began to grow a womanish form, he became even more correct and formal, and would offer compliments on my clothes or my stitchery in the same studied way that he greeted the high keep's tenants at Aedonmansa, when he called each man by his name -- learned from the Seneschal's accounting books -- as he filed past and wished each a good year.

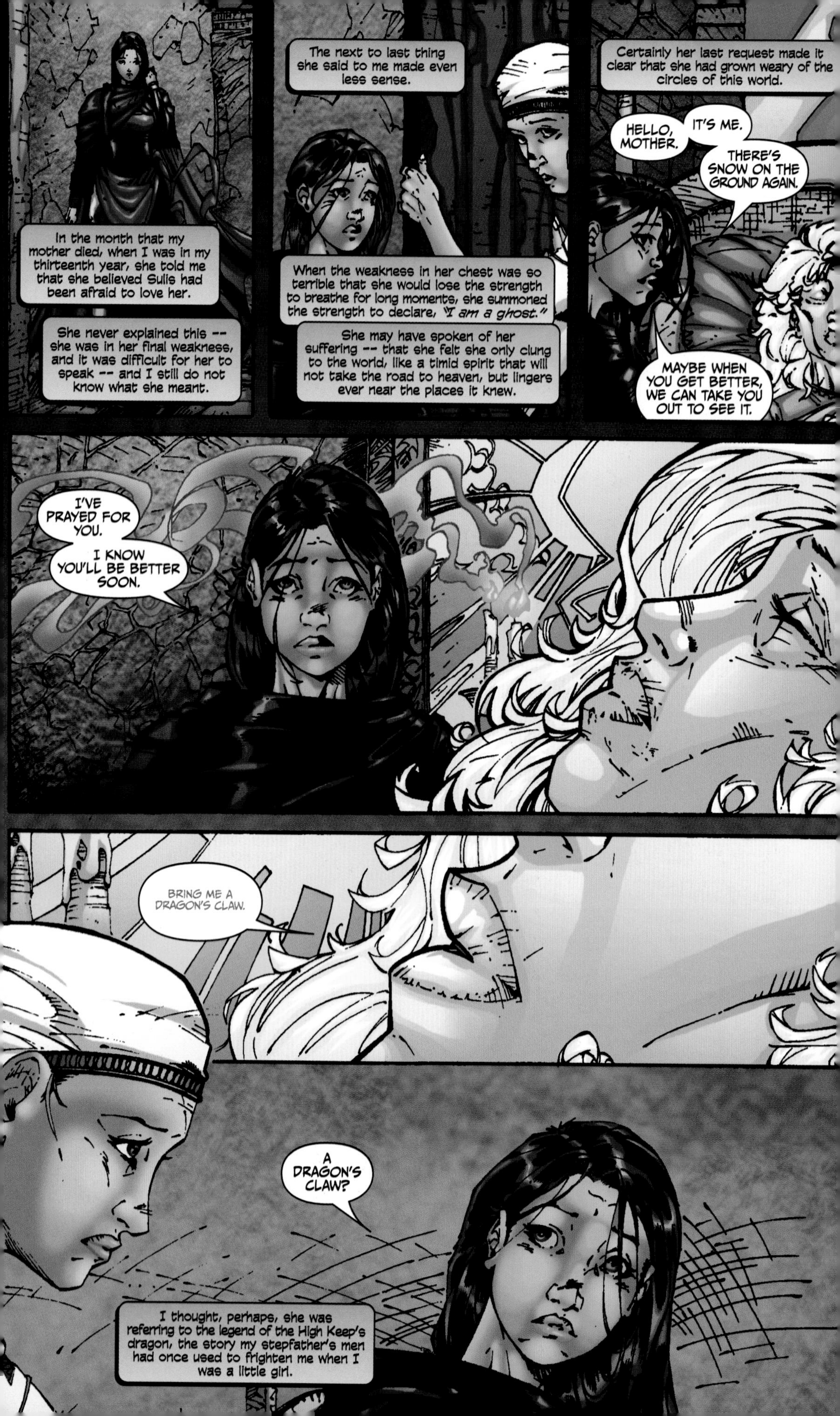
In the month that my mother died, when I was in my thirteenth year, she told me that she believed Sulis had been afraid to love her.
She never explained this -- she was in her final weakness, and it was difficult for her to speak -- and I still do not know what she meant.
The next to last thing she said to me made even less sense.
When the weakness in her chest was so terrible that she would lose the strength to breathe for long moments, she summoned the strength to declare, "I am a ghost."
She may have spoken of her suffering -- that she felt she only clung to the world, like a timid spirit that will not take the road to heaven, but lingers ever near the places it knew.
Certainly her last request made it clear that she had grown weary of the circles of this world.
HELLO, MOTHER.
IT'S ME.
THERE'S SNOW ON THE GROUND AGAIN.
MAYBE WHEN YOU GET BETTER, WE CAN TAKE YOU OUT TO SEE IT.
I'VE PRAYED FOR YOU.
I KNOW YOU'LL BE BETTER SOON.
BRING ME A DRAGON'S CLAW.
A DRAGON'S CLAW?
I thought, perhaps, she was referring to the legend of the High Keep's dragon, the story my stepfather's men had once used to frighten me when I was a little girl.

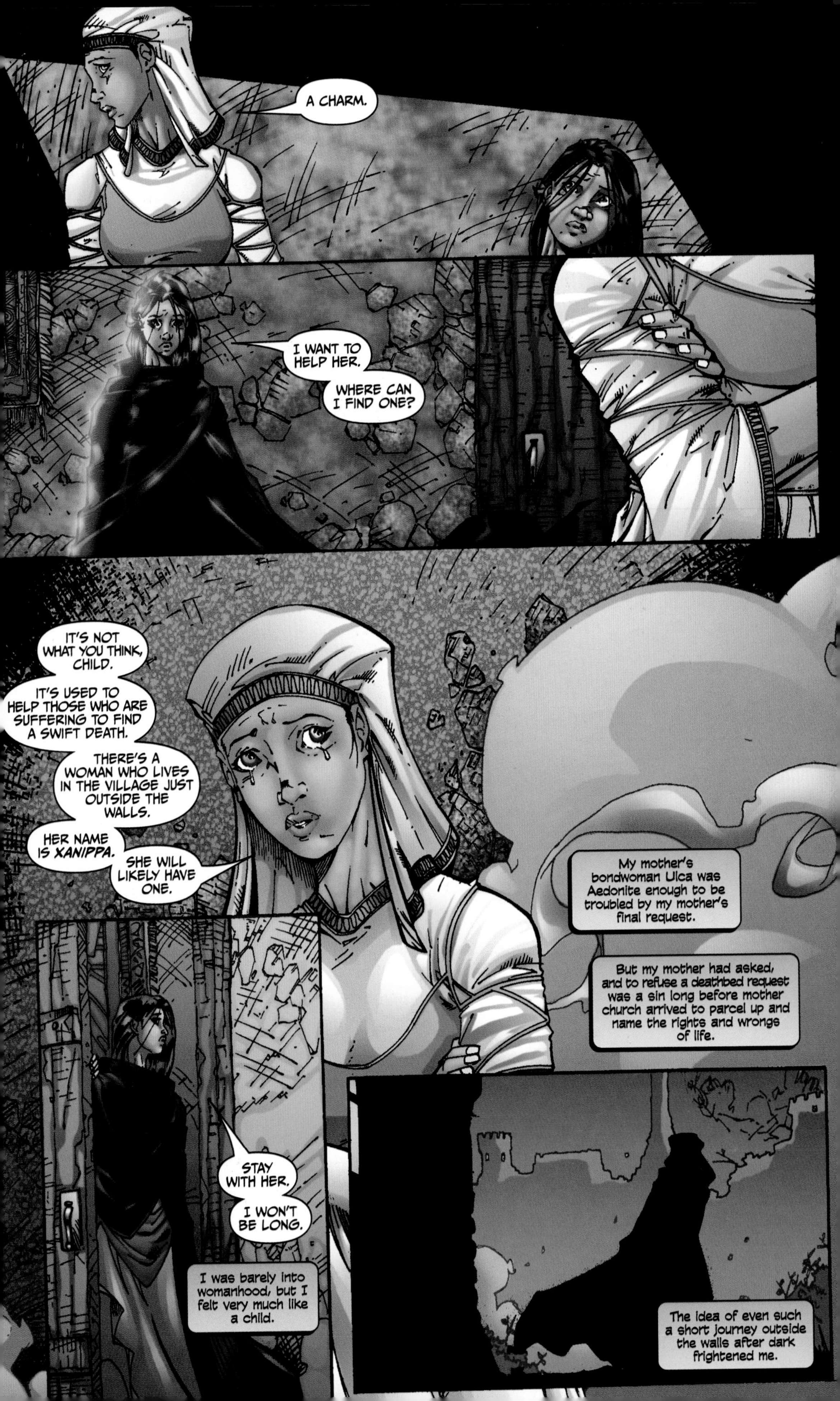

A CHARM.
I WANT TO HELP HER.
WHERE CAN I FIND ONE?
IT'S NOT WHAT YOU THINK, CHILD.
IT'S USED TO HELP THOSE WHO ARE SUFFERING TO FIND A SWIFT DEATH.
THERE'S A WOMAN WHO LIVES IN THE VILLAGE JUST OUTSIDE THE WALLS.
HER NAME IS XANIPPA.
SHE WILL LIKELY HAVE ONE.
My mother's bondwoman Ulca was Aedonite enough to be troubled by my mother's final request.
But my mother had asked, and to refuse a deathbed request was a sin long before mother church arrived to parcel up and name the rights and wrongs of life.
STAY WITH HER.
I WON'T BE LONG.
I was barely into womanhood, but I felt very much like a child.
The idea of even such a short journey outside the walls after dark frightened me.

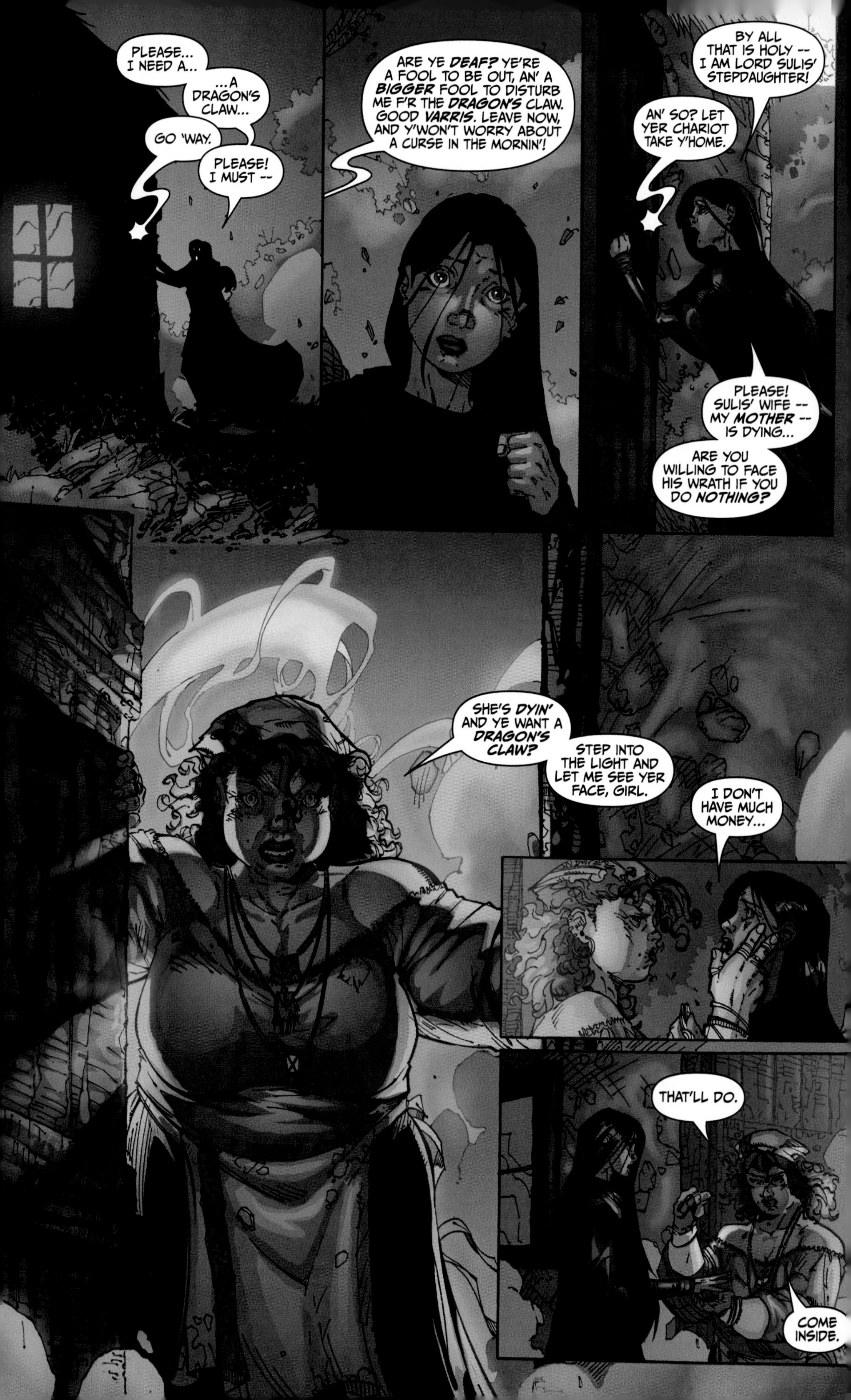
PLEASE... I NEED A...
...A DRAGON'S CLAW...
GO 'WAY.
PLEASE! I MUST --
ARE YE DEAF? YE'RE A FOOL TO BE OUT, AN' A BIGGER FOOL TO DISTURB ME F'R THE DRAGON'S CLAW. GOOD VARRIS. LEAVE NOW, AND Y'WON'T WORRY ABOUT A CURSE IN THE MORNIN'!
BY ALL THAT IS HOLY -- I AM LORD SULIS' STEPDAUGHTER!
AN' SO? LET YER CHARIOT TAKE Y'HOME.
PLEASE! SULIS' WIFE -- MY MOTHER -- IS DYING...
ARE YOU WILLING TO FACE HIS WRATH IF YOU DO NOTHING?
SHE'S DYIN' AND YE WANT A DRAGON'S CLAW?
STEP INTO THE LIGHT AND LET ME SEE YER FACE, GIRL.
I DON'T HAVE MUCH MONEY...
THAT'LL DO.
COME INSIDE.

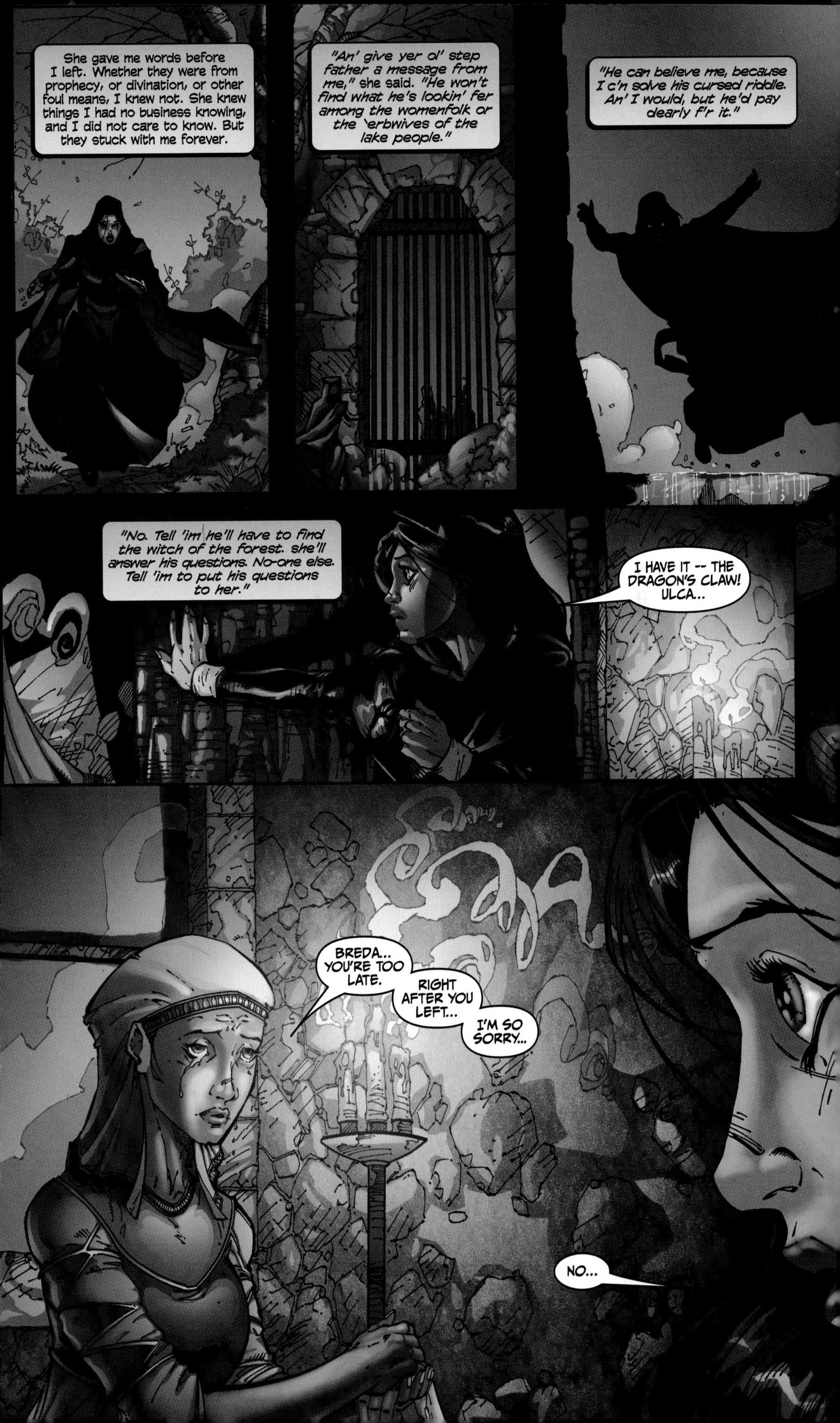
She gave me words before I left. Whether they were from prophecy, or divination, or other foul means, I knew not. She knew things I had no business knowing, and I did not care to know. But they stuck with me forever.
"An' give yer ol' step father a message from me," she said. "He won't find what he's lookin' fer among the womenfolk or the `erbwives of the lake people."
"He can believe me, because I c'n solve his cursed riddle. An' I would, but he'd pay dearly f'r it."
"No. Tell 'im he'll have to find the witch of the forest. she'll answer his questions. No-one else. Tell 'im to put his questions to her."
I HAVE IT -- THE DRAGON'S CLAW! ULCA...
BREDA... YOU'RE TOO LATE.
RIGHT AFTER YOU LEFT...
I'M SO SORRY...
NO...

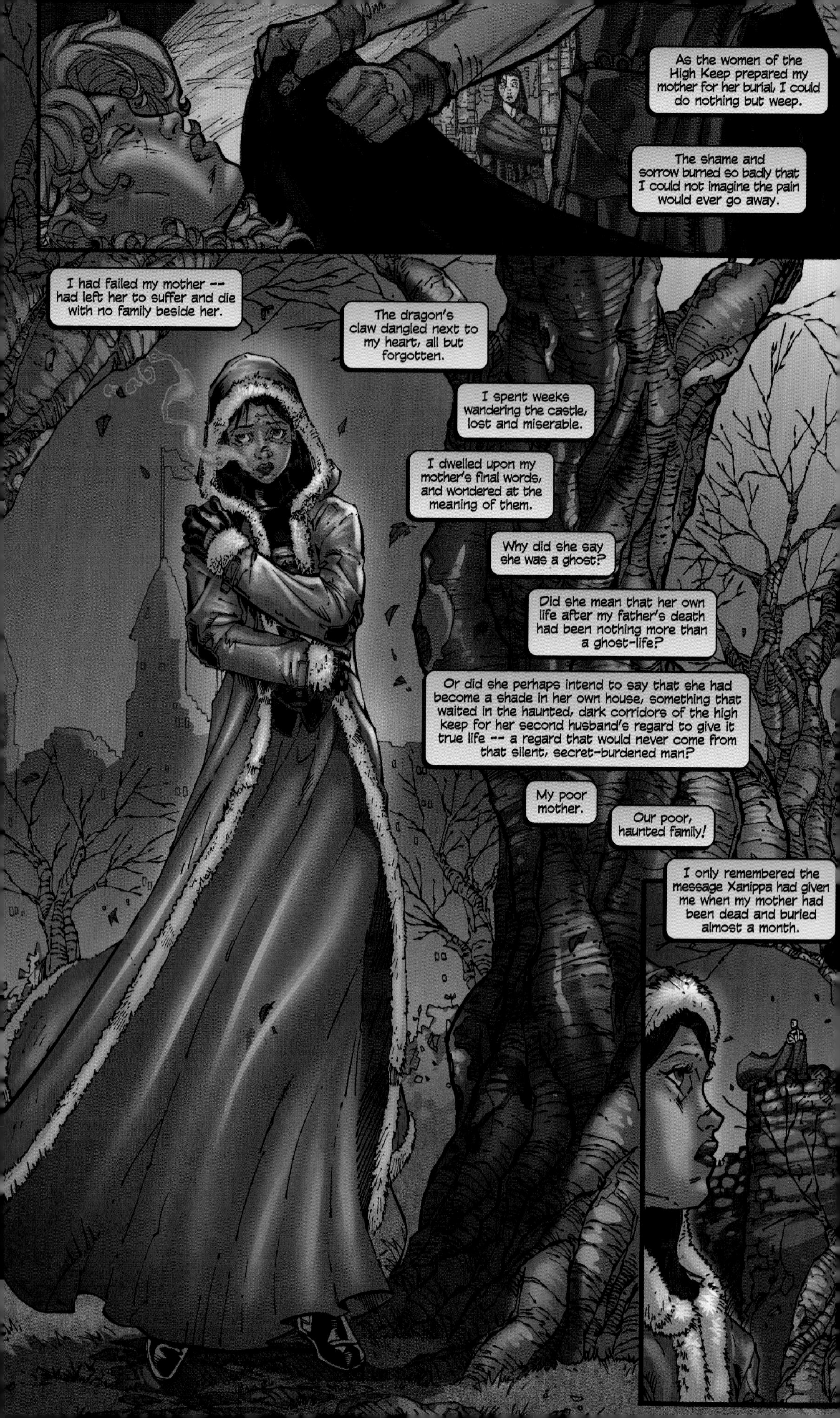

As the women of the High Keep prepared my mother for her burial, I could do nothing but weep.
The shame and sorrow burned so badly that I could not imagine the pain would ever go away.
I had failed my mother -- had left her to suffer and die with no family beside her.
The dragon's claw dangled next to my heart, all but forgotten.
I spent weeks wandering the castle, lost and miserable.
I dwelled upon my mother's final words, and wondered at the meaning of them.
Why did she say she was a ghost?
Did she mean that her own life after my father's death had been nothing more than a ghost-life?
Or did she perhaps intend to say that she had become a shade in her own house, something that waited in the haunted, dark corridors of the high keep for her second husband's regard to give it true life -- a regard that would never come from that silent, secret-burdened man?
My poor mother.
Our poor, haunted family!
I only remembered the message Xanippa had given me when my mother had been dead and buried almost a month.

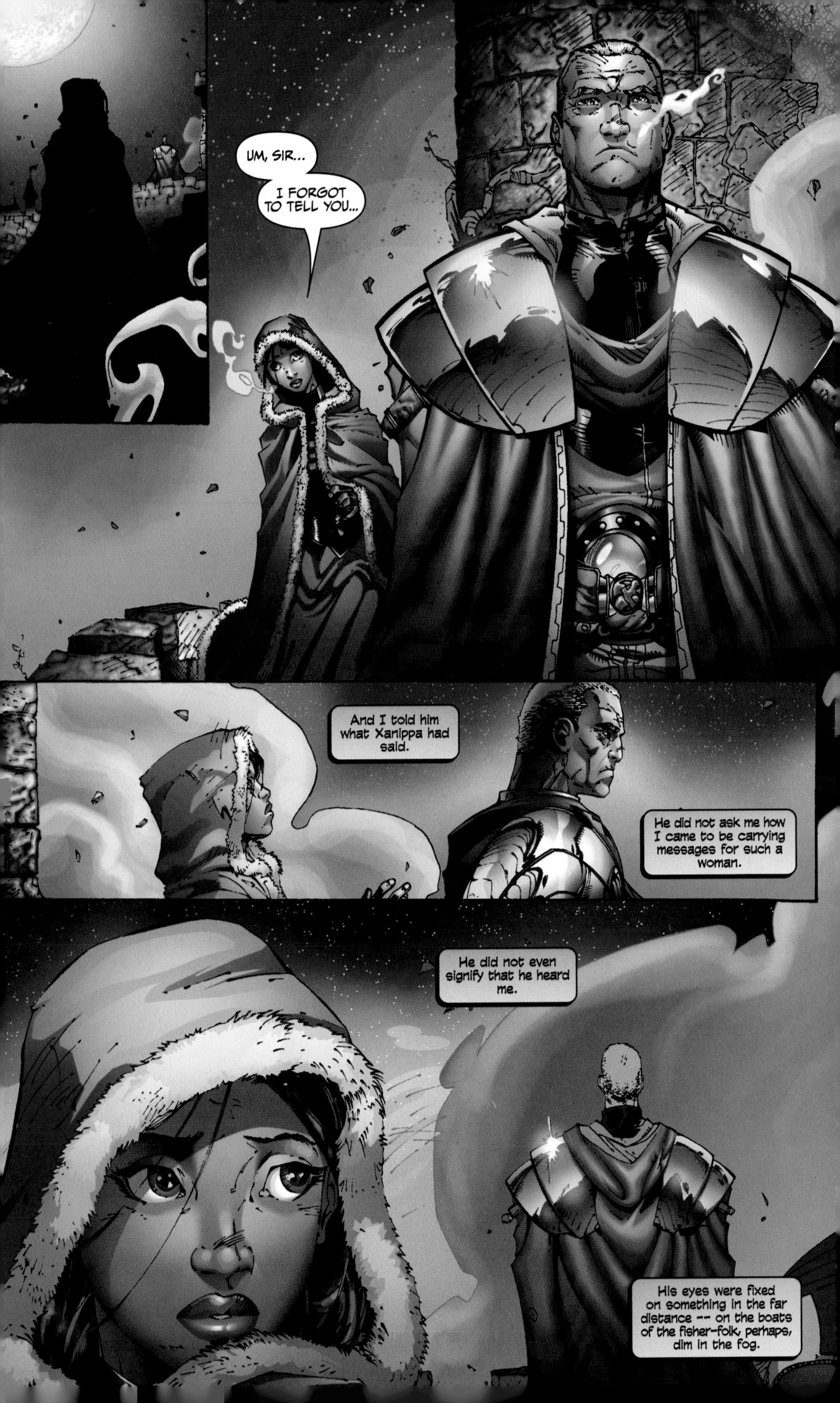
UM, SIR...
I FORGOT TO TELL YOU...
And I told him what Xanippa had said.
He did not ask me how I came to be carrying messages for such a woman.
He did not even signify that he heard me.
His eyes were fixed on something in the far distance -- on the boats of the fisher-folk, perhaps, dim in the fog.

Sulis grew even more distant in the year after my mother died, as though losing her had finally untethered him from the daily tasks he had always performed in such a stiff, practiced way.

He spent less and less time seeing to the matters of government, and instead sat reading for hours -- sometimes all through the night, wrapped in heavy robes against the midnight chill, burning candles faster than the rest of the house put together.

It was in the season after my mother's death, on a day when I found him reading in the gray light that steamed into the throne room, that Lord Sulis truly looked at me for the one and only time I remember.

When I shyly asked what he was doing, he allowed me to examine the book in his lap.

A beautiful illustrated history of the prophet Varris with the heron of Honsa Sulis worked in gilt on the binding.

Poor, poor man...

How he must have suffered.

All because he stayed true to his God.

The Lord must have given him sweet welcome to Heaven.

The picture of Varris jumped a little -- I had startled my stepfather into a flinch.

His brown eyes were so wide with feelings I could not recognize that for a moment I was terrified he would strike me.

THEY HAVE TAKEN EVERYTHING FROM ME, BREDA.

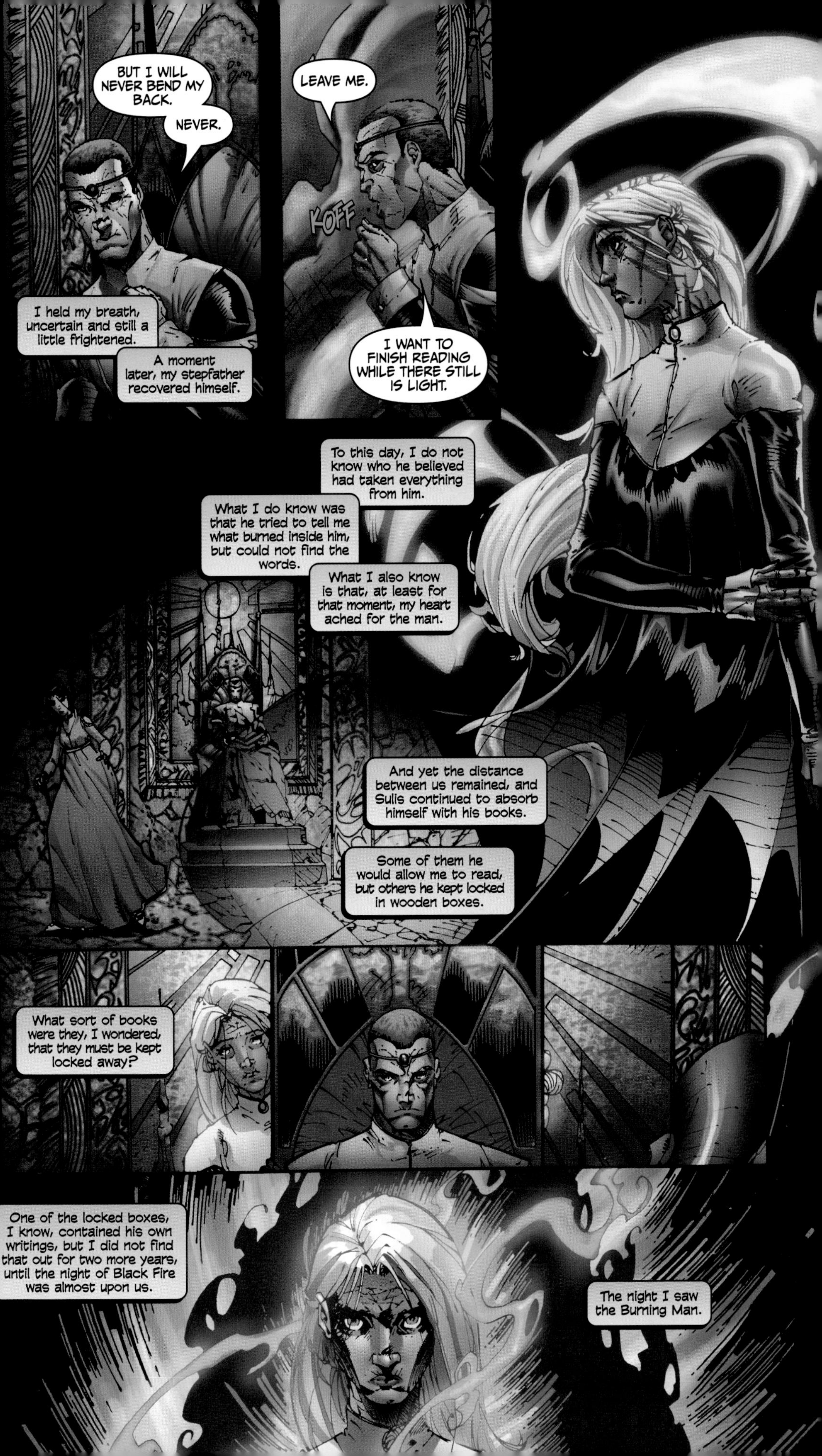

BUT I WILL NEVER BEND MY BACK.
NEVER.
I held my breath, uncertain and still a little frightened.
A moment later, my stepfather recovered himself.
LEAVE ME.
KOFF
I WANT TO FINISH READING WHILE THERE STILL IS LIGHT.
To this day, I do not know who he believed had taken everything from him.
What I do know was that he tried to tell me what burned inside him, but could not find the words.
What I also know is that, at least for that moment, my heart ached for the man.
And yet the distance between us remained, and Sulis continued to absorb himself with his books.
Some of them he would allow me to read, but others he kept locked in wooden boxes.
What sort of books were they, I wondered, that they must be kept locked away?
One of the locked boxes, I know, contained his own writings, but I did not find that out for two more years, until the night of Black Fire was almost upon us.
The night I saw the Burning Man.

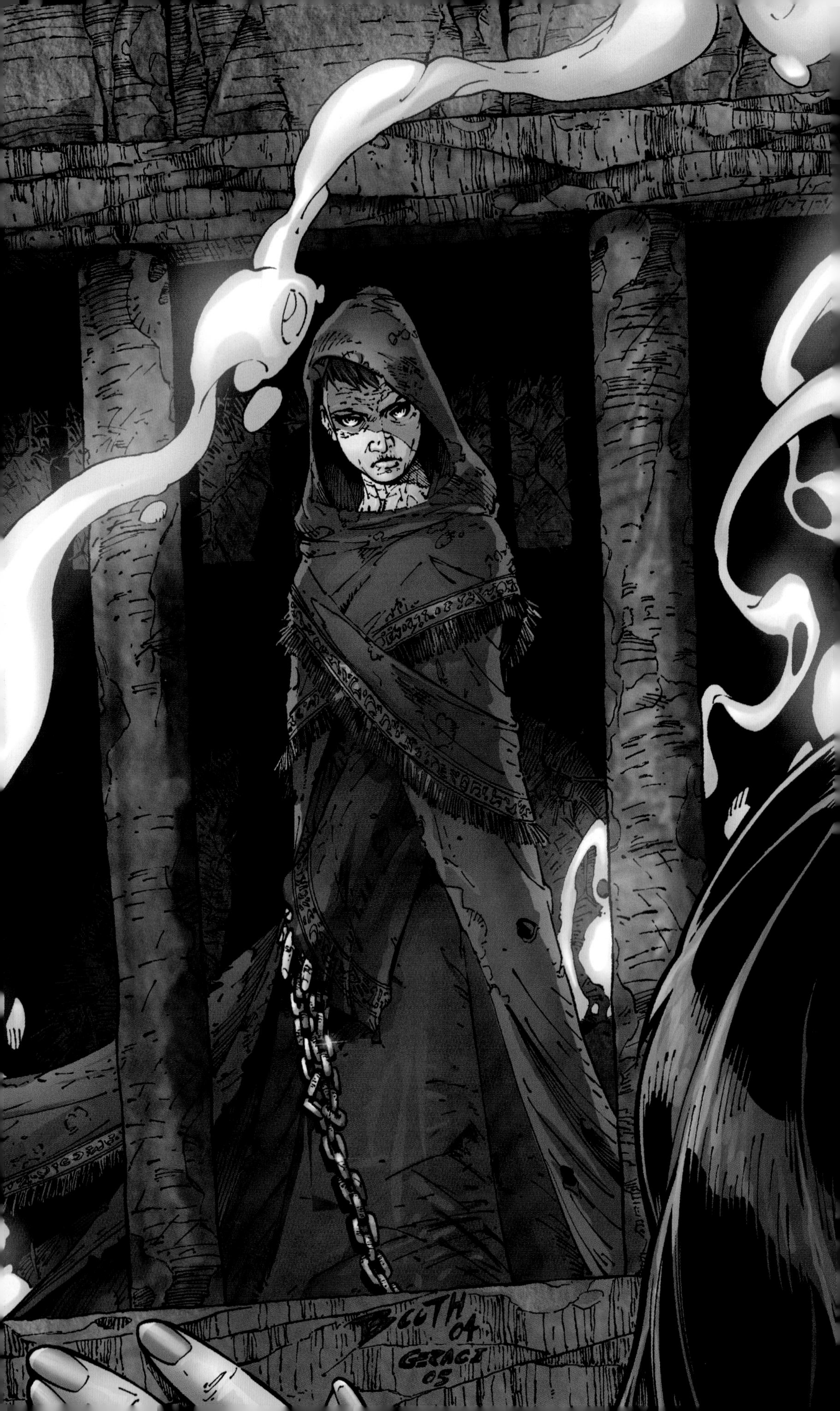
BOOTH 04
GRACE 05

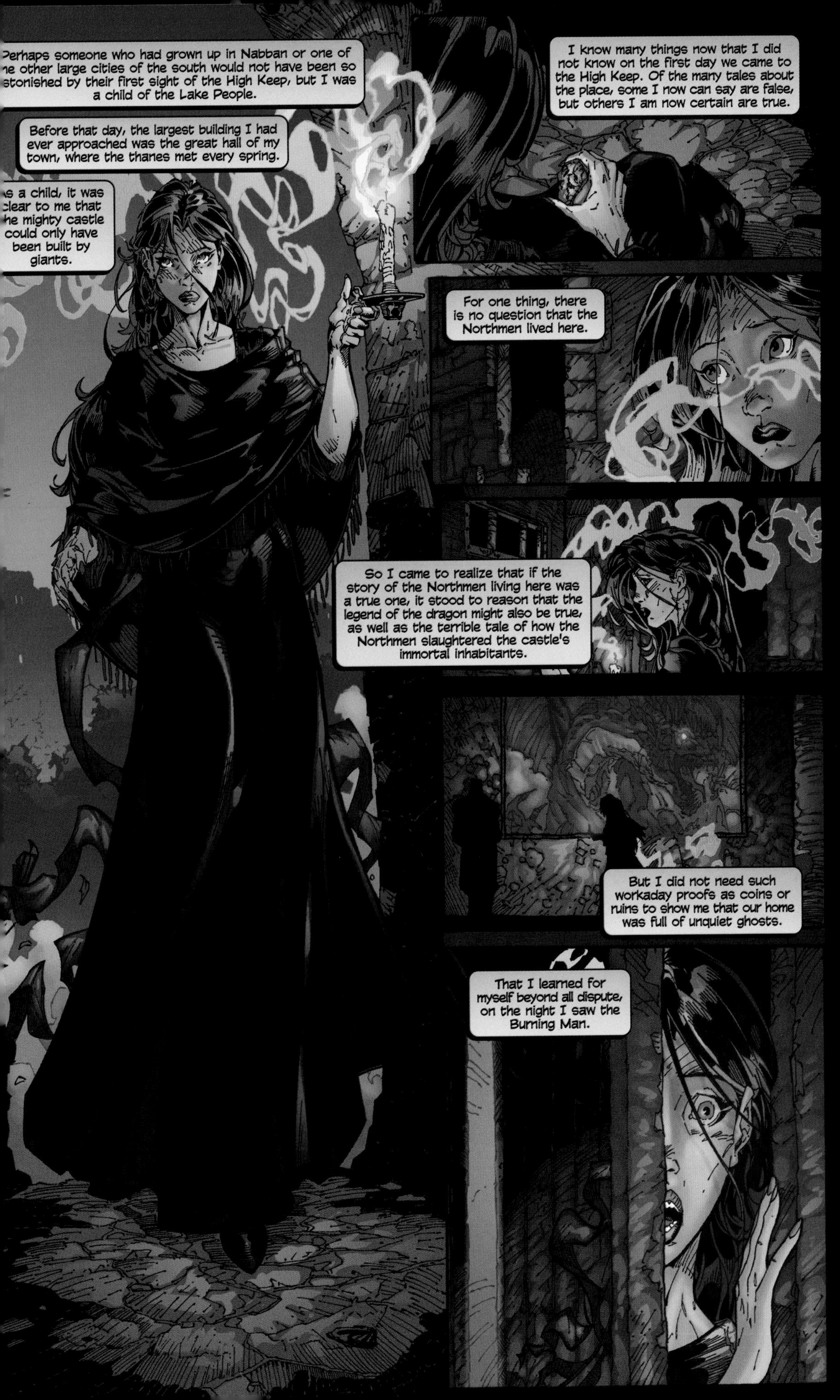

Perhaps someone who had grown up in Nabban or one of the other large cities of the south would not have been so stonished by their first sight of the High Keep, but I was a child of the Lake People.
Before that day, the largest building I had ever approached was the great hall of my town, where the thanes met every spring.
As a child, it was clear to me that the mighty castle could only have been built by giants.
I know many things now that I did not know on the first day we came to the High Keep. Of the many tales about the place, some I now can say are false, but others I am now certain are true.
For one thing, there is no question that the Northmen lived here.
So I came to realize that if the story of the Northmen living here was a true one, it stood to reason that the legend of the dragon might also be true, as well as the terrible tale of how the Northmen slaughtered the castle's immortal inhabitants.
But I did not need such workaday proofs as coins or ruins to show me that our home was full of unquiet ghosts.
That I learned for myself beyond all dispute, on the night I saw the Burning Man.

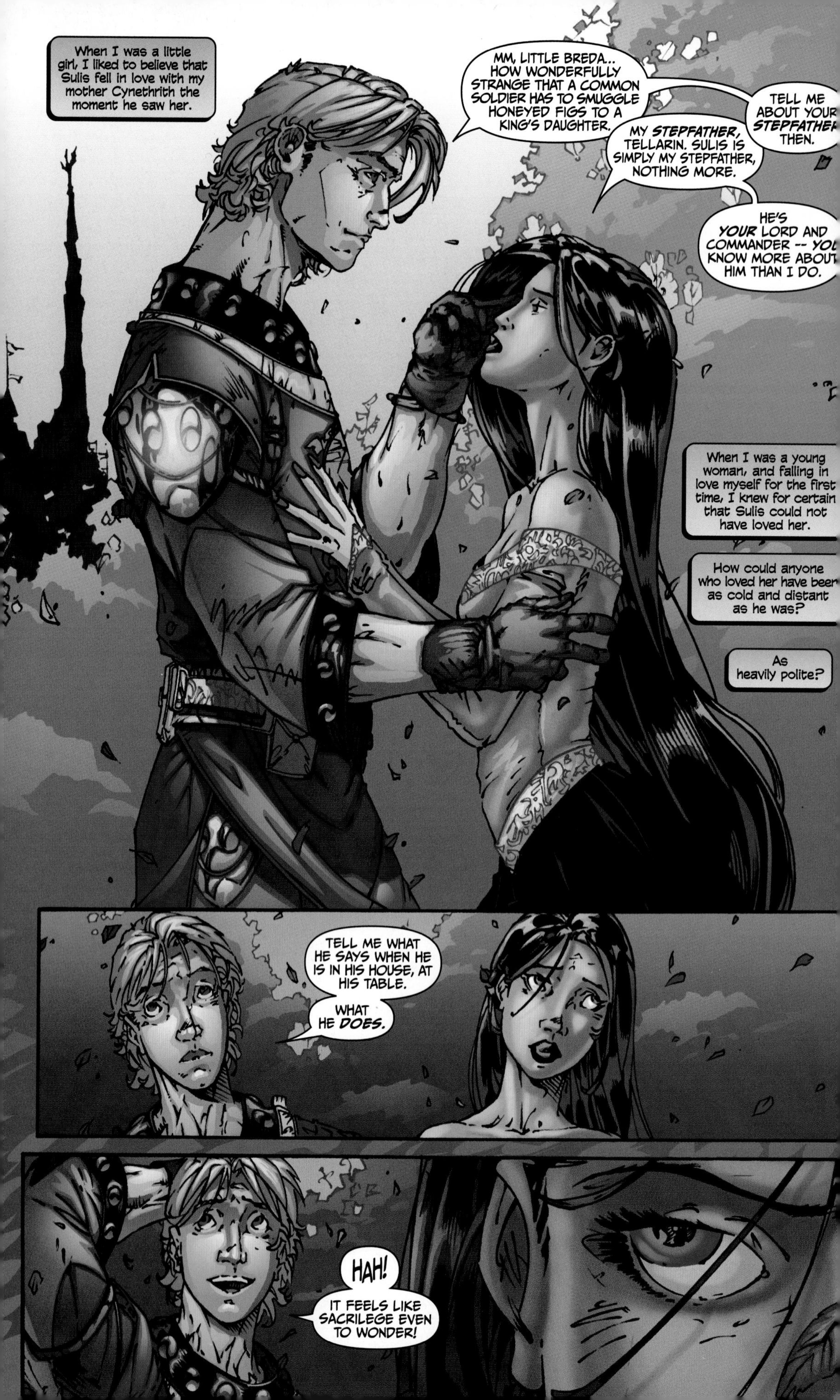

When I was a little girl, I liked to believe that Sulis fell in love with my mother Cynethrith the moment he saw her.
MM, LITTLE BREDA... HOW WONDERFULLY STRANGE THAT A COMMON SOLDIER HAS TO SMUGGLE HONEYED FIGS TO A KING'S DAUGHTER.
MY STEPFATHER, TELLARIN. SULIS IS SIMPLY MY STEPFATHER, NOTHING MORE.
TELL ME ABOUT YOUR STEPFATHER THEN.
HE'S YOUR LORD AND COMMANDER -- YOU KNOW MORE ABOUT HIM THAN I DO.
When I was a young woman, and falling in love myself for the first time, I knew for certain that Sulis could not have loved her.
How could anyone who loved her have been as cold and distant as he was?
As heavily polite?
TELL ME WHAT HE SAYS WHEN HE IS IN HIS HOUSE, AT HIS TABLE.
WHAT HE DOES.
HAH!
IT FEELS LIKE SACRILEGE EVEN TO WONDER!

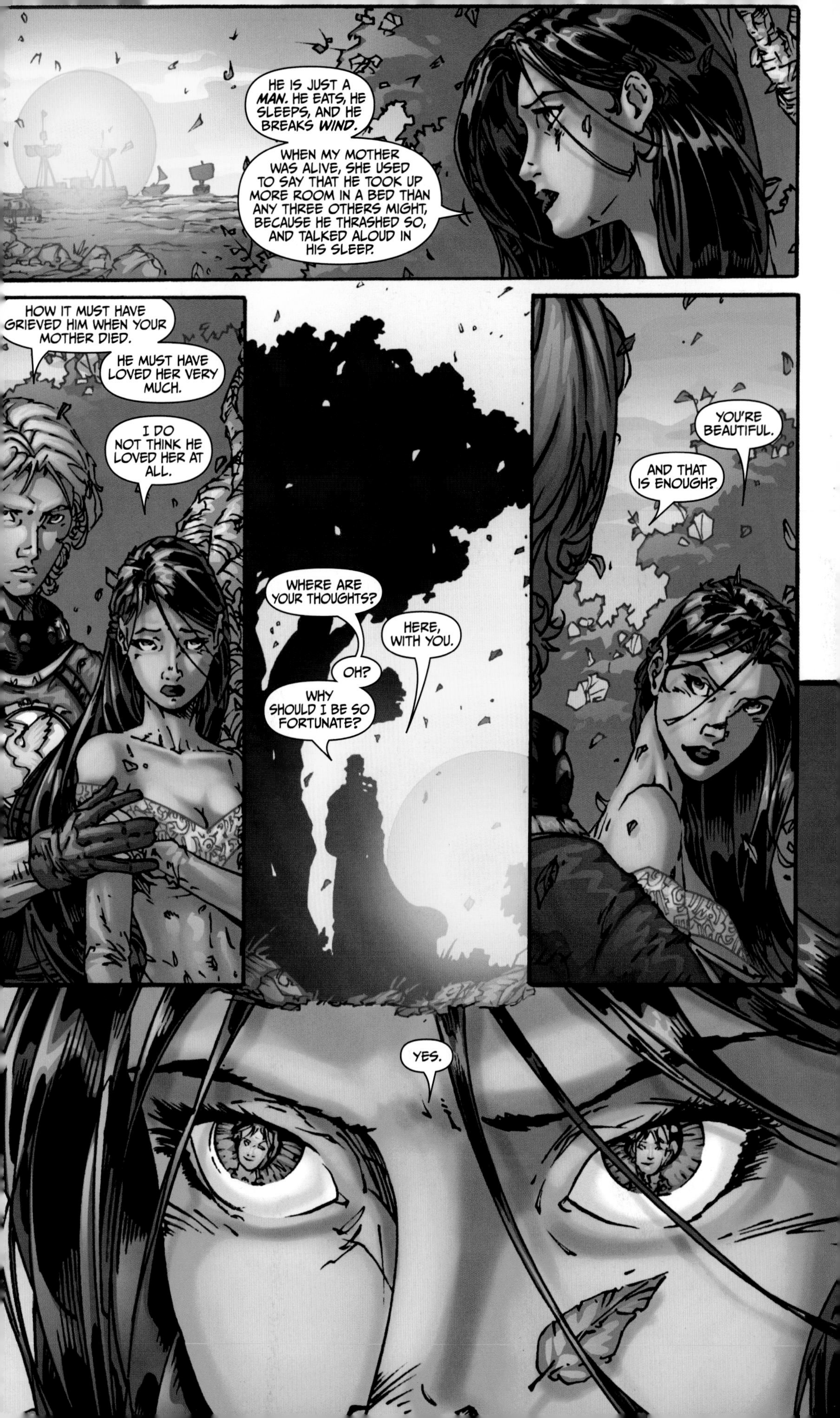
HE IS JUST A MAN. HE EATS, HE SLEEPS, AND HE BREAKS WIND.
WHEN MY MOTHER WAS ALIVE, SHE USED TO SAY THAT HE TOOK UP MORE ROOM IN A BED THAN ANY THREE OTHERS MIGHT, BECAUSE HE THRASHED SO, AND TALKED ALOUD IN HIS SLEEP.
HOW IT MUST HAVE GRIEVED HIM WHEN YOUR MOTHER DIED.
HE MUST HAVE LOVED HER VERY MUCH.
I DO NOT THINK HE LOVED HER AT ALL.
WHERE ARE YOUR THOUGHTS?
HERE, WITH YOU.
OH?
WHY SHOULD I BE SO FORTUNATE?
YOU'RE BEAUTIFUL.
AND THAT IS ENOUGH?
YES.

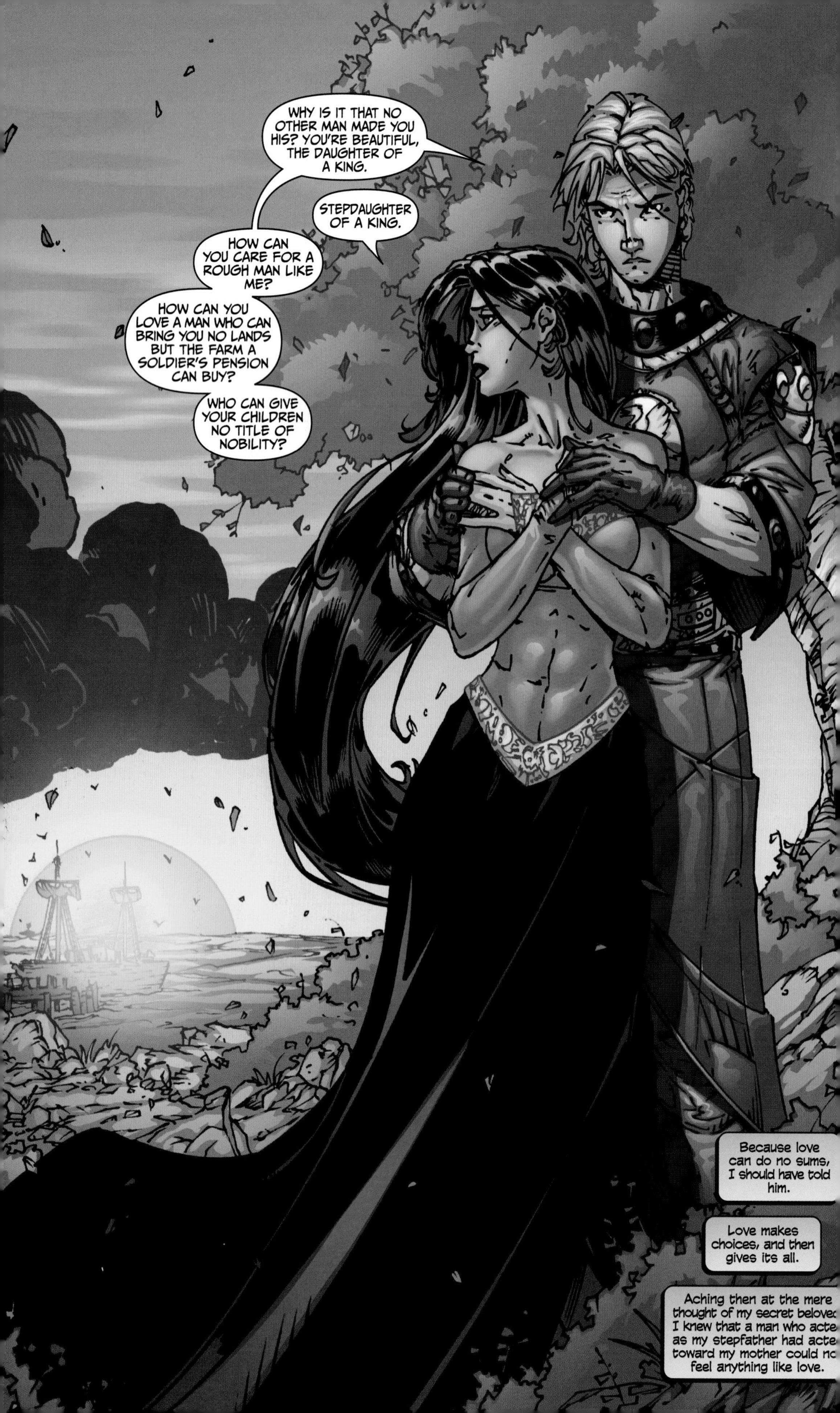
WHY IS IT THAT NO OTHER MAN MADE YOU HIS? YOU'RE BEAUTIFUL, THE DAUGHTER OF A KING.
STEPDAUGHTER OF A KING.
HOW CAN YOU CARE FOR A ROUGH MAN LIKE ME?
HOW CAN YOU LOVE A MAN WHO CAN BRING YOU NO LANDS BUT THE FARM A SOLDIER'S PENSION CAN BUY?
WHO CAN GIVE YOUR CHILDREN NO TITLE OF NOBILITY?
Because love can do no sums, I should have told him.
Love makes choices, and then gives its all.
Aching then at the mere thought of my secret belove
I knew that a man who acte
as my stepfather had acte
toward my mother could no
feel anything like love.

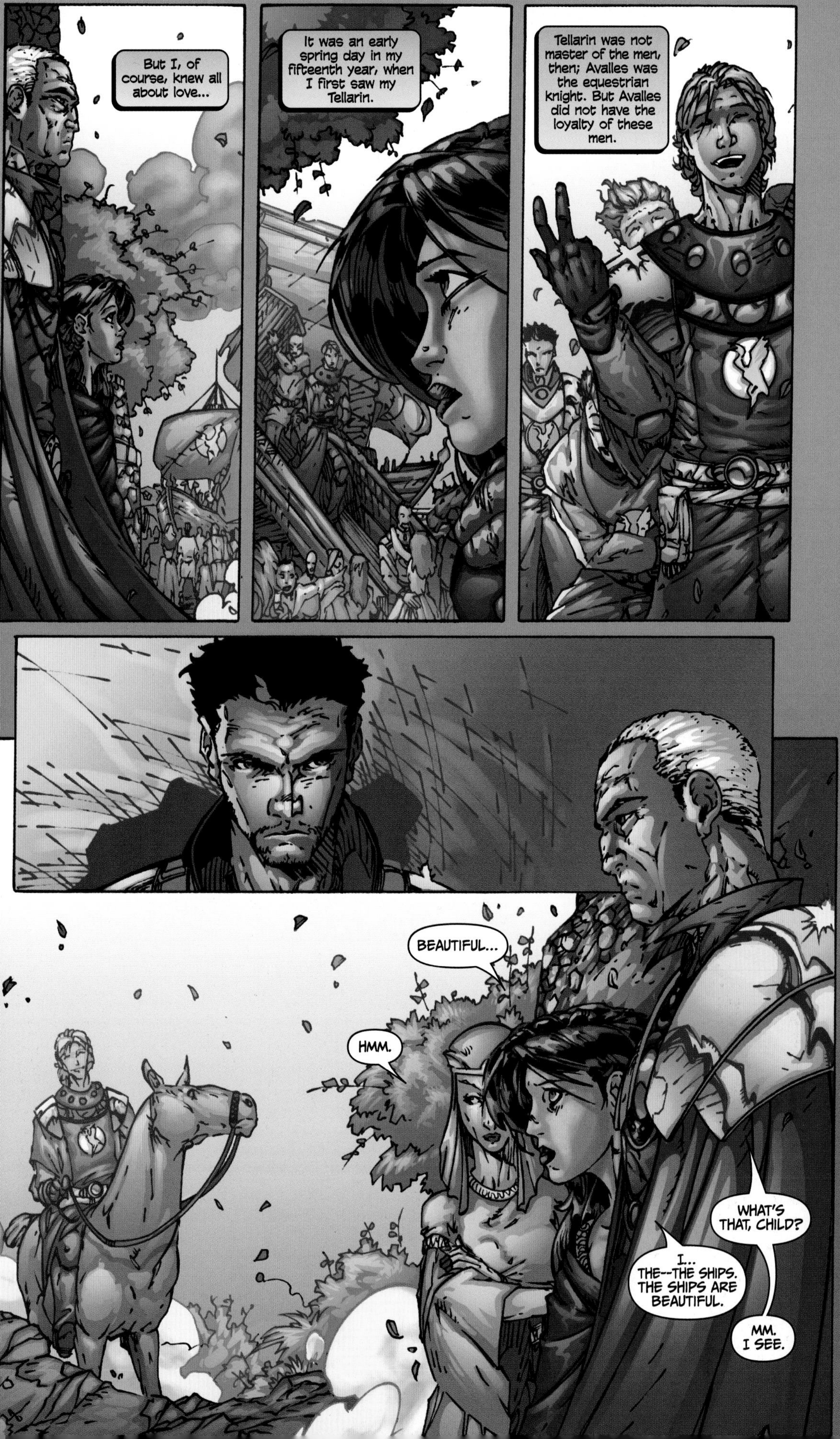
But I, of course, knew all about love...
It was an early spring day in my fifteenth year, when I first saw my Tellarin.
Tellarin was not master of the men, then; Avalles was the equestrian knight. But Avalles did not have the loyalty of these men.
BEAUTIFUL...
HMM.
WHAT'S THAT, CHILD?
I... THE--THE SHIPS. THE SHIPS ARE BEAUTIFUL.
MM. I SEE.

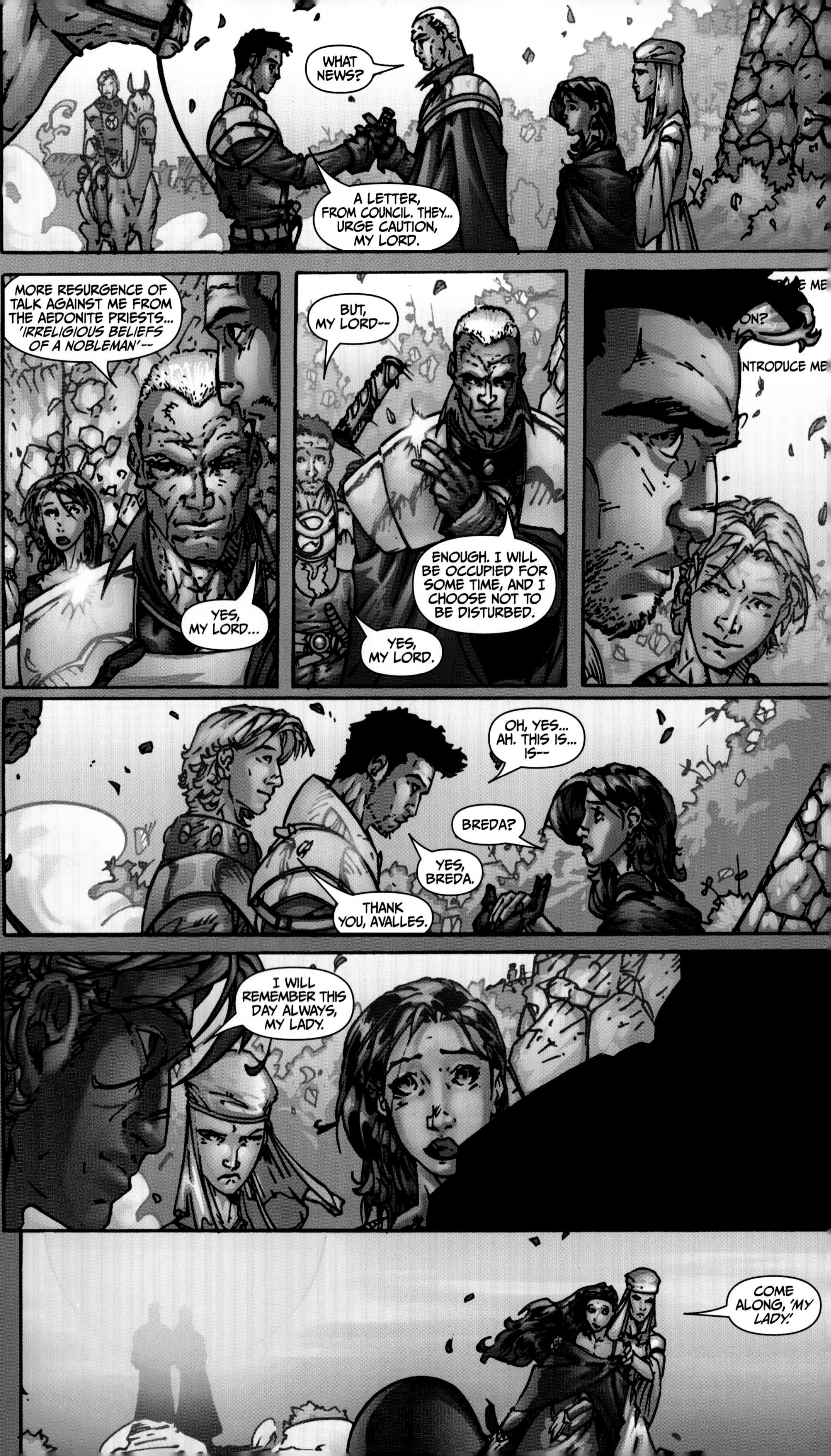
WHAT NEWS?
A LETTER, FROM COUNCIL. THEY... URGE CAUTION, MY LORD.
MORE RESURGENCE OF TALK AGAINST ME FROM THE AEDONITE PRIESTS... *'IRRELIGIOUS BELIEFS OF A NOBLEMAN'*--
YES, MY LORD...
BUT, MY LORD--
ENOUGH. I WILL BE OCCUPIED FOR SOME TIME, AND I CHOOSE NOT TO BE DISTURBED.
YES, MY LORD.
OH, YES... AH. THIS IS... IS--
BREDA?
YES, BREDA.
THANK YOU, AVALLES.
I WILL REMEMBER THIS DAY ALWAYS, MY LADY.
COME ALONG, *'MY LADY.'*

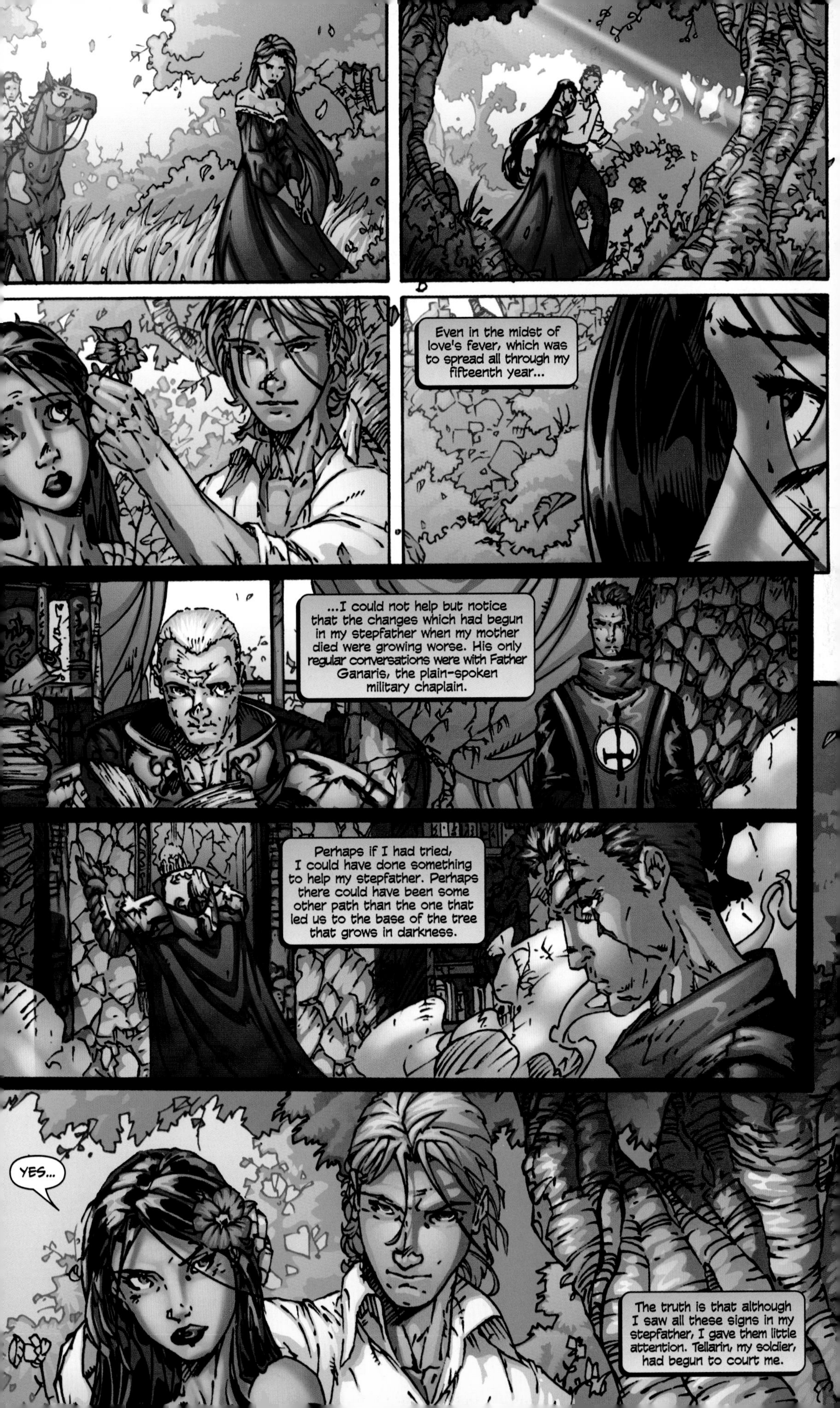

Even in the midst of love's fever, which was to spread all through my fifteenth year...
...I could not help but notice that the changes which had begun in my stepfather when my mother died were growing worse. His only regular conversations were with Father Ganaris, the plain-spoken military chaplain.
Perhaps if I had tried, I could have done something to help my stepfather. Perhaps there could have been some other path than the one that led us to the base of the tree that grows in darkness.
YES...
The truth is that although I saw all these signs in my stepfather, I gave them little attention. Tellarin, my soldier, had begun to court me.

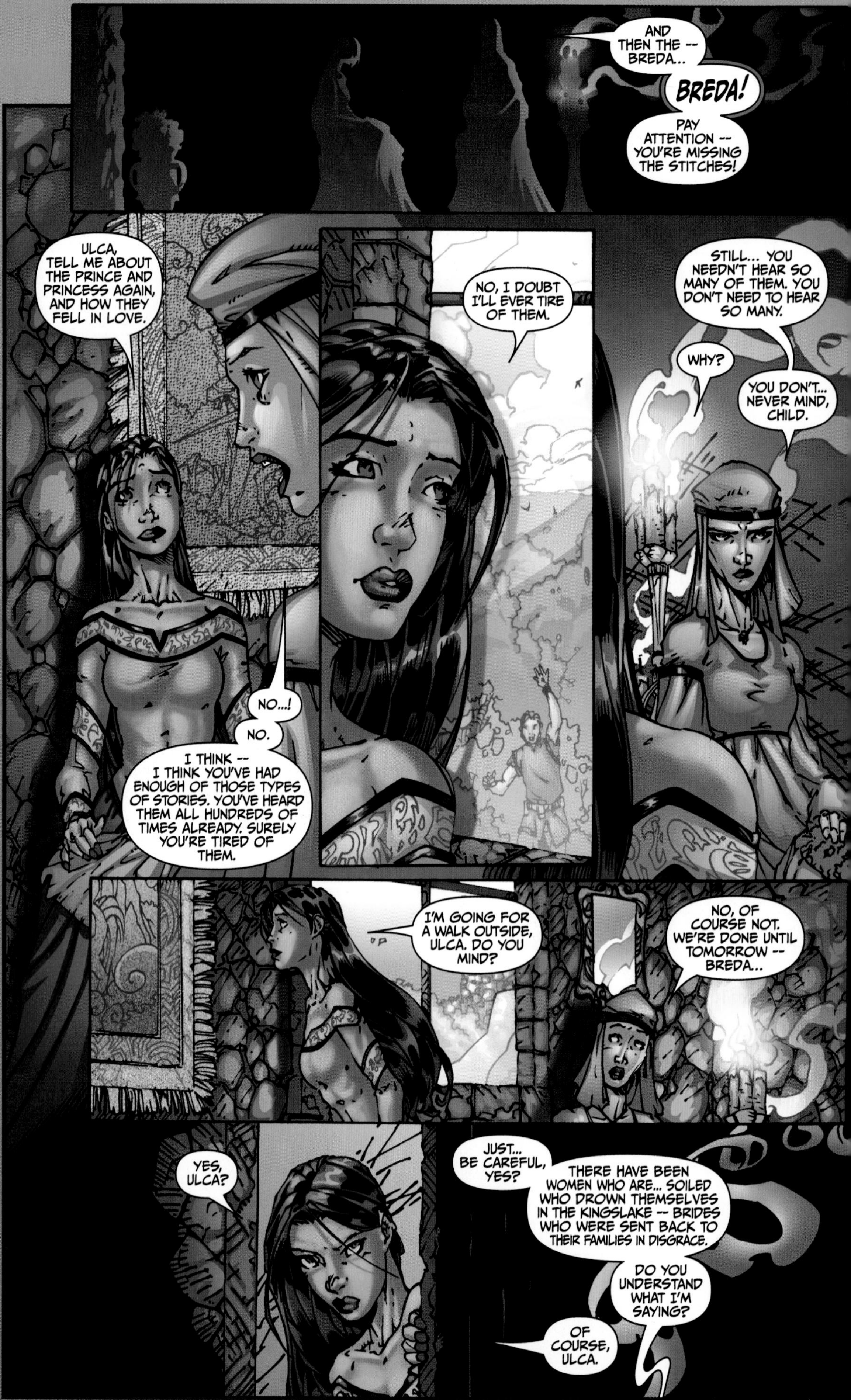
AND THEN THE -- BREDA...
BREDA!
PAY ATTENTION -- YOU'RE MISSING THE STITCHES!
ULCA, TELL ME ABOUT THE PRINCE AND PRINCESS AGAIN, AND HOW THEY FELL IN LOVE.
NO...!
NO.
I THINK -- I THINK YOU'VE HAD ENOUGH OF THOSE TYPES OF STORIES. YOU'VE HEARD THEM ALL HUNDREDS OF TIMES ALREADY. SURELY YOU'RE TIRED OF THEM.
NO, I DOUBT I'LL EVER TIRE OF THEM.
STILL... YOU NEEDN'T HEAR SO MANY OF THEM. YOU DON'T NEED TO HEAR SO MANY.
WHY?
YOU DON'T... NEVER MIND, CHILD.
I'M GOING FOR A WALK OUTSIDE, ULCA. DO YOU MIND?
NO, OF COURSE NOT. WE'RE DONE UNTIL TOMORROW -- BREDA...
YES, ULCA?
JUST... BE CAREFUL, YES?
THERE HAVE BEEN WOMEN WHO ARE... SOILED WHO DROWN THEMSELVES IN THE KINGSLAKE -- BRIDES WHO WERE SENT BACK TO THEIR FAMILIES IN DISGRACE.
DO YOU UNDERSTAND WHAT I'M SAYING?
OF COURSE, ULCA.

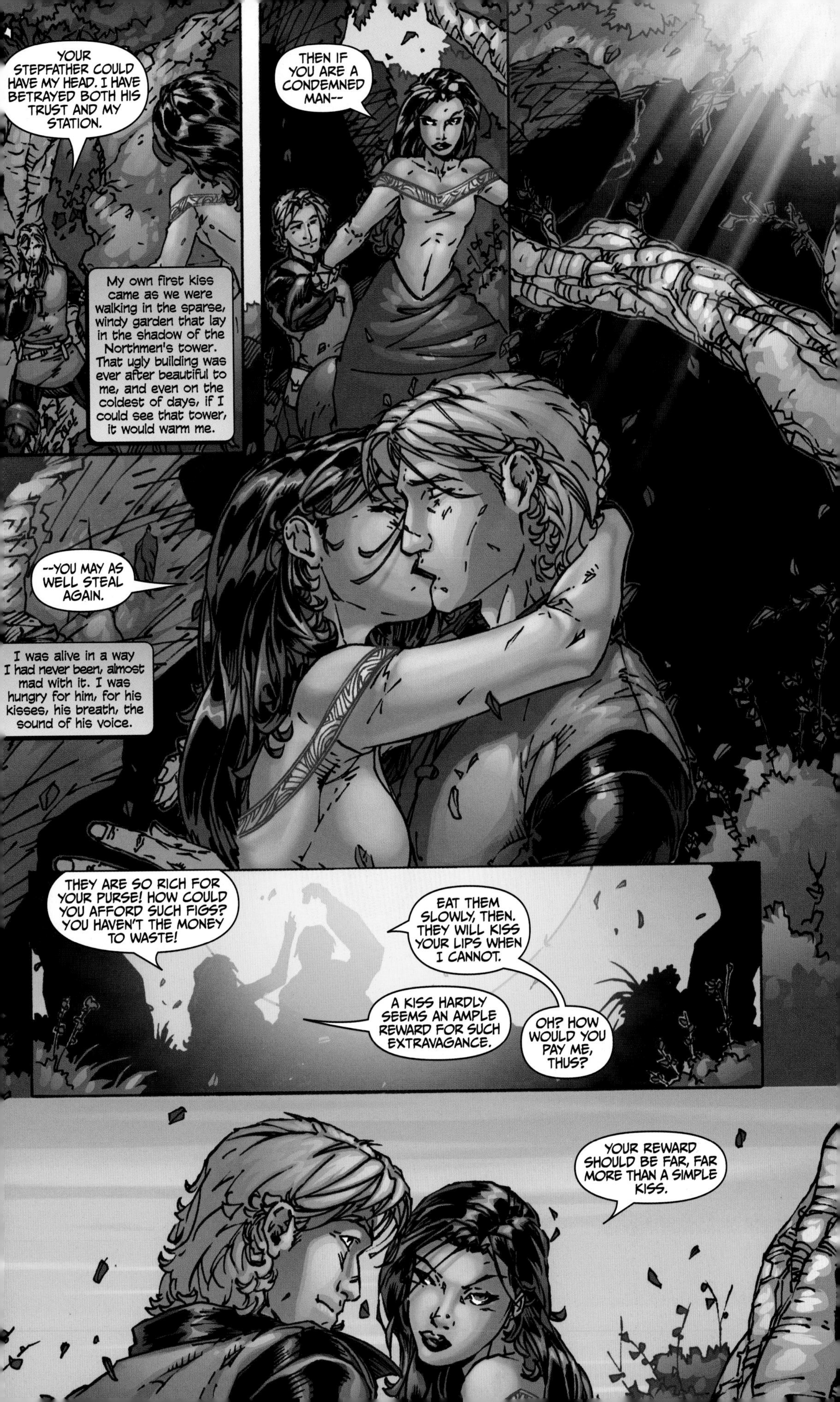

YOUR STEPFATHER COULD HAVE MY HEAD. I HAVE BETRAYED BOTH HIS TRUST AND MY STATION.
THEN IF YOU ARE A CONDEMNED MAN--
My own first kiss came as we were walking in the sparse, windy garden that lay in the shadow of the Northmen's tower. That ugly building was ever after beautiful to me, and even on the coldest of days, if I could see that tower, it would warm me.
--YOU MAY AS WELL STEAL AGAIN.
I was alive in a way I had never been, almost mad with it. I was hungry for him, for his kisses, his breath, the sound of his voice.
THEY ARE SO RICH FOR YOUR PURSE! HOW COULD YOU AFFORD SUCH FIGS? YOU HAVEN'T THE MONEY TO WASTE!
EAT THEM SLOWLY, THEN. THEY WILL KISS YOUR LIPS WHEN I CANNOT.
A KISS HARDLY SEEMS AN AMPLE REWARD FOR SUCH EXTRAVAGANCE.
OH? HOW WOULD YOU PAY ME, THUS?
YOUR REWARD SHOULD BE FAR, FAR MORE THAN A SIMPLE KISS.

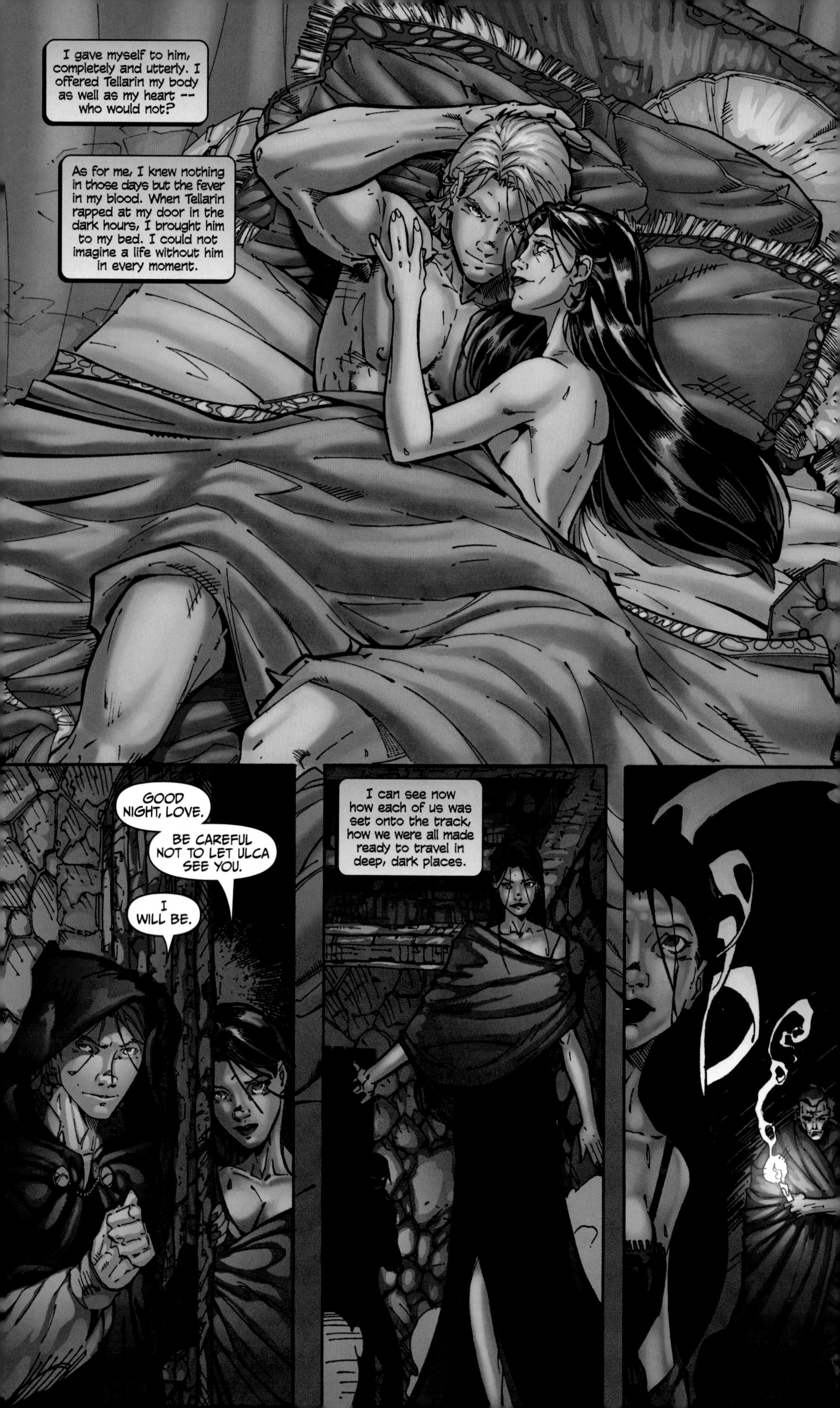
I gave myself to him, completely and utterly. I offered Tellarin my body as well as my heart -- who would not?
As for me, I knew nothing in those days but the fever in my blood. When Tellarin rapped at my door in the dark hours, I brought him to my bed. I could not imagine a life without him in every moment.
GOOD NIGHT, LOVE.
BE CAREFUL NOT TO LET ULCA SEE YOU.
I WILL BE.
I can see now how each of us was set onto the track, how we were all made ready to travel in deep, dark places.

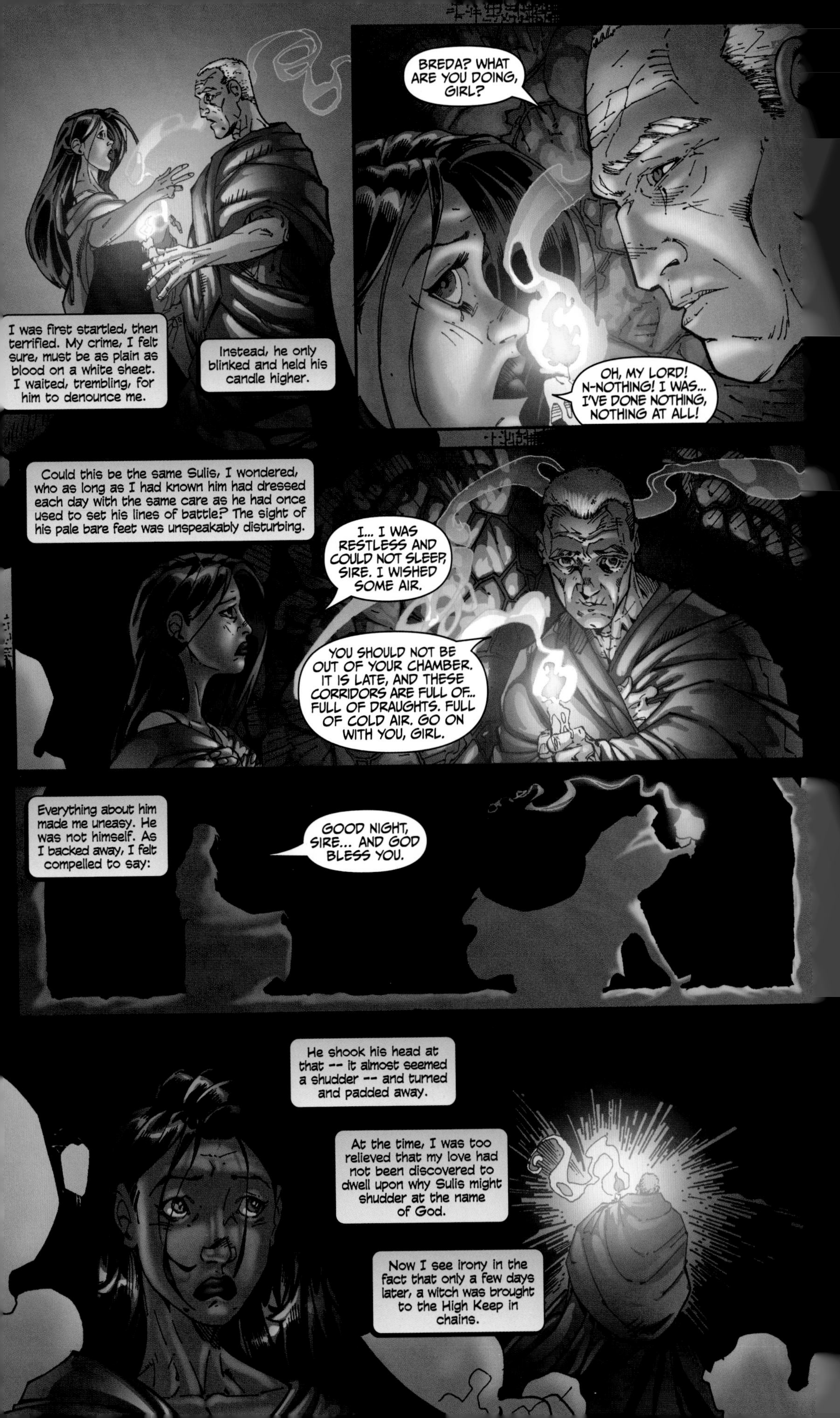
I was first startled, then terrified. My crime, I felt sure, must be as plain as blood on a white sheet. I waited, trembling, for him to denounce me.
Instead, he only blinked and held his candle higher.
BREDA? WHAT ARE YOU DOING, GIRL?
OH, MY LORD! N-NOTHING! I WAS... I'VE DONE NOTHING, NOTHING AT ALL!
Could this be the same Sulis, I wondered, who as long as I had known him had dressed each day with the same care as he had once used to set his lines of battle? The sight of his pale bare feet was unspeakably disturbing.
I... I WAS RESTLESS AND COULD NOT SLEEP, SIRE. I WISHED SOME AIR.
YOU SHOULD NOT BE OUT OF YOUR CHAMBER. IT IS LATE, AND THESE CORRIDORS ARE FULL OF... FULL OF DRAUGHTS. FULL OF COLD AIR. GO ON WITH YOU, GIRL.
Everything about him made me uneasy. He was not himself. As I backed away, I felt compelled to say:
GOOD NIGHT, SIRE... AND GOD BLESS YOU.
He shook his head at that -- it almost seemed a shudder -- and turned and padded away.
At the time, I was too relieved that my love had not been discovered to dwell upon why Sulis might shudder at the name of God.
Now I see irony in the fact that only a few days later, a witch was brought to the High Keep in chains.

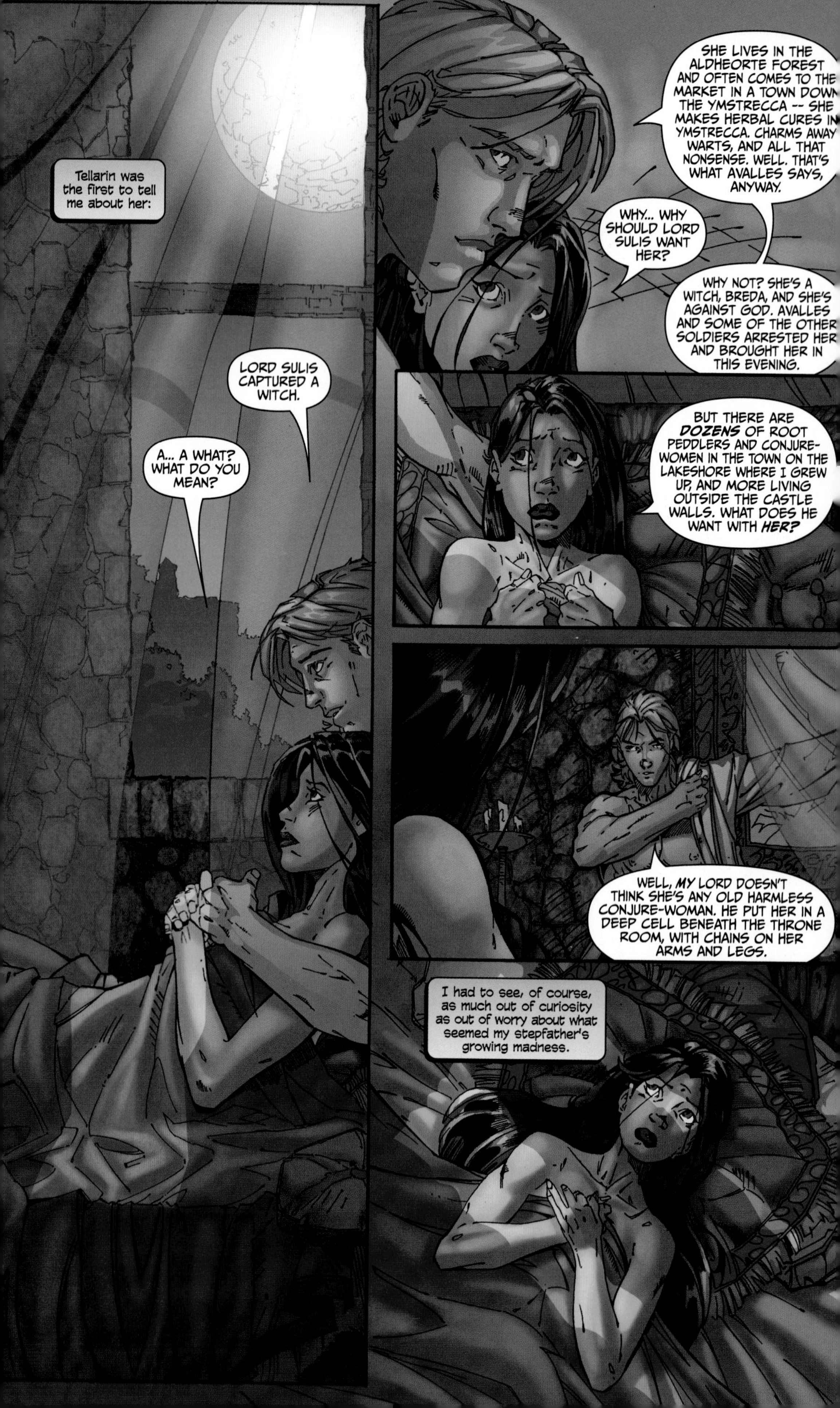
Tellarin was the first to tell me about her:
LORD SULIS CAPTURED A WITCH.
A... A WHAT? WHAT DO YOU MEAN?
SHE LIVES IN THE ALDHEORTE FOREST AND OFTEN COMES TO THE MARKET IN A TOWN DOWN THE YMSTRECCA -- SHE MAKES HERBAL CURES IN YMSTRECCA. CHARMS AWAY WARTS, AND ALL THAT NONSENSE. WELL. THAT'S WHAT AVALLES SAYS, ANYWAY.
WHY... WHY SHOULD LORD SULIS WANT HER?
WHY NOT? SHE'S A WITCH, BREDA, AND SHE'S AGAINST GOD. AVALLES AND SOME OF THE OTHER SOLDIERS ARRESTED HER AND BROUGHT HER IN THIS EVENING.
BUT THERE ARE DOZENS OF ROOT PEDDLERS AND CONJURE-WOMEN IN THE TOWN ON THE LAKESHORE WHERE I GREW UP, AND MORE LIVING OUTSIDE THE CASTLE WALLS. WHAT DOES HE WANT WITH HER?
WELL, MY LORD DOESN'T THINK SHE'S ANY OLD HARMLESS CONJURE-WOMAN. HE PUT HER IN A DEEP CELL BENEATH THE THRONE ROOM, WITH CHAINS ON HER ARMS AND LEGS.
I had to see, of course, as much out of curiosity as out of worry about what seemed my stepfather's growing madness.

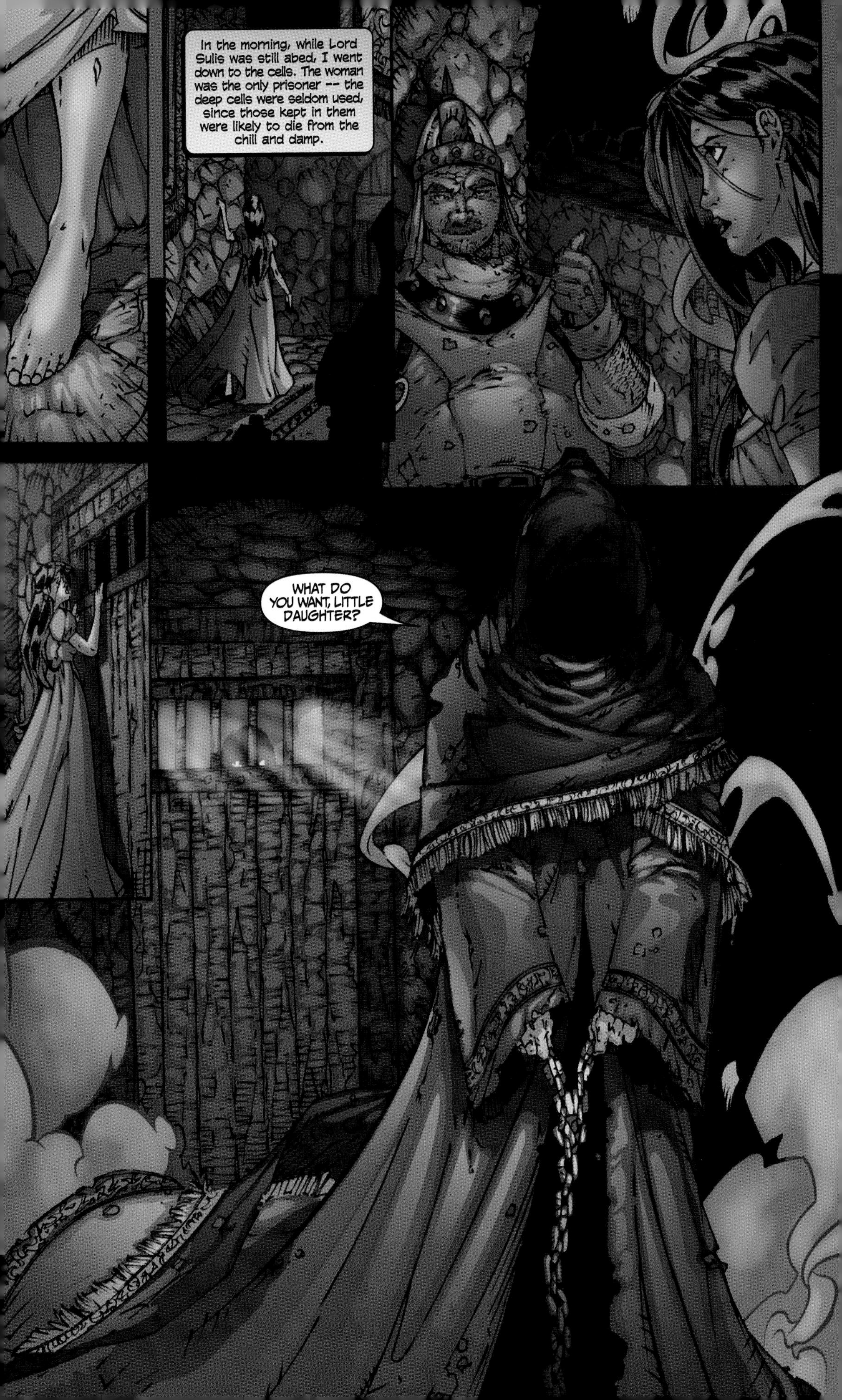
In the morning, while Lord Sulis was still abed, I went down to the cells. The woman was the only prisoner -- the deep cells were seldom used, since those kept in them were likely to die from the chill and damp.
WHAT DO YOU WANT, LITTLE DAUGHTER?

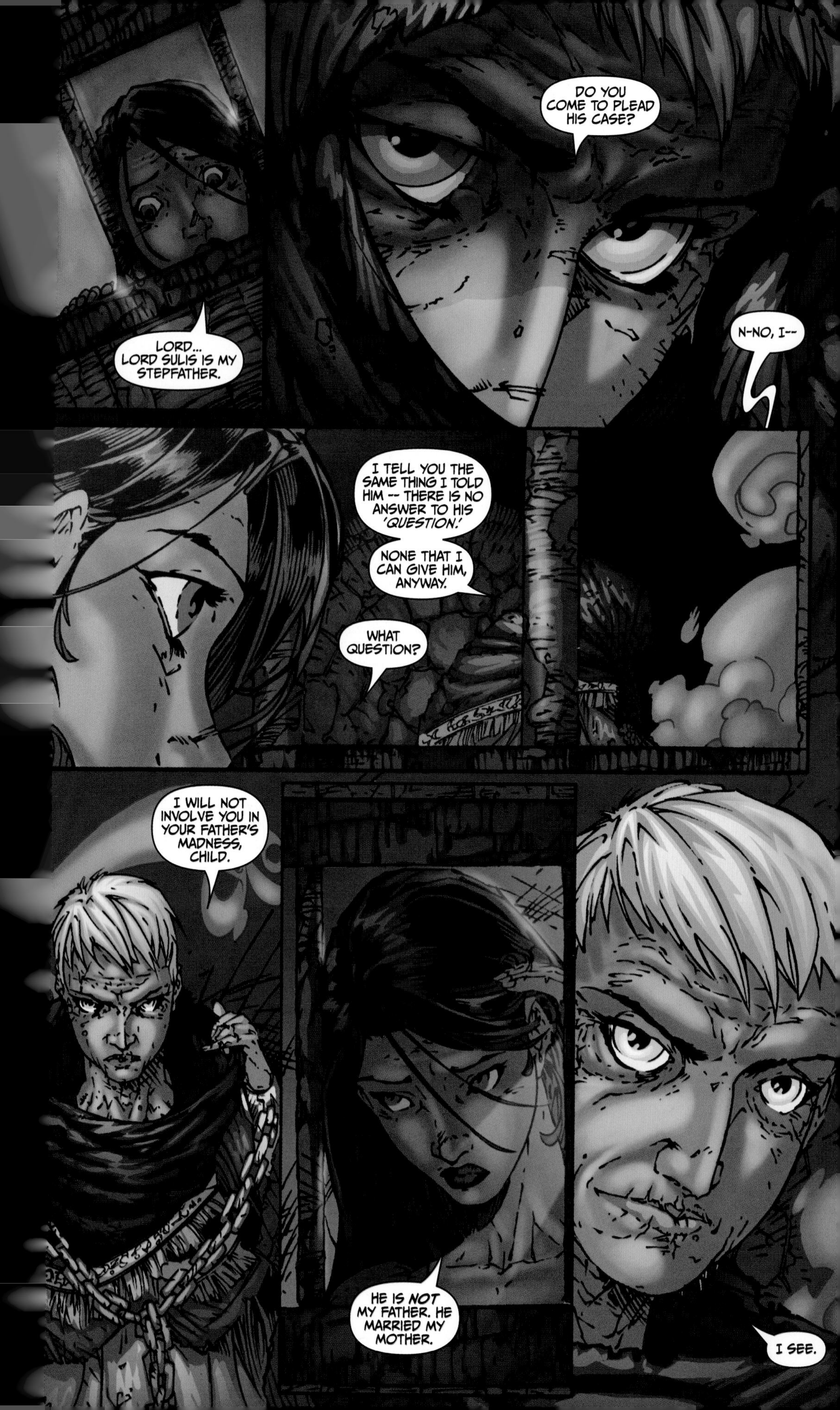

DO YOU COME TO PLEAD HIS CASE?
LORD... LORD SULIS IS MY STEPFATHER.
N-NO, I--
I TELL YOU THE SAME THING I TOLD HIM -- THERE IS NO ANSWER TO HIS 'QUESTION.'
NONE THAT I CAN GIVE HIM, ANYWAY.
WHAT QUESTION?
I WILL NOT INVOLVE YOU IN YOUR FATHER'S MADNESS, CHILD.
HE IS NOT MY FATHER. HE MARRIED MY MOTHER.
I SEE.

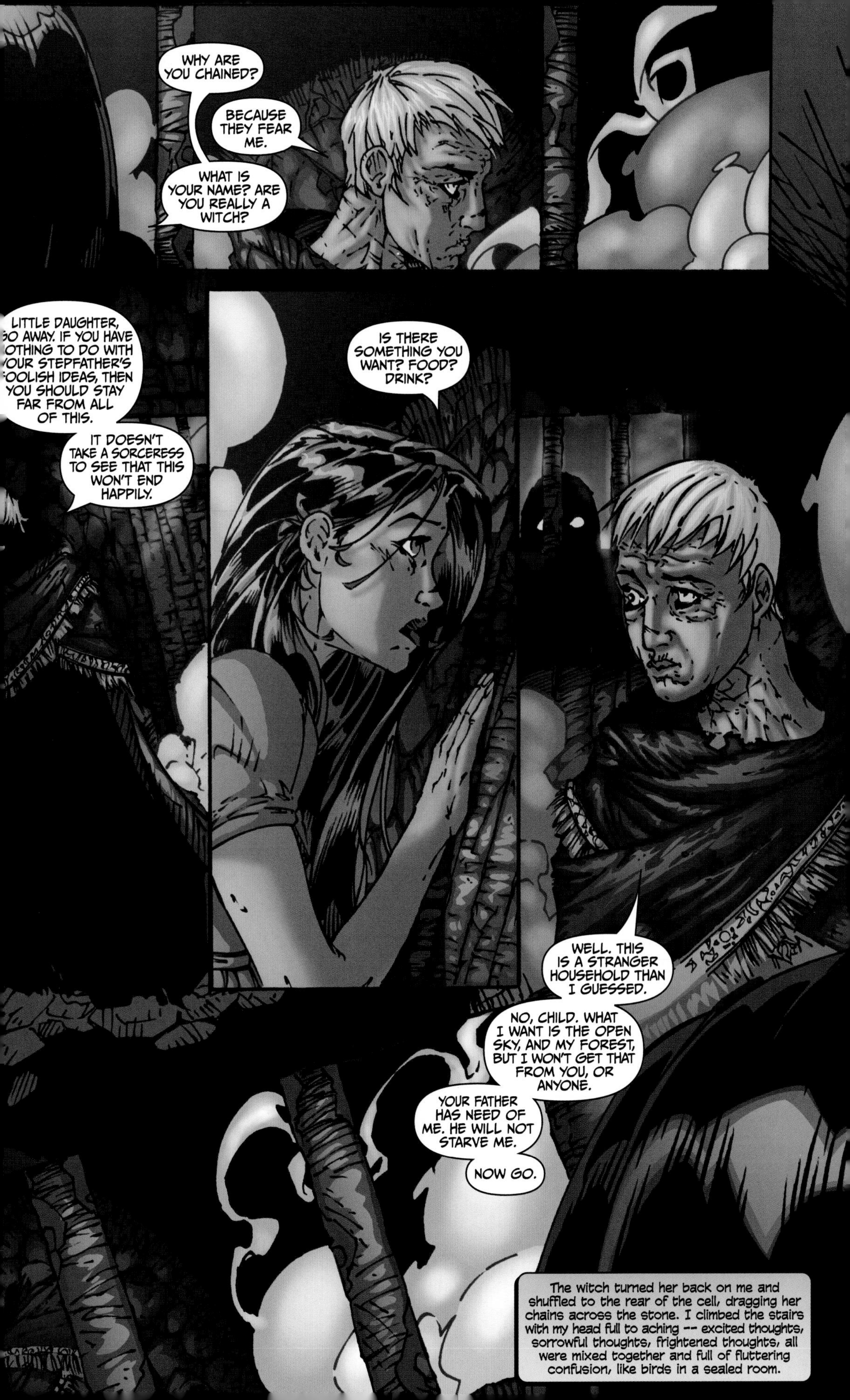

WHY ARE YOU CHAINED?
BECAUSE THEY FEAR ME.
WHAT IS YOUR NAME? ARE YOU REALLY A WITCH?
LITTLE DAUGHTER, GO AWAY. IF YOU HAVE NOTHING TO DO WITH YOUR STEPFATHER'S FOOLISH IDEAS, THEN YOU SHOULD STAY FAR FROM ALL OF THIS.
IT DOESN'T TAKE A SORCERESS TO SEE THAT THIS WON'T END HAPPILY.
IS THERE SOMETHING YOU WANT? FOOD? DRINK?
WELL. THIS IS A STRANGER HOUSEHOLD THAN I GUESSED.
NO, CHILD. WHAT I WANT IS THE OPEN SKY, AND MY FOREST, BUT I WON'T GET THAT FROM YOU, OR ANYONE.
YOUR FATHER HAS NEED OF ME. HE WILL NOT STARVE ME.
NOW GO.
The witch turned her back on me and shuffled to the rear of the cell, dragging her chains across the stone. I climbed the stairs with my head full to aching -- excited thoughts, sorrowful thoughts, frightened thoughts, all were mixed together and full of fluttering confusion, like birds in a sealed room.

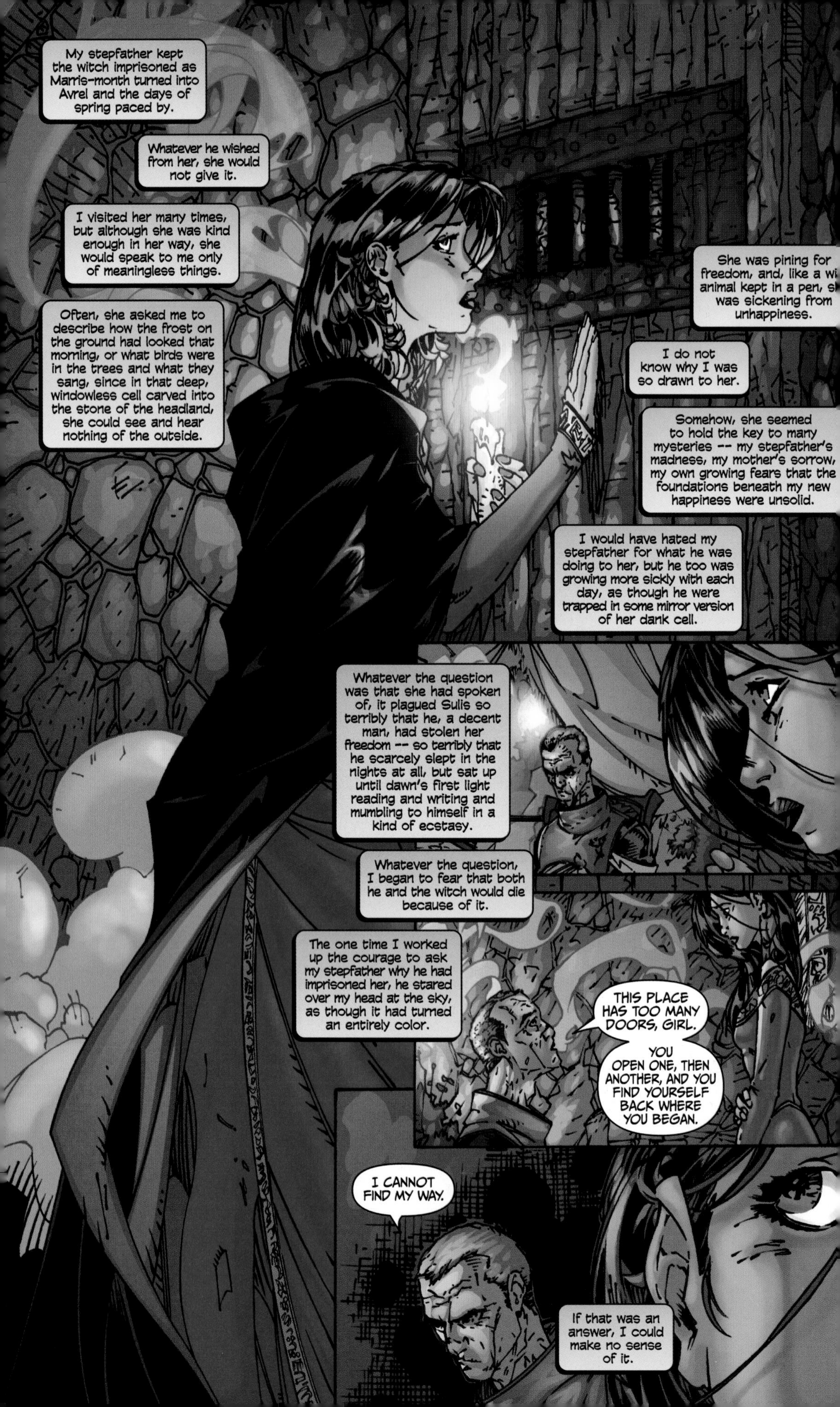

My stepfather kept the witch imprisoned as Marris-month turned into Avrel and the days of spring paced by.
Whatever he wished from her, she would not give it.
I visited her many times, but although she was kind enough in her way, she would speak to me only of meaningless things.
Often, she asked me to describe how the frost on the ground had looked that morning, or what birds were in the trees and what they sang, since in that deep, windowless cell carved into the stone of the headland, she could see and hear nothing of the outside.
She was pining for freedom, and, like a wi animal kept in a pen, s was sickening from unhappiness.
I do not know why I was so drawn to her.
Somehow, she seemed to hold the key to many mysteries -- my stepfather's madness, my mother's sorrow, my own growing fears that the foundations beneath my new happiness were unsolid.
I would have hated my stepfather for what he was doing to her, but he too was growing more sickly with each day, as though he were trapped in some mirror version of her dark cell.
Whatever the question was that she had spoken of, it plagued Sulis so terribly that he, a decent man, had stolen her freedom -- so terribly that he scarcely slept in the nights at all, but sat up until dawn's first light reading and writing and mumbling to himself in a kind of ecstasy.
Whatever the question, I began to fear that both he and the witch would die because of it.
The one time I worked up the courage to ask my stepfather why he had imprisoned her, he stared over my head at the sky, as though it had turned an entirely color.
THIS PLACE HAS TOO MANY DOORS, GIRL.
YOU OPEN ONE, THEN ANOTHER, AND YOU FIND YOURSELF BACK WHERE YOU BEGAN.
I CANNOT FIND MY WAY.
If that was an answer, I could make no sense of it.

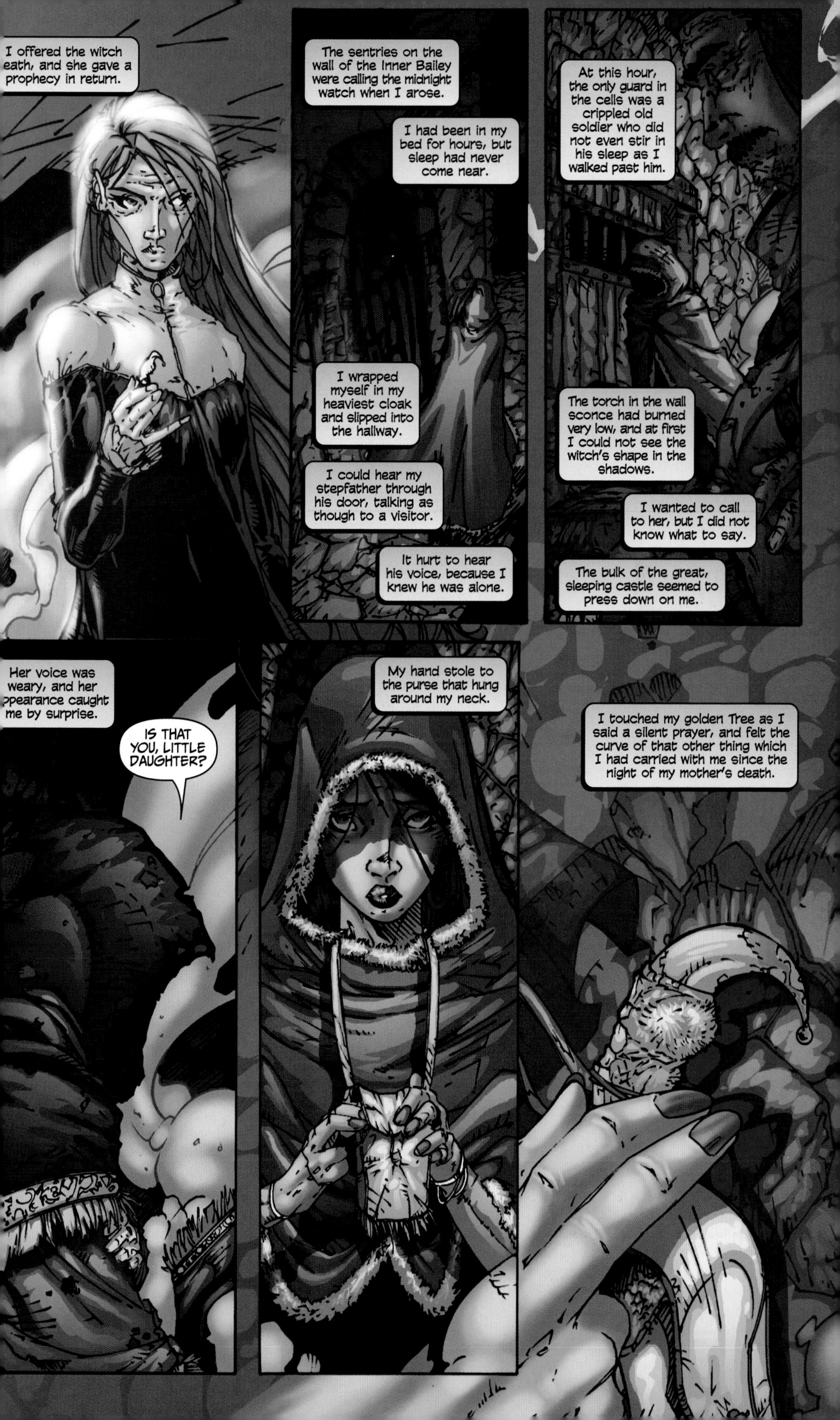
I offered the witch eath, and she gave a prophecy in return.
The sentries on the wall of the Inner Bailey were calling the midnight watch when I arose.
I had been in my bed for hours, but sleep had never come near.
I wrapped myself in my heaviest cloak and slipped into the hallway.
I could hear my stepfather through his door, talking as though to a visitor.
It hurt to hear his voice, because I knew he was alone.
At this hour, the only guard in the cells was a crippled old soldier who did not even stir in his sleep as I walked past him.
The torch in the wall sconce had burned very low, and at first I could not see the witch's shape in the shadows.
I wanted to call to her, but I did not know what to say.
The bulk of the great, sleeping castle seemed to press down on me.
Her voice was weary, and her ppearance caught me by surprise.
IS THAT YOU, LITTLE DAUGHTER?
My hand stole to the purse that hung around my neck.
I touched my golden Tree as I said a silent prayer, and felt the curve of that other thing which I had carried with me since the night of my mother's death.

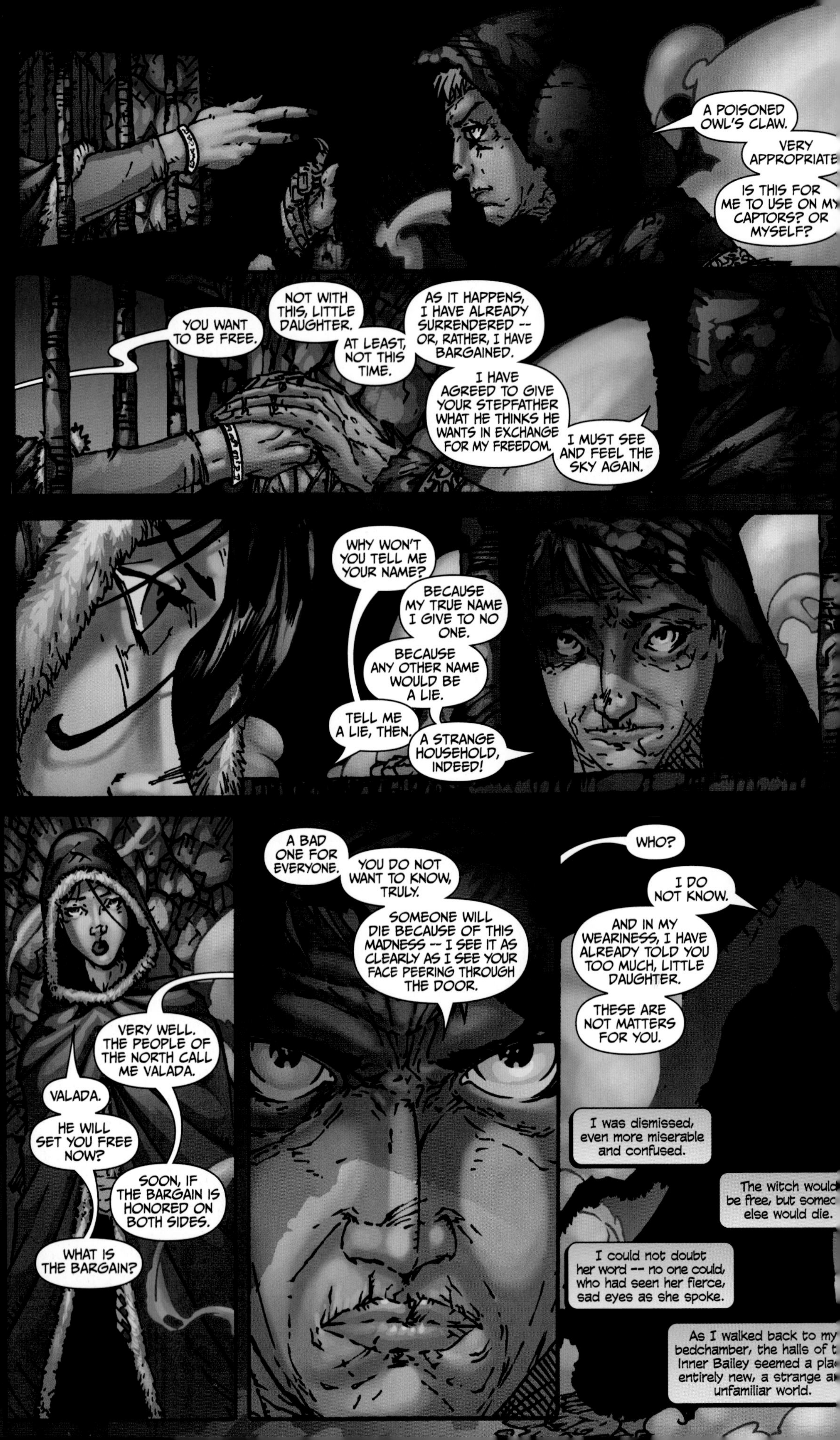
A POISONED OWL'S CLAW.
VERY APPROPRIATE
IS THIS FOR ME TO USE ON MY CAPTORS? OR MYSELF?
YOU WANT TO BE FREE.
NOT WITH THIS, LITTLE DAUGHTER.
AT LEAST, NOT THIS TIME.
AS IT HAPPENS, I HAVE ALREADY SURRENDERED -- OR, RATHER, I HAVE BARGAINED.
I HAVE AGREED TO GIVE YOUR STEPFATHER WHAT HE THINKS HE WANTS IN EXCHANGE FOR MY FREEDOM.
I MUST SEE AND FEEL THE SKY AGAIN.
WHY WON'T YOU TELL ME YOUR NAME?
BECAUSE MY TRUE NAME I GIVE TO NO ONE.
BECAUSE ANY OTHER NAME WOULD BE A LIE.
TELL ME A LIE, THEN.
A STRANGE HOUSEHOLD, INDEED!
VERY WELL. THE PEOPLE OF THE NORTH CALL ME VALADA.
VALADA.
HE WILL SET YOU FREE NOW?
SOON, IF THE BARGAIN IS HONORED ON BOTH SIDES.
WHAT IS THE BARGAIN?
A BAD ONE FOR EVERYONE.
YOU DO NOT WANT TO KNOW, TRULY.
SOMEONE WILL DIE BECAUSE OF THIS MADNESS -- I SEE IT AS CLEARLY AS I SEE YOUR FACE PEERING THROUGH THE DOOR.
WHO?
I DO NOT KNOW.
AND IN MY WEARINESS, I HAVE ALREADY TOLD YOU TOO MUCH, LITTLE DAUGHTER.
THESE ARE NOT MATTERS FOR YOU.
I was dismissed, even more miserable and confused.
The witch would be free, but somec else would die.
I could not doubt her word -- no one could, who had seen her fierce, sad eyes as she spoke.
As I walked back to my bedchamber, the halls of t Inner Bailey seemed a pla entirely new, a strange a unfamiliar world.

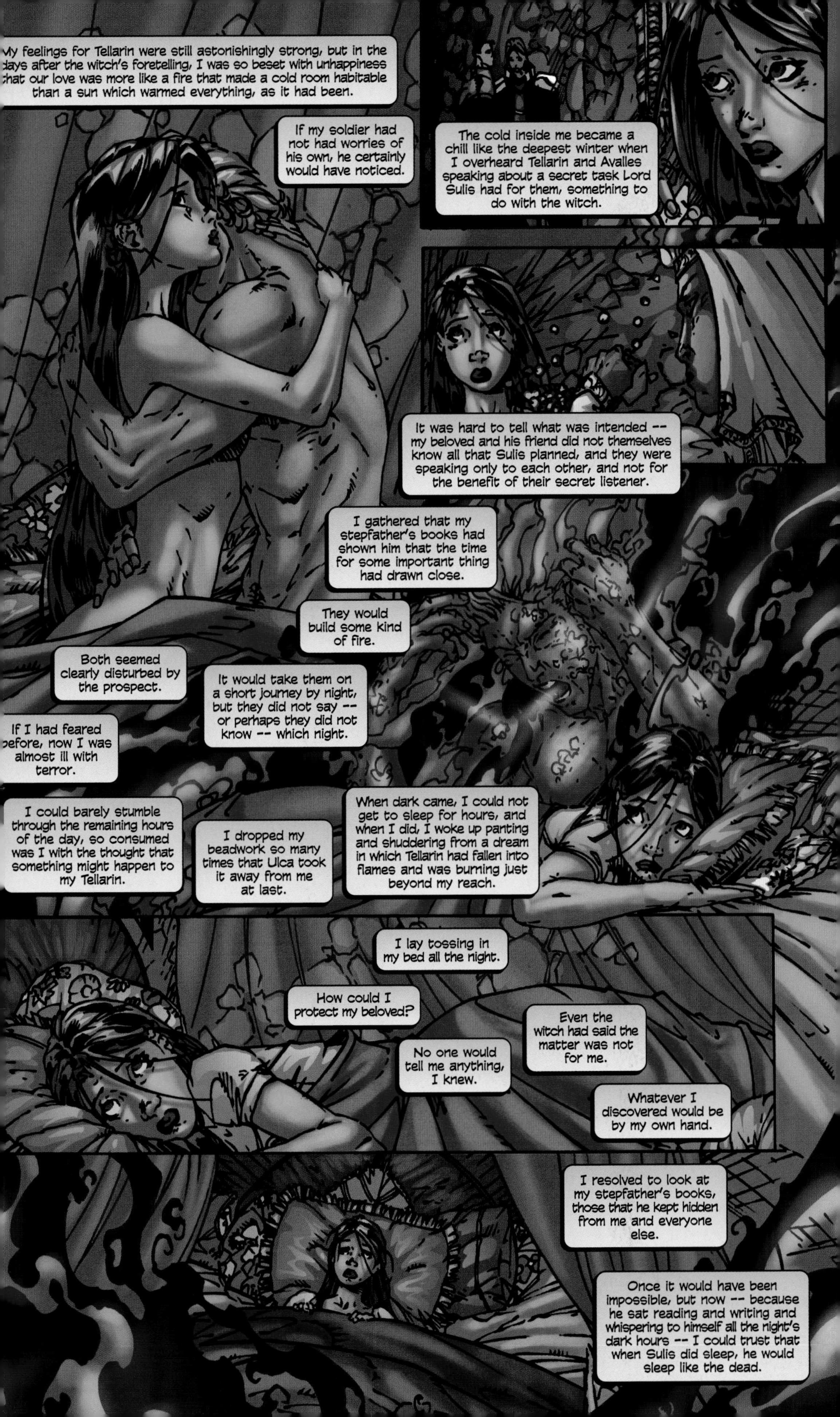
My feelings for Tellarin were still astonishingly strong, but in the days after the witch's foretelling, I was so beset with unhappiness that our love was more like a fire that made a cold room habitable than a sun which warmed everything, as it had been.
If my soldier had not had worries of his own, he certainly would have noticed.
The cold inside me became a chill like the deepest winter when I overheard Tellarin and Avalles speaking about a secret task Lord Sulis had for them, something to do with the witch.
It was hard to tell what was intended -- my beloved and his friend did not themselves know all that Sulis planned, and they were speaking only to each other, and not for the benefit of their secret listener.
I gathered that my stepfather's books had shown him that the time for some important thing had drawn close.
They would build some kind of fire.
Both seemed clearly disturbed by the prospect.
It would take them on a short journey by night, but they did not say -- or perhaps they did not know -- which night.
If I had feared before, now I was almost ill with terror.
I could barely stumble through the remaining hours of the day, so consumed was I with the thought that something might happen to my Tellarin.
I dropped my beadwork so many times that Ulca took it away from me at last.
When dark came, I could not get to sleep for hours, and when I did, I woke up panting and shuddering from a dream in which Tellarin had fallen into flames and was burning just beyond my reach.
I lay tossing in my bed all the night.
How could I protect my beloved?
No one would tell me anything, I knew.
Even the witch had said the matter was not for me.
Whatever I discovered would be by my own hand.
I resolved to look at my stepfather's books, those that he kept hidden from me and everyone else.
Once it would have been impossible, but now -- because he sat reading and writing and whispering to himself all the night's dark hours -- I could trust that when Sulis did sleep, he would sleep like the dead.

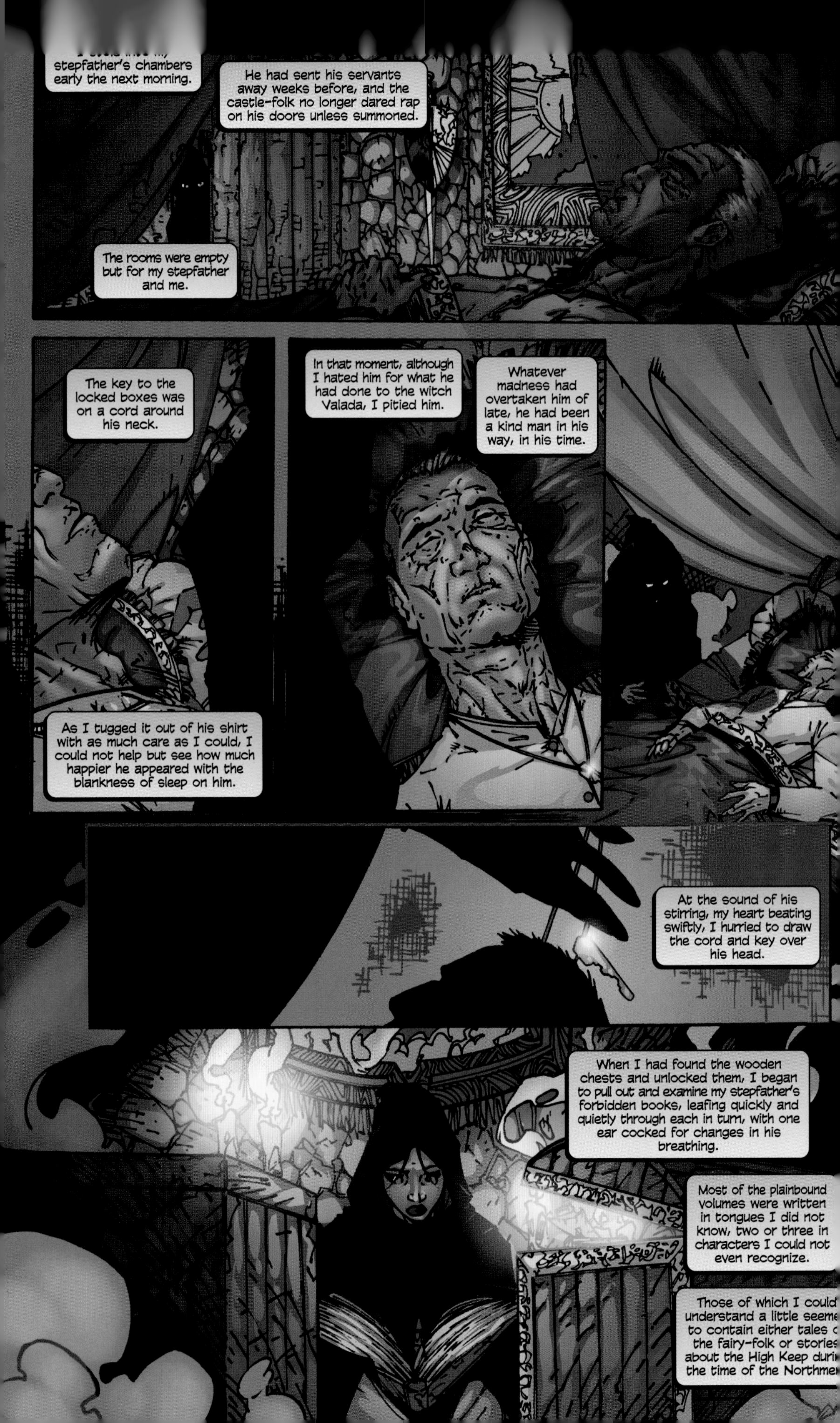

stepfather's chambers early the next morning.
He had sent his servants away weeks before, and the castle-folk no longer dared rap on his doors unless summoned.
The rooms were empty but for my stepfather and me.
The key to the locked boxes was on a cord around his neck.
As I tugged it out of his shirt with as much care as I could, I could not help but see how much happier he appeared with the blankness of sleep on him.
In that moment, although I hated him for what he had done to the witch Valada, I pitied him.
Whatever madness had overtaken him of late, he had been a kind man in his way, in his time.
At the sound of his stirring, my heart beating swiftly, I hurried to draw the cord and key over his head.
When I had found the wooden chests and unlocked them, I began to pull out and examine my stepfather's forbidden books, leafing quickly and quietly through each in turn, with one ear cocked for changes in his breathing.
Most of the plainbound volumes were written in tongues I did not know, two or three in characters I could not even recognize.
Those of which I could understand a little seeme
to contain either tales
the fairy-folk or stories
about the High Keep duri
the time of the Northme

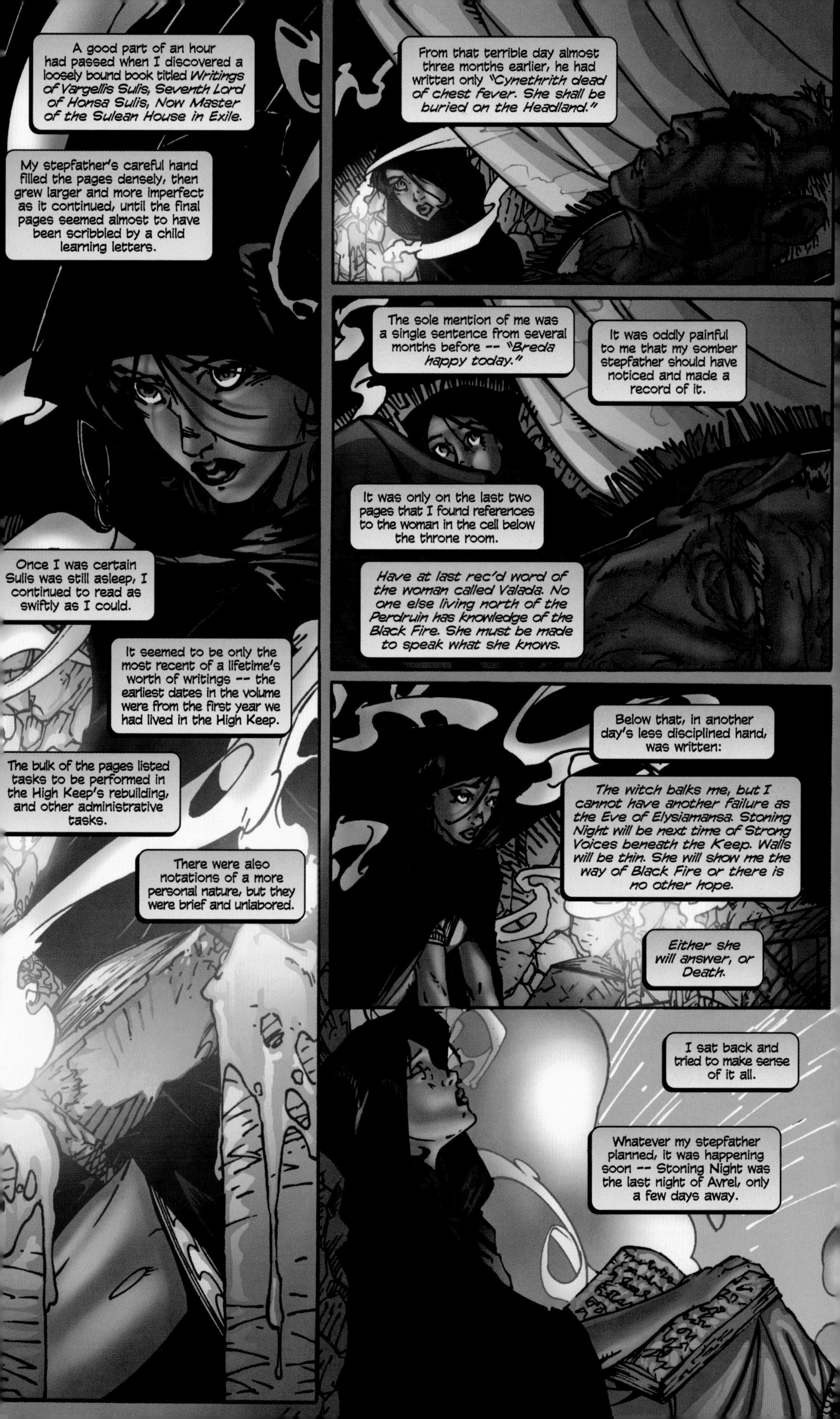
A good part of an hour had passed when I discovered a loosely bound book titled *Writings of Vargellis Sulis, Seventh Lord of Honsa Sulis, Now Master of the Sulean House in Exile.*
My stepfather's careful hand filled the pages densely, then grew larger and more imperfect as it continued, until the final pages seemed almost to have been scribbled by a child learning letters.
Once I was certain Sulis was still asleep, I continued to read as swiftly as I could.
It seemed to be only the most recent of a lifetime's worth of writings -- the earliest dates in the volume were from the first year we had lived in the High Keep.
The bulk of the pages listed tasks to be performed in the High Keep's rebuilding, and other administrative tasks.
There were also notations of a more personal nature, but they were brief and unlabored.
From that terrible day almost three months earlier, he had written only *"Cynethrith dead of chest fever. She shall be buried on the Headland."*
The sole mention of me was a single sentence from several months before -- *"Breda happy today."*
It was oddly painful to me that my somber stepfather should have noticed and made a record of it.
It was only on the last two pages that I found references to the woman in the cell below the throne room.
Have at last rec'd word of the woman called Valada. No one else living north of the Perdruin has knowledge of the Black Fire. She must be made to speak what she knows.
Below that, in another day's less disciplined hand, was written:
The witch balks me, but I cannot have another failure as the Eve of Elysiamansa. Stoning Night will be next time of Strong Voices beneath the Keep. Walls will be thin. She will show me the way of Black Fire or there is no other hope.
Either she will answer, or Death.
I sat back and tried to make sense of it all.
Whatever my stepfather planned, it was happening soon -- Stoning Night was the last night of Avrel, only a few days away.

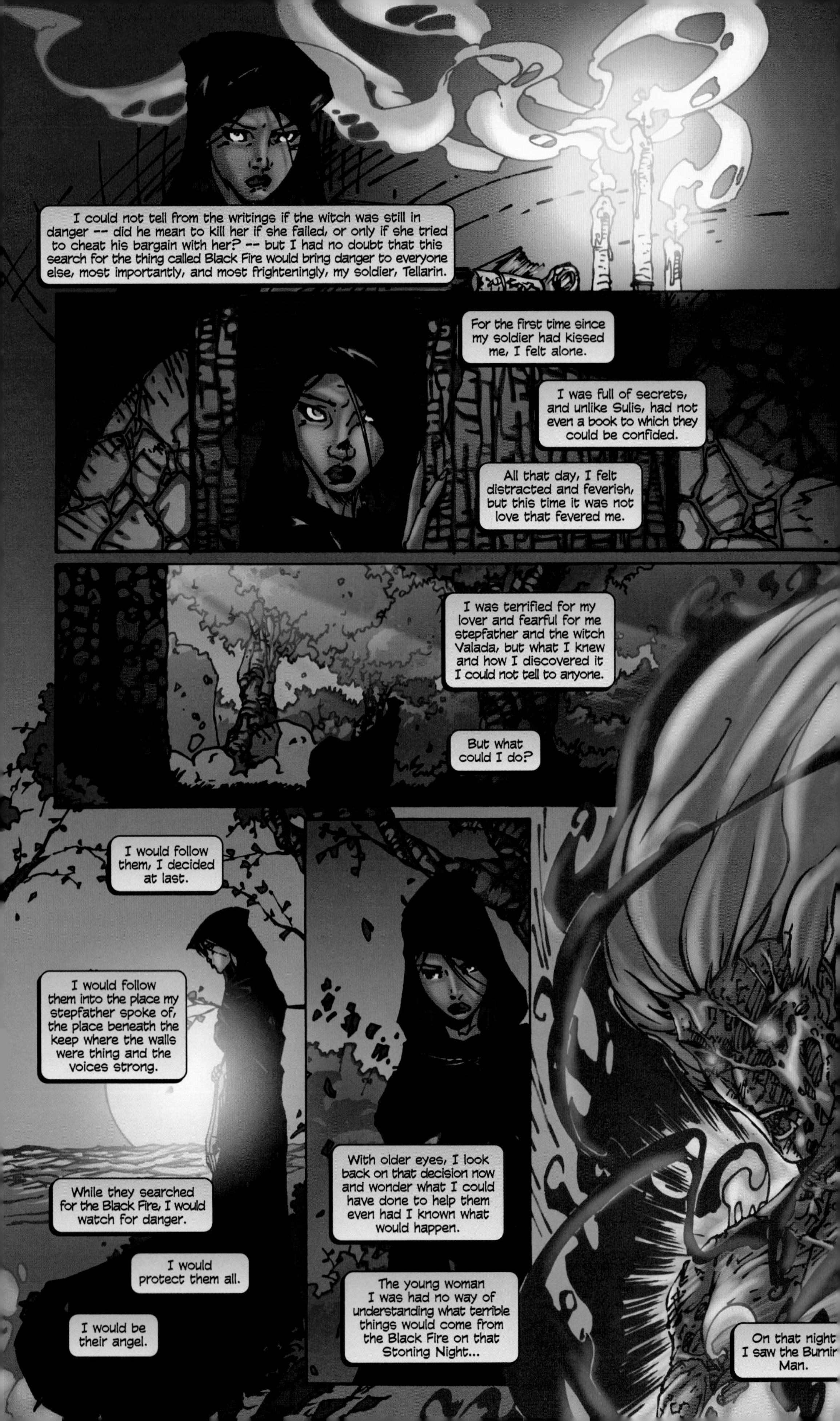
I could not tell from the writings if the witch was still in danger -- did he mean to kill her if she failed, or only if she tried to cheat his bargain with her? -- but I had no doubt that this search for the thing called Black Fire would bring danger to everyone else, most importantly, and most frighteningly, my soldier, Tellarin.
For the first time since my soldier had kissed me, I felt alone.
I was full of secrets, and unlike Sulis, had not even a book to which they could be confided.
All that day, I felt distracted and feverish, but this time it was not love that fevered me.
I was terrified for my lover and fearful for me stepfather and the witch Valada, but what I knew and how I discovered it I could not tell to anyone.
But what could I do?
I would follow them, I decided at last.
I would follow them into the place my stepfather spoke of, the place beneath the keep where the walls were thing and the voices strong.
While they searched for the Black Fire, I would watch for danger.
I would protect them all.
I would be their angel.
With older eyes, I look back on that decision now and wonder what I could have done to help them even had I known what would happen.
The young woman I was had no way of understanding what terrible things would come from the Black Fire on that Stoning Night...
On that night I saw the Burnir Man.

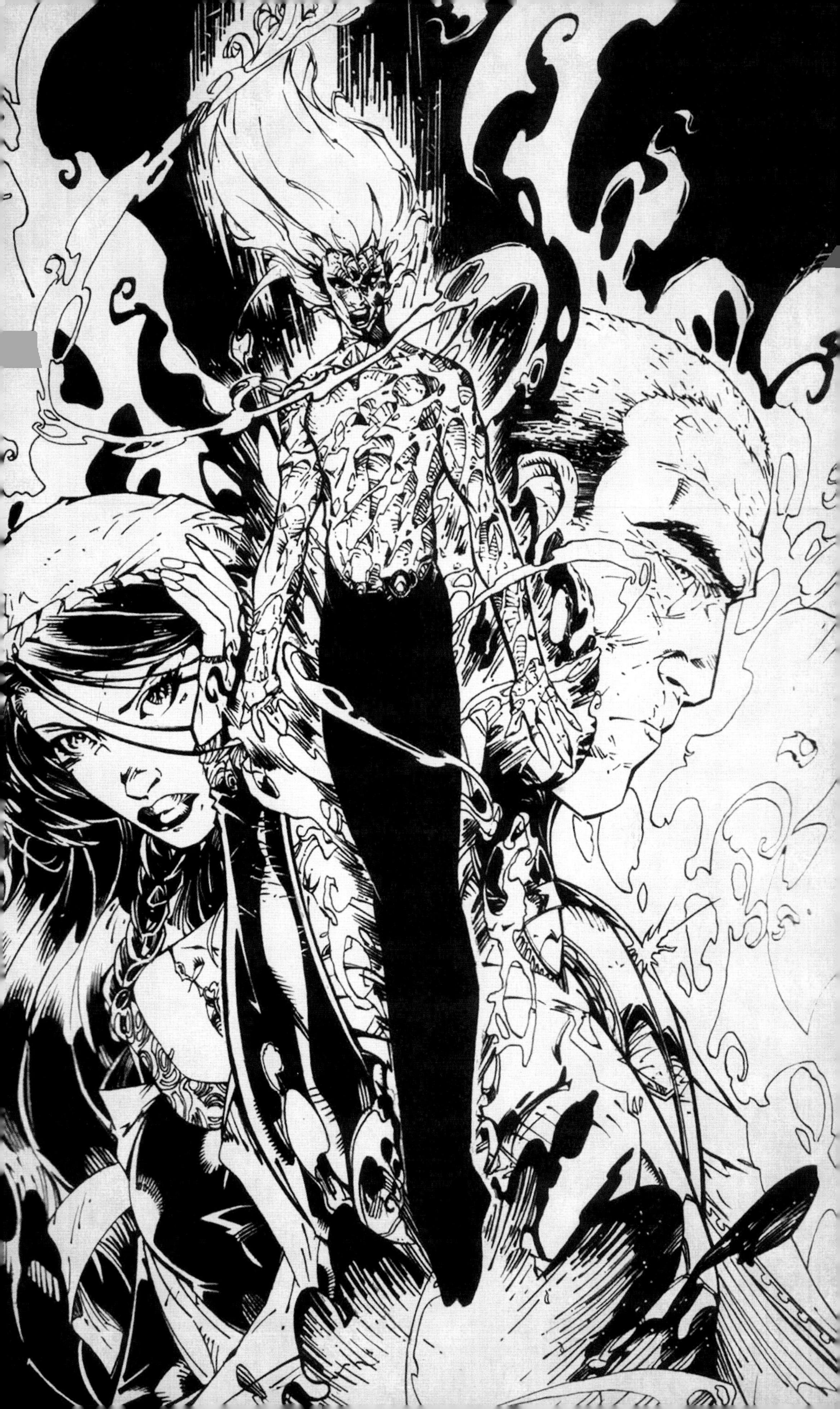

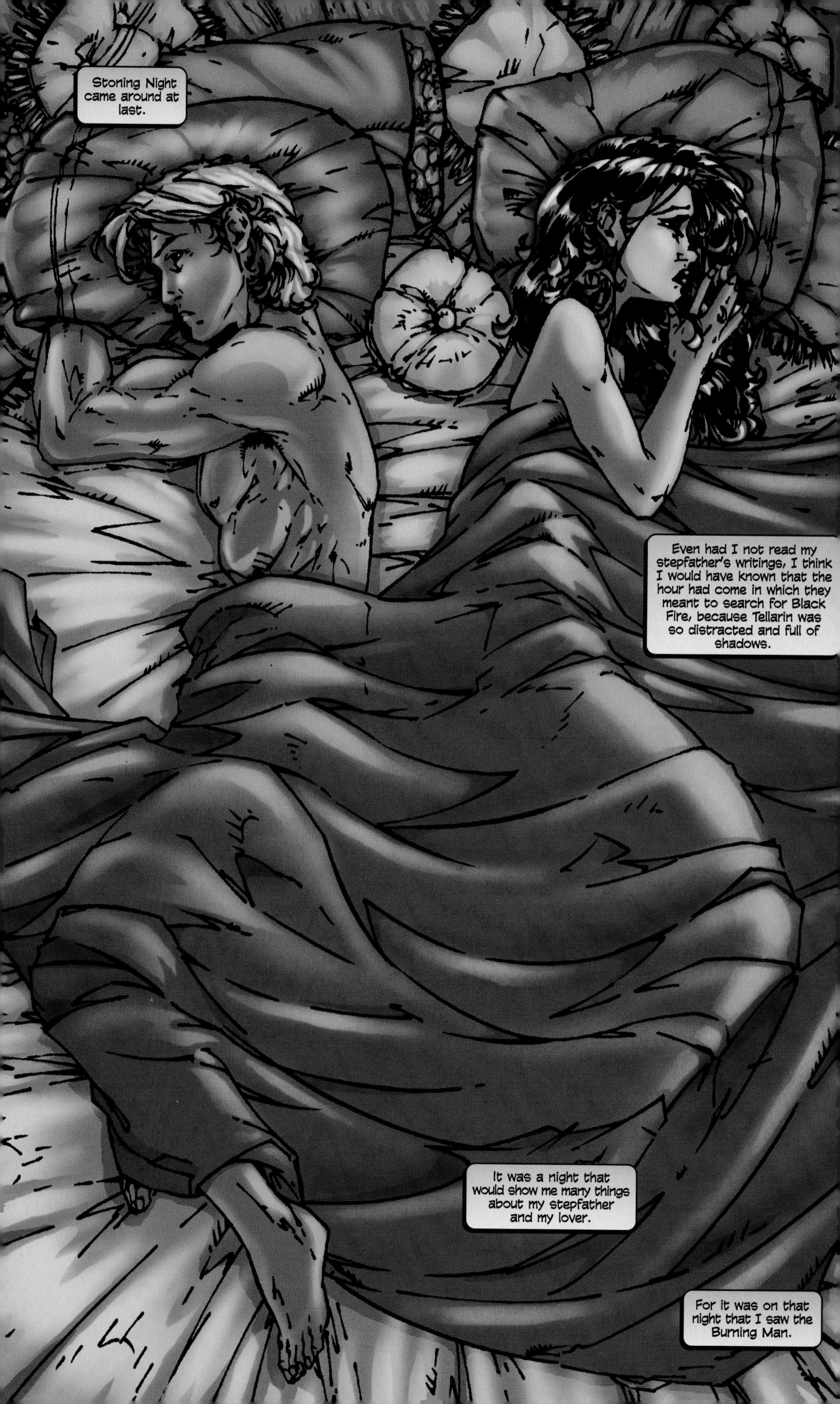
Stoning Night came around at last.
Even had I not read my stepfather's writings, I think I would have known that the hour had come in which they meant to search for Black Fire, because Tellarin was so distracted and full of shadows.
It was a night that would show me many things about my stepfather and my lover.
For it was on that night that I saw the Burning Man.

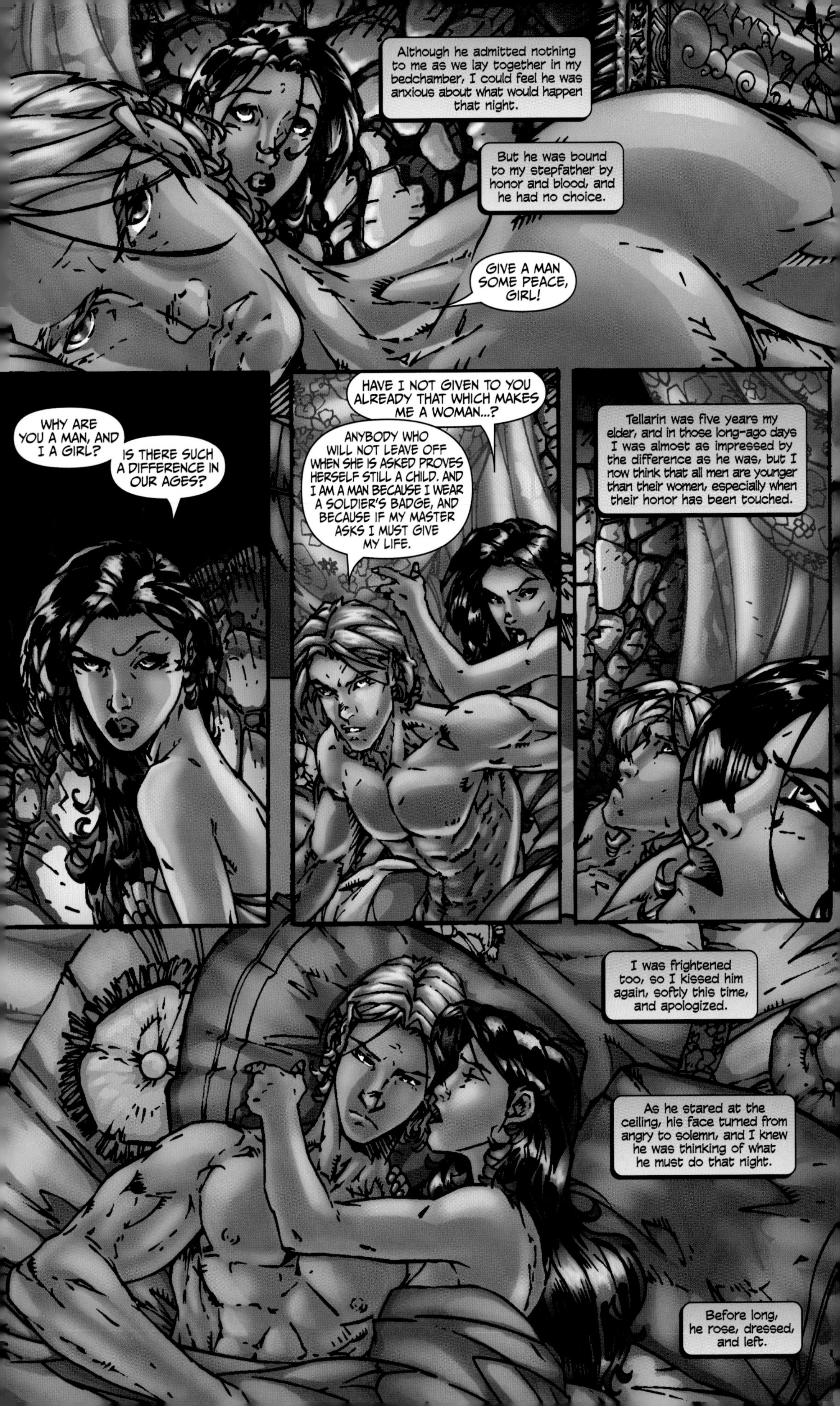
Although he admitted nothing to me as we lay together in my bedchamber, I could feel he was anxious about what would happen that night.
But he was bound to my stepfather by honor and blood, and he had no choice.
GIVE A MAN SOME PEACE, GIRL!
WHY ARE YOU A MAN, AND I A GIRL?
IS THERE SUCH A DIFFERENCE IN OUR AGES?
HAVE I NOT GIVEN TO YOU ALREADY THAT WHICH MAKES ME A WOMAN...?
ANYBODY WHO WILL NOT LEAVE OFF WHEN SHE IS ASKED PROVES HERSELF STILL A CHILD. AND I AM A MAN BECAUSE I WEAR A SOLDIER'S BADGE, AND BECAUSE IF MY MASTER ASKS I MUST GIVE MY LIFE.
Tellarin was five years my elder, and in those long-ago days I was almost as impressed by the difference as he was, but I now think that all men are younger than their women, especially when their honor has been touched.
I was frightened too, so I kissed him again, softly this time, and apologized.
As he stared at the ceiling, his face turned from angry to solemn, and I knew he was thinking of what he must do that night.
Before long, he rose, dressed, and left.

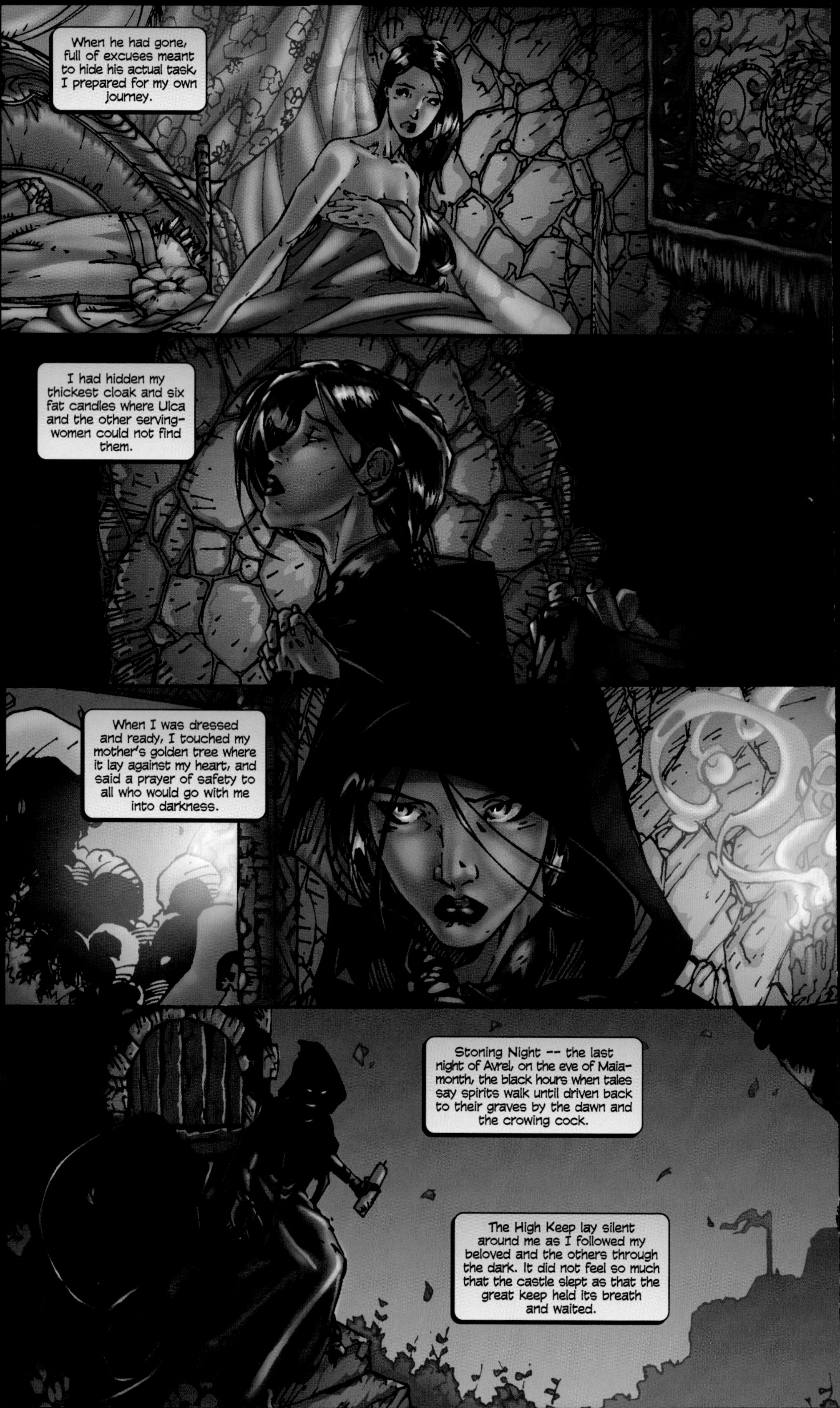

When he had gone, full of excuses meant to hide his actual task, I prepared for my own journey.
I had hidden my thickest cloak and six fat candles where Ulca and the other serving-women could not find them.
When I was dressed and ready, I touched my mother's golden tree where it lay against my heart, and said a prayer of safety to all who would go with me into darkness.
Stoning Night -- the last night of Avrel, on the eve of Maia-month, the black hours when tales say spirits walk until driven back to their graves by the dawn and the crowing cock.
The High Keep lay silent around me as I followed my beloved and the others through the dark. It did not feel so much that the castle slept as that the great keep held its breath and waited.

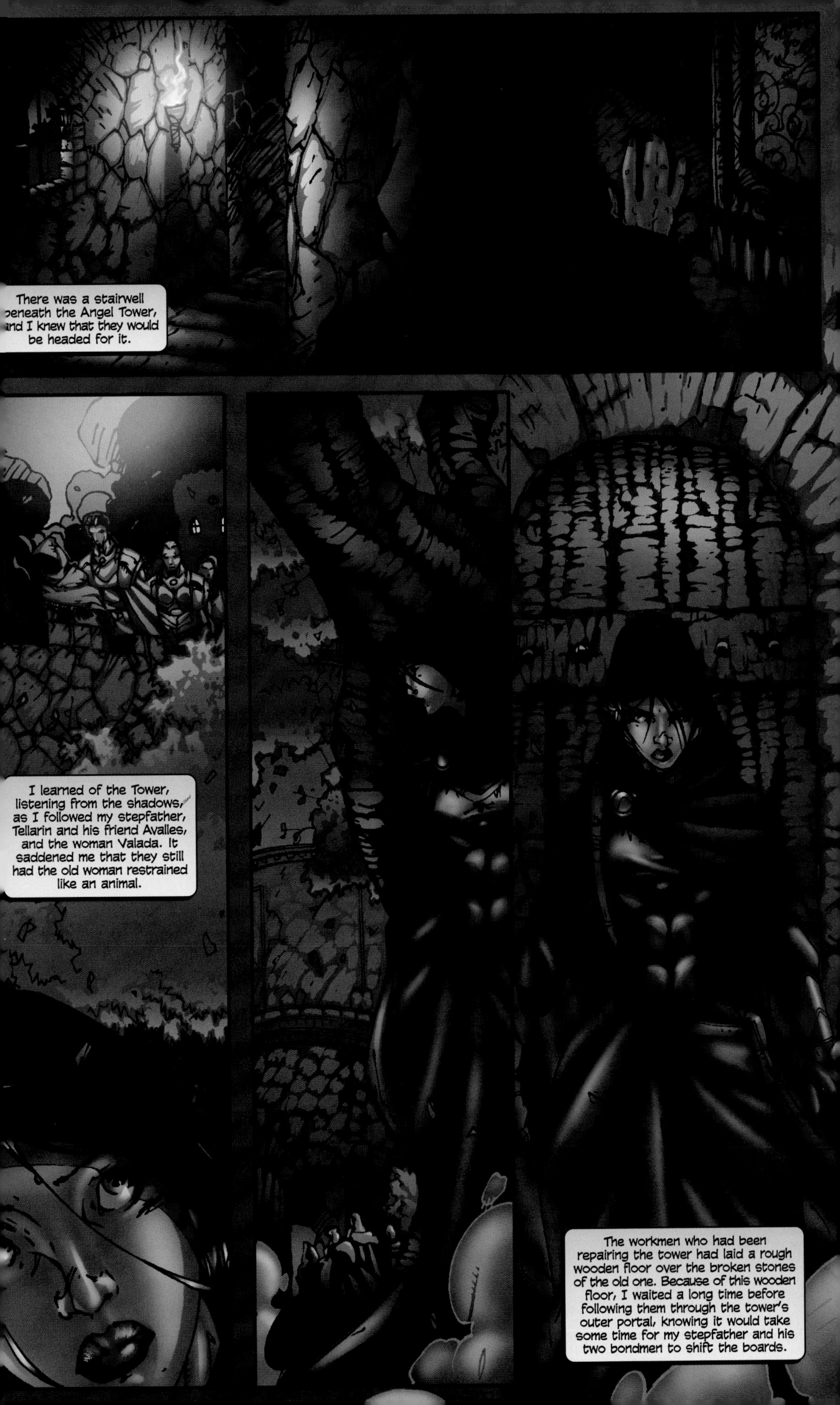
There was a stairwell beneath the Angel Tower, and I knew that they would be headed for it.
I learned of the Tower, listening from the shadows, as I followed my stepfather, Tellarin and his friend Avalles, and the woman Valada. It saddened me that they still had the old woman restrained like an animal.
The workmen who had been repairing the tower had laid a rough wooden floor over the broken stones of the old one. Because of this wooden floor, I waited a long time before following them through the tower's outer portal, knowing it would take some time for my stepfather and his two bondmen to shift the boards.

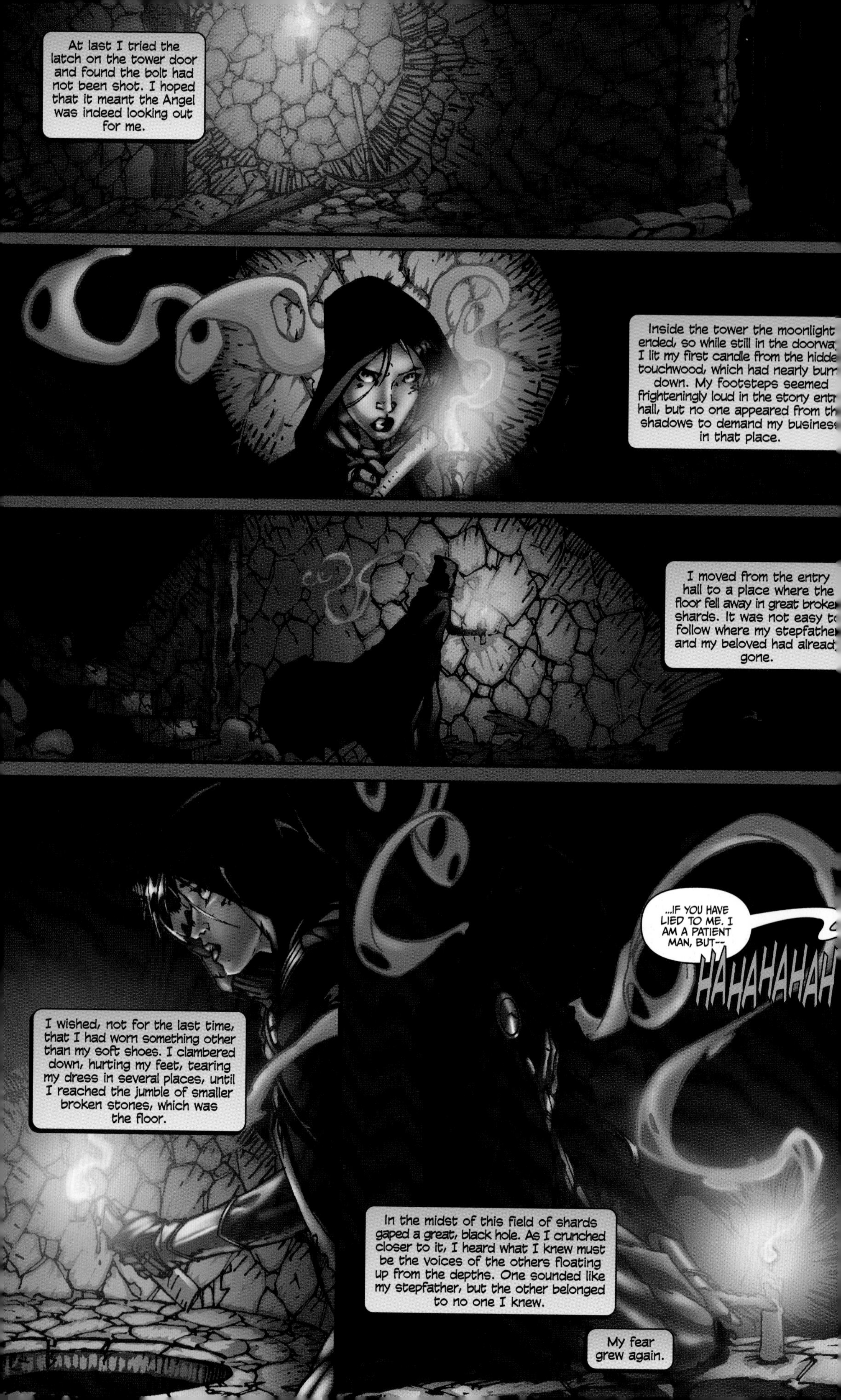
At last I tried the latch on the tower door and found the bolt had not been shot. I hoped that it meant the Angel was indeed looking out for me.
Inside the tower the moonlight ended, so while still in the doorwa I lit my first candle from the hidde touchwood, which had nearly burn down. My footsteps seemed frighteningly loud in the stony entr hall, but no one appeared from th shadows to demand my busines in that place.
I moved from the entry hall to a place where the floor fell away in great broke shards. It was not easy t follow where my stepfathe and my beloved had alread gone.
I wished, not for the last time, that I had worn something other than my soft shoes. I clambered down, hurting my feet, tearing my dress in several places, until I reached the jumble of smaller broken stones, which was the floor.
...IF YOU HAVE LIED TO ME. I AM A PATIENT MAN, BUT--
HAHAHAHAH
In the midst of this field of shards gaped a great, black hole. As I crunched closer to it, I heard what I knew must be the voices of the others floating up from the depths. One sounded like my stepfather, but the other belonged to no one I knew.
My fear grew again.

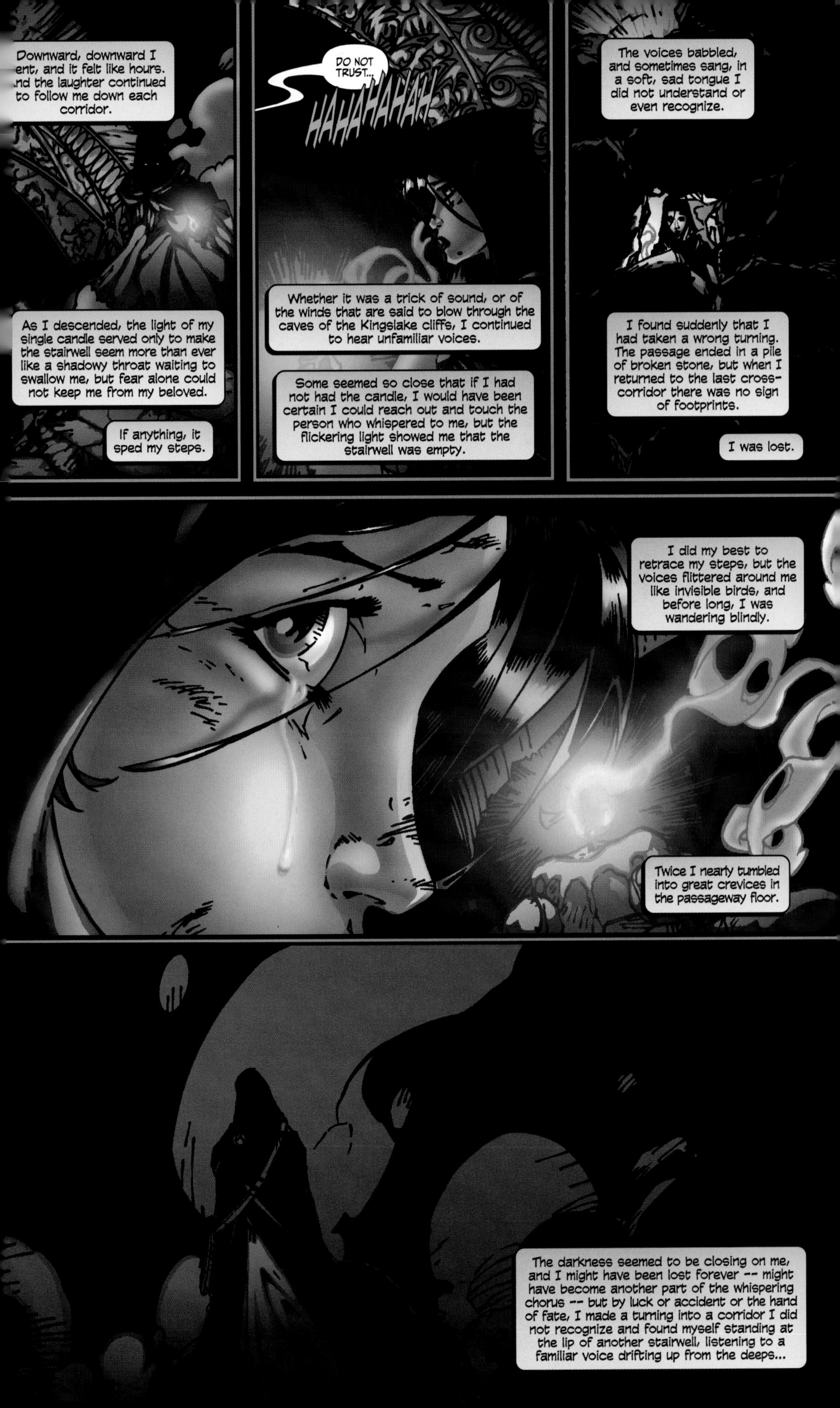

Downward, downward I
ent, and it felt like hours.
nd the laughter continued
to follow me down each
corridor.
As I descended, the light of my single candle served only to make the stairwell seem more than ever like a shadowy throat waiting to swallow me, but fear alone could not keep me from my beloved.
If anything, it sped my steps.
DO NOT TRUST...
HAHAHAHAH
Whether it was a trick of sound, or of the winds that are said to blow through the caves of the Kingslake cliffs, I continued to hear unfamiliar voices.
Some seemed so close that if I had not had the candle, I would have been certain I could reach out and touch the person who whispered to me, but the flickering light showed me that the stairwell was empty.
The voices babbled, and sometimes sang, in a soft, sad tongue I did not understand or even recognize.
I found suddenly that I had taken a wrong turning. The passage ended in a pile of broken stone, but when I returned to the last cross-corridor there was no sign of footprints.
I was lost.
I did my best to retrace my steps, but the voices flittered around me like invisible birds, and before long, I was wandering blindly.
Twice I nearly tumbled into great crevices in the passageway floor.
The darkness seemed to be closing on me, and I might have been lost forever -- might have become another part of the whispering chorus -- but by luck or accident or the hand of fate, I made a turning into a corridor I did not recognize and found myself standing at the lip of another stairwell, listening to a familiar voice drifting up from the deeps...

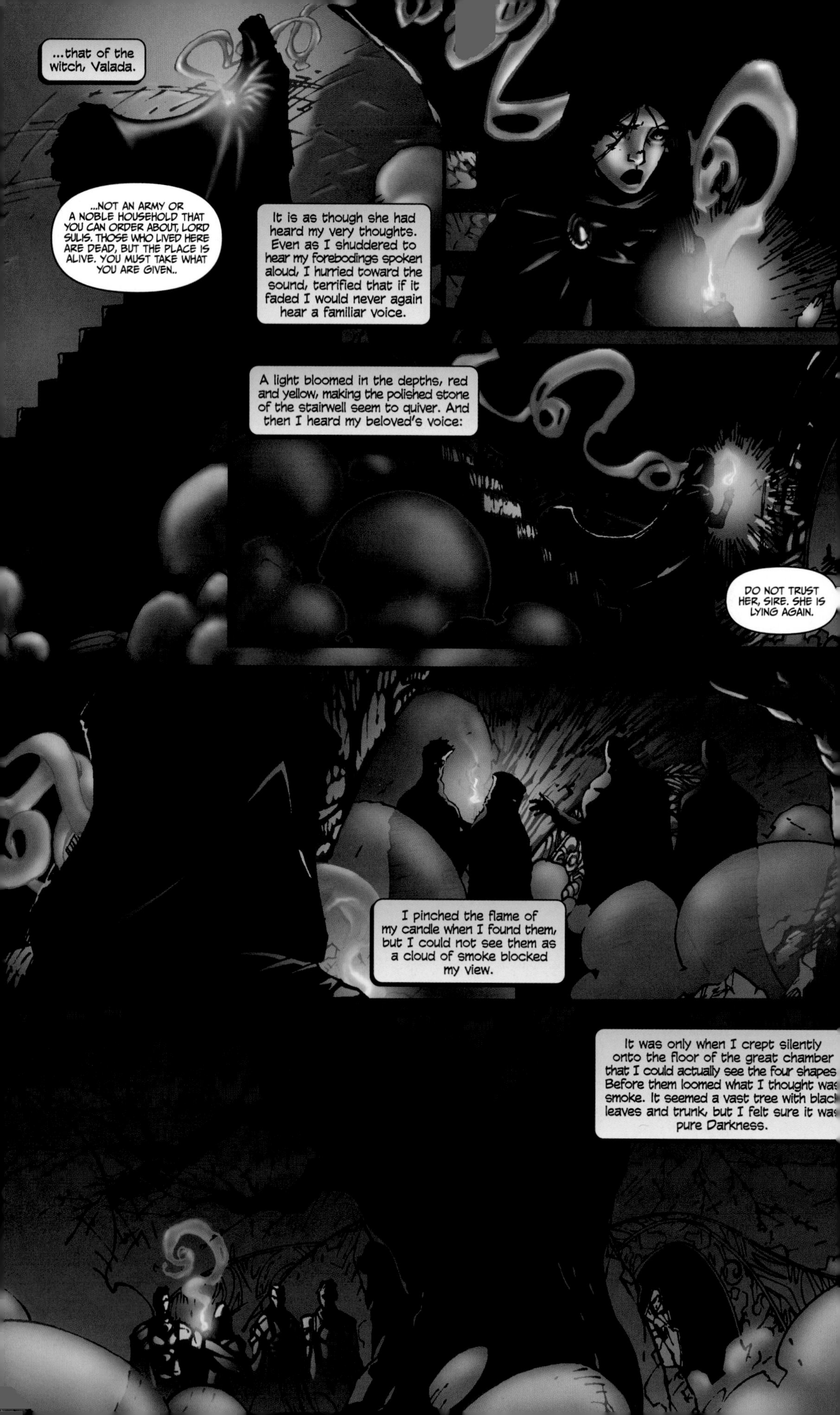
...that of the witch, Valada.
...NOT AN ARMY OR A NOBLE HOUSEHOLD THAT YOU CAN ORDER ABOUT, LORD SULIS. THOSE WHO LIVED HERE ARE DEAD, BUT THE PLACE IS ALIVE. YOU MUST TAKE WHAT YOU ARE GIVEN..
It is as though she had heard my very thoughts. Even as I shuddered to hear my forebodings spoken aloud, I hurried toward the sound, terrified that if it faded I would never again hear a familiar voice.
A light bloomed in the depths, red and yellow, making the polished stone of the stairwell seem to quiver. And then I heard my beloved's voice:
DO NOT TRUST HER, SIRE. SHE IS LYING AGAIN.
I pinched the flame of my candle when I found them, but I could not see them as a cloud of smoke blocked my view.
It was only when I crept silently onto the floor of the great chamber that I could actually see the four shapes. Before them loomed what I thought was smoke. It seemed a vast tree with black leaves and trunk, but I felt sure it was pure Darkness.

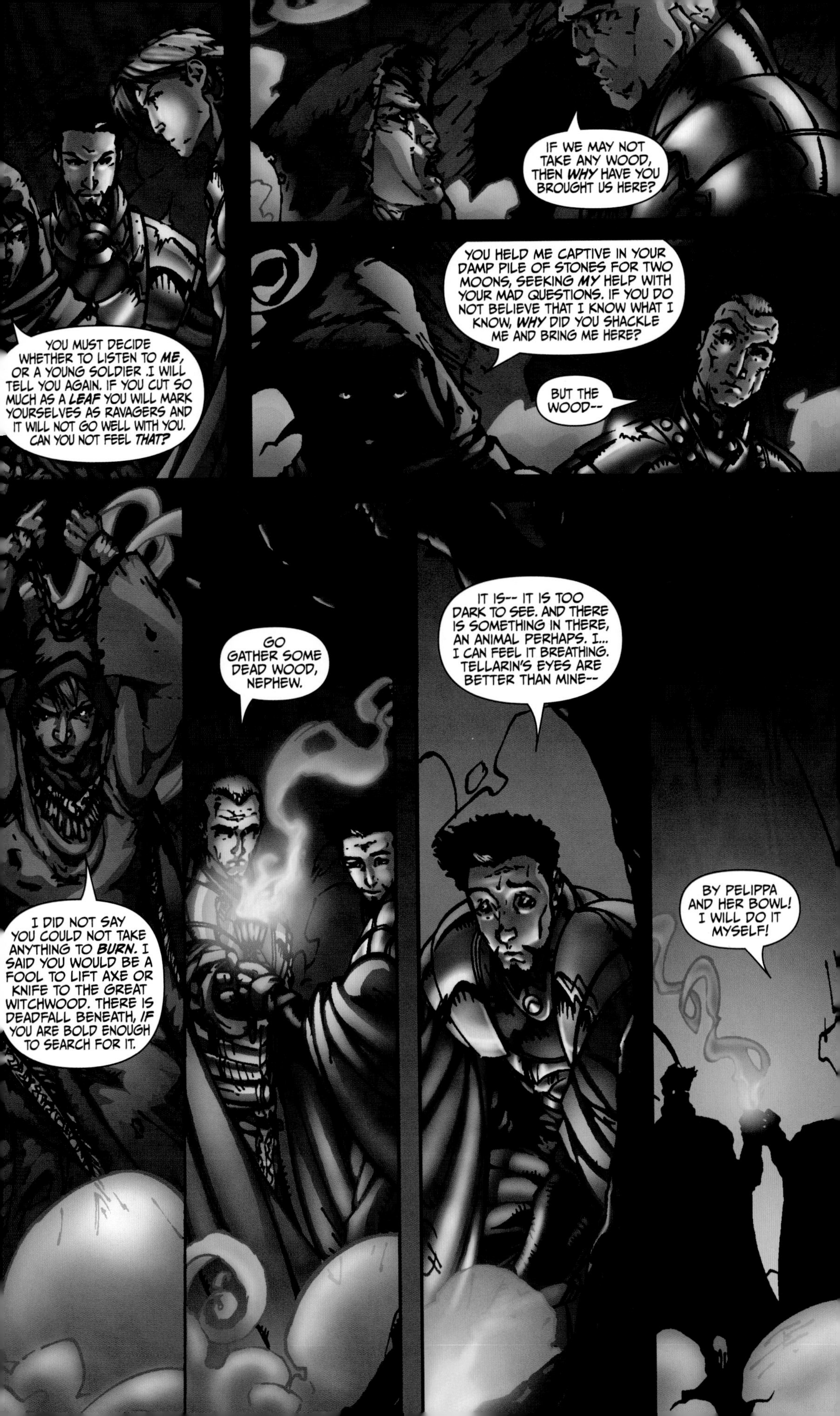
IF WE MAY NOT TAKE ANY WOOD, THEN WHY HAVE YOU BROUGHT US HERE?
YOU MUST DECIDE WHETHER TO LISTEN TO ME, OR A YOUNG SOLDIER .I WILL TELL YOU AGAIN. IF YOU CUT SO MUCH AS A LEAF YOU WILL MARK YOURSELVES AS RAVAGERS AND IT WILL NOT GO WELL WITH YOU. CAN YOU NOT FEEL THAT?
YOU HELD ME CAPTIVE IN YOUR DAMP PILE OF STONES FOR TWO MOONS, SEEKING MY HELP WITH YOUR MAD QUESTIONS. IF YOU DO NOT BELIEVE THAT I KNOW WHAT I KNOW, WHY DID YOU SHACKLE ME AND BRING ME HERE?
BUT THE WOOD--
I DID NOT SAY YOU COULD NOT TAKE ANYTHING TO BURN. I SAID YOU WOULD BE A FOOL TO LIFT AXE OR KNIFE TO THE GREAT WITCHWOOD. THERE IS DEADFALL BENEATH, IF YOU ARE BOLD ENOUGH TO SEARCH FOR IT.
GO GATHER SOME DEAD WOOD, NEPHEW.
IT IS-- IT IS TOO DARK TO SEE. AND THERE IS SOMETHING IN THERE, AN ANIMAL PERHAPS. I... I CAN FEEL IT BREATHING. TELLARIN'S EYES ARE BETTER THAN MINE--
BY PELIPPA AND HER BOWL! I WILL DO IT MYSELF!

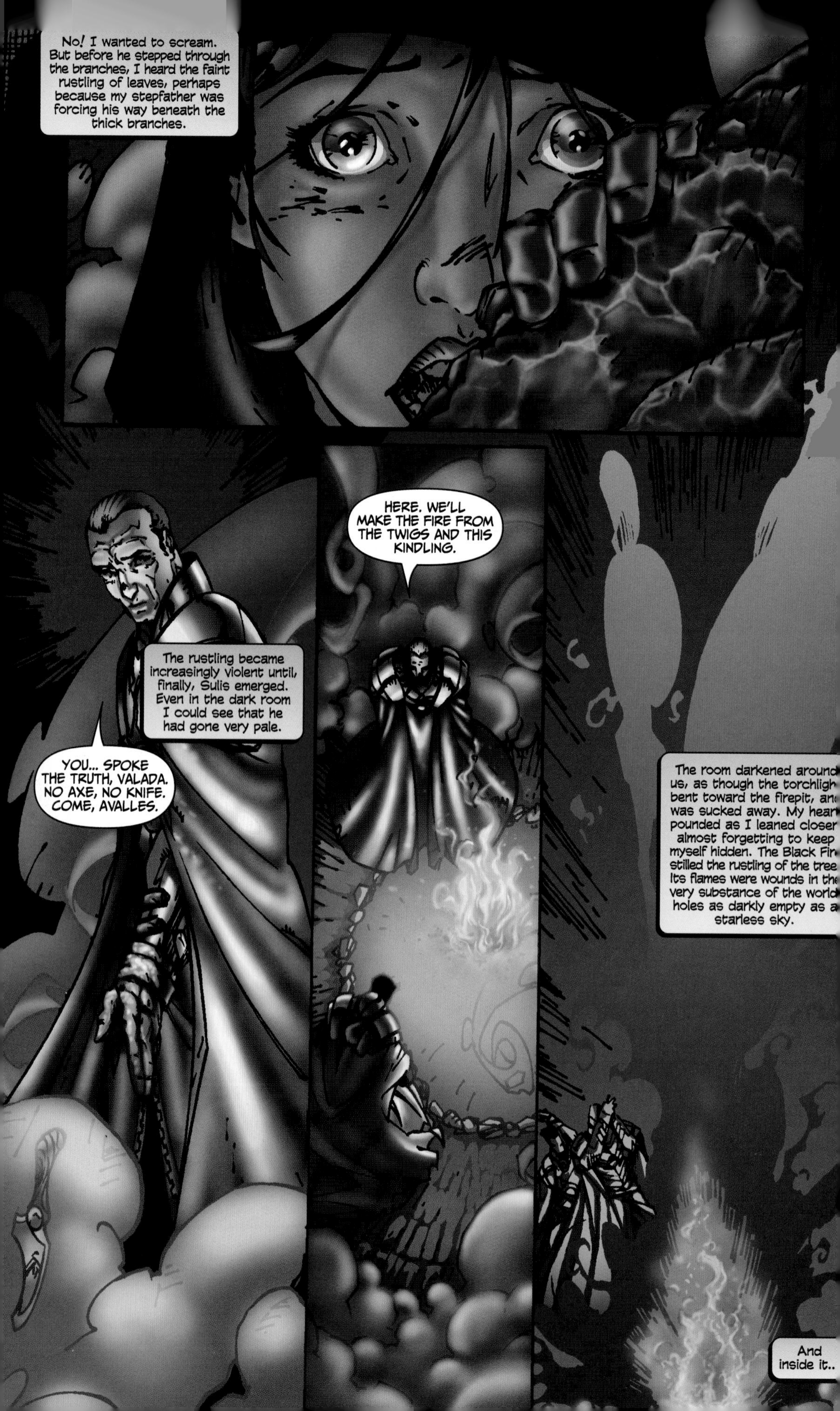
No! I wanted to scream. But before he stepped through the branches, I heard the faint rustling of leaves, perhaps because my stepfather was forcing his way beneath the thick branches.
The rustling became increasingly violent until, finally, Sulis emerged. Even in the dark room I could see that he had gone very pale.
YOU... SPOKE THE TRUTH, VALADA. NO AXE, NO KNIFE. COME, AVALLES.
HERE. WE'LL MAKE THE FIRE FROM THE TWIGS AND THIS KINDLING.
The room darkened around us, as though the torchligh bent toward the firepit, an was sucked away. My hear pounded as I leaned closer almost forgetting to keep myself hidden. The Black Fir stilled the rustling of the tree Its flames were wounds in the very substance of the world holes as darkly empty as a starless sky.
And inside it..

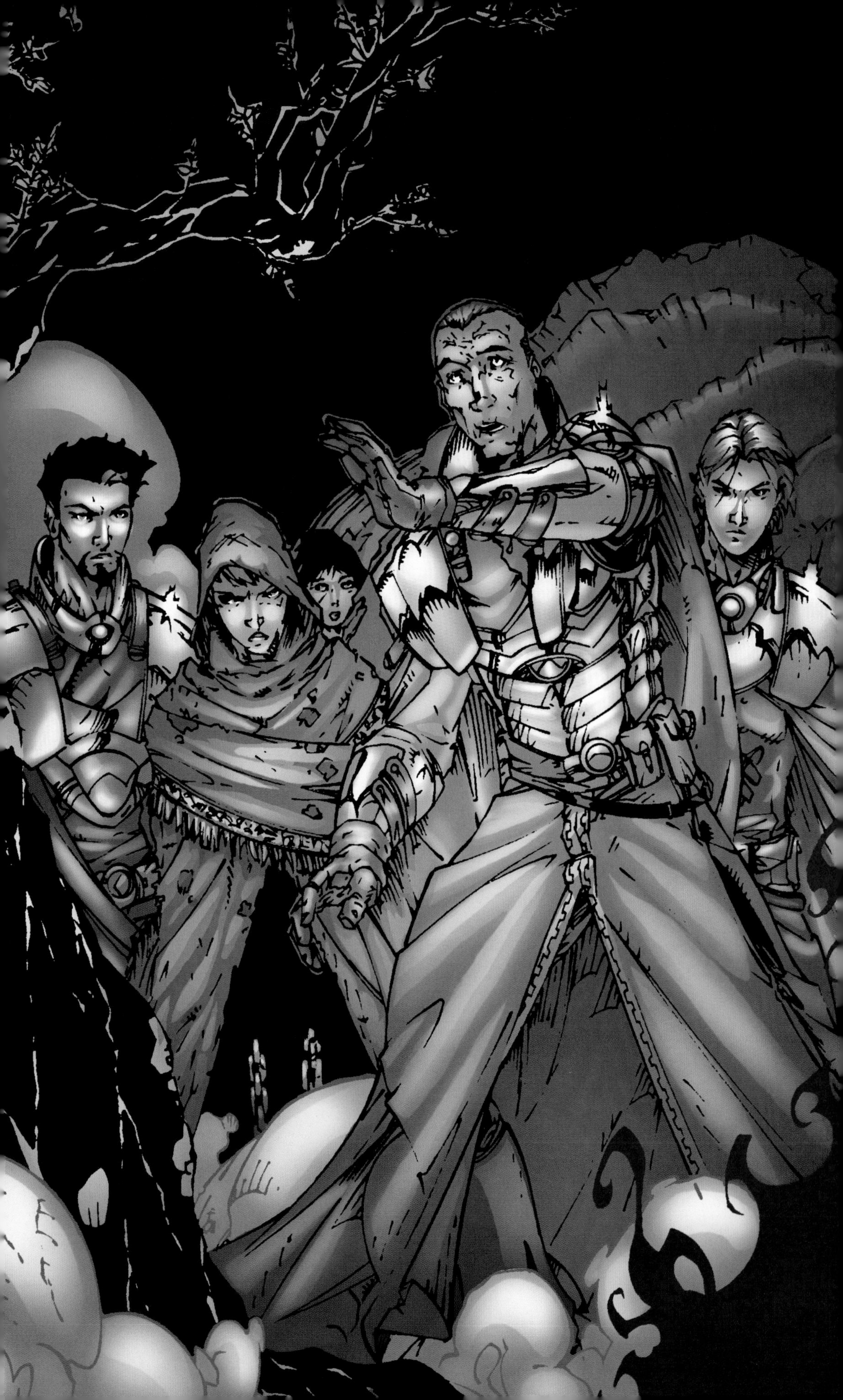

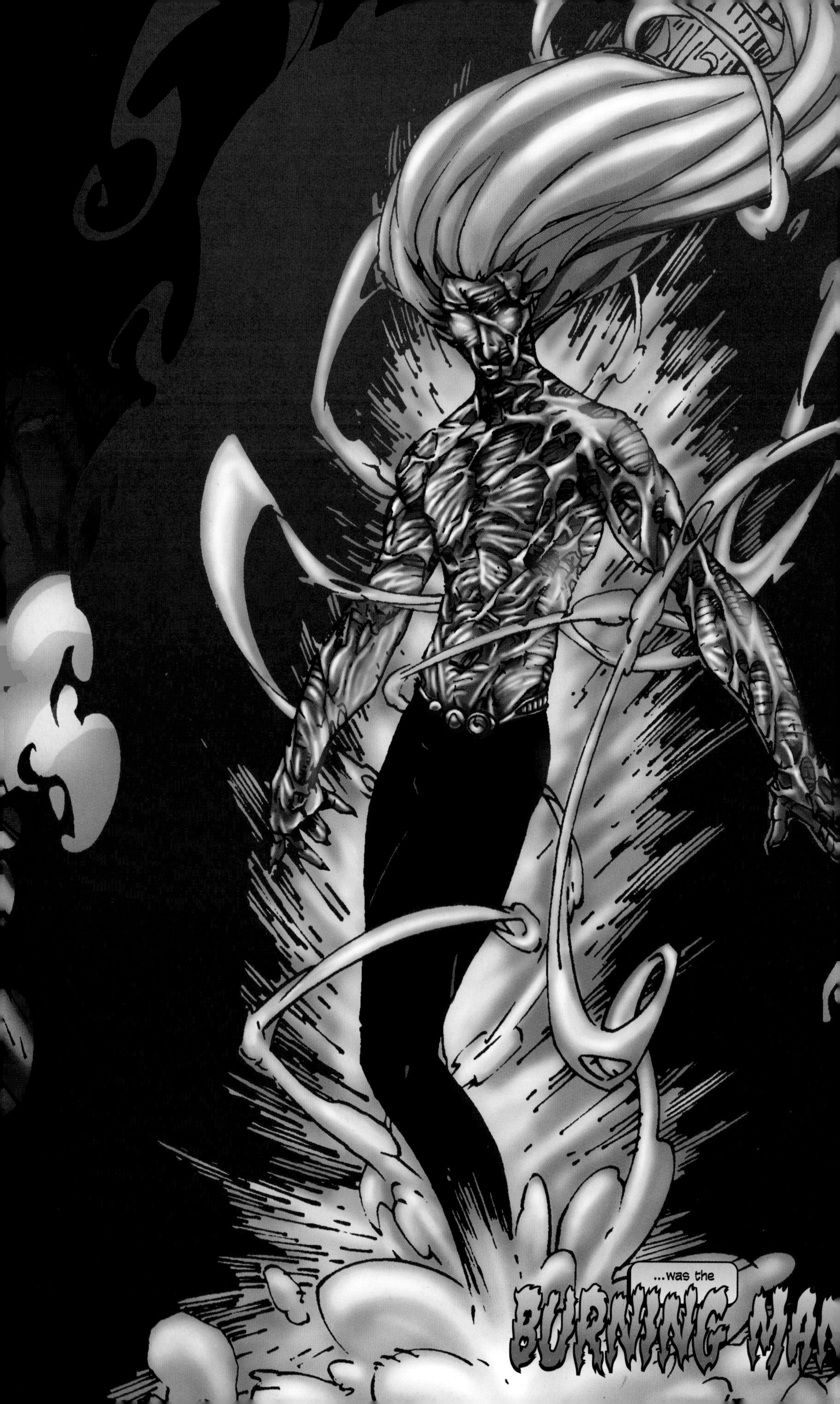
...was the
BURNING MAN

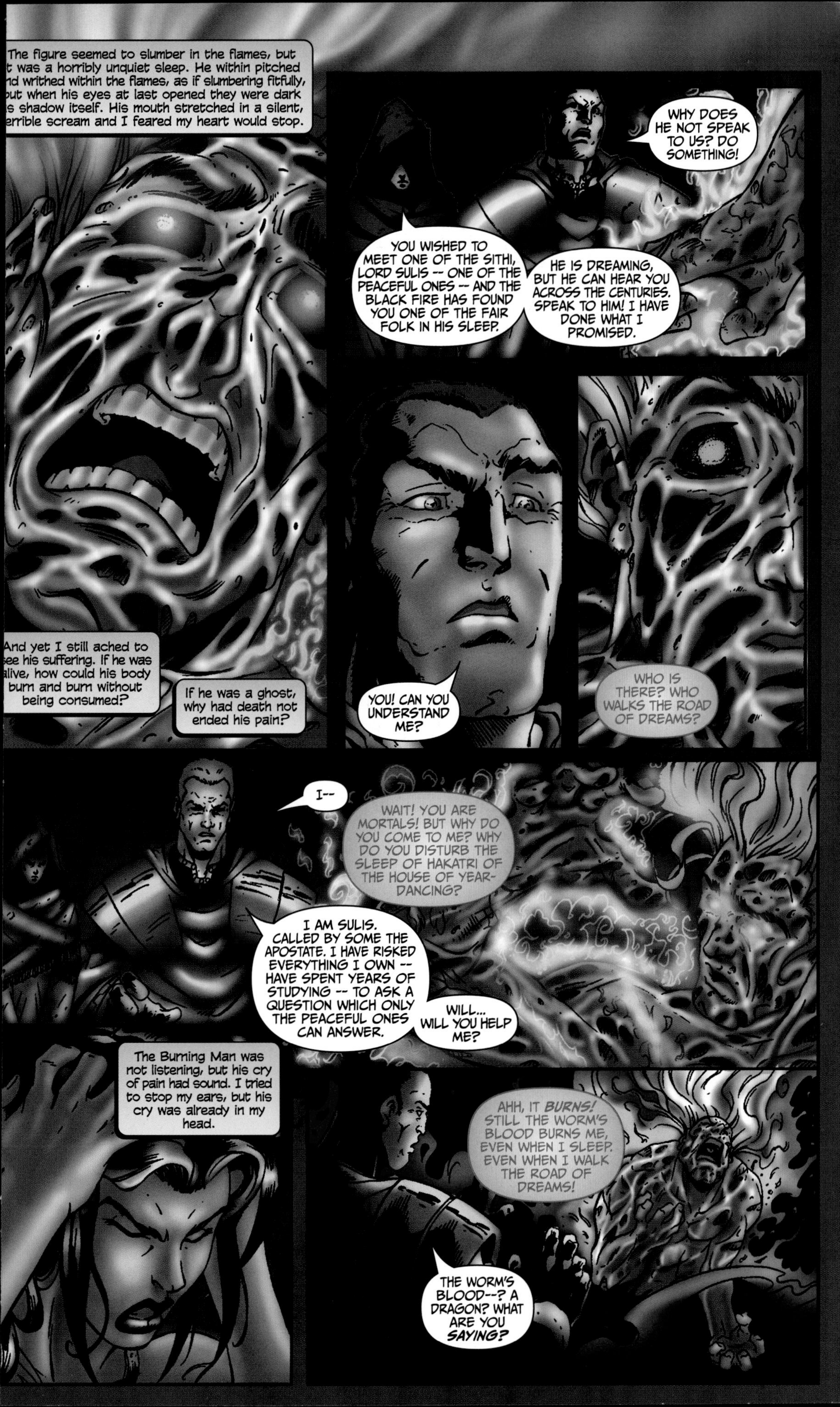

The figure seemed to slumber in the flames, but t was a horribly unquiet sleep. He within pitched nd writhed within the flames, as if slumbering fitfully, out when his eyes at last opened they were dark s shadow itself. His mouth stretched in a silent, errible scream and I feared my heart would stop.
WHY DOES HE NOT SPEAK TO US? DO SOMETHING!
YOU WISHED TO MEET ONE OF THE SITHI, LORD SULIS -- ONE OF THE PEACEFUL ONES -- AND THE BLACK FIRE HAS FOUND YOU ONE OF THE FAIR FOLK IN HIS SLEEP.
HE IS DREAMING, BUT HE CAN HEAR YOU ACROSS THE CENTURIES. SPEAK TO HIM! I HAVE DONE WHAT I PROMISED.
And yet I still ached to see his suffering. If he was alive, how could his body burn and burn without being consumed?
If he was a ghost, why had death not ended his pain?
YOU! CAN YOU UNDERSTAND ME?
WHO IS THERE? WHO WALKS THE ROAD OF DREAMS?
I--
WAIT! YOU ARE MORTALS! BUT WHY DO YOU COME TO ME? WHY DO YOU DISTURB THE SLEEP OF HAKATRI OF THE HOUSE OF YEAR-DANCING?
I AM SULIS. CALLED BY SOME THE APOSTATE. I HAVE RISKED EVERYTHING I OWN -- HAVE SPENT YEARS OF STUDYING -- TO ASK A QUESTION WHICH ONLY THE PEACEFUL ONES CAN ANSWER.
WILL... WILL YOU HELP ME?
The Burning Man was not listening, but his cry of pain had sound. I tried to stop my ears, but his cry was already in my head.
AHH, IT BURNS! STILL THE WORM'S BLOOD BURNS ME, EVEN WHEN I SLEEP. EVEN WHEN I WALK THE ROAD OF DREAMS!
THE WORM'S BLOOD--? A DRAGON? WHAT ARE YOU SAYING?

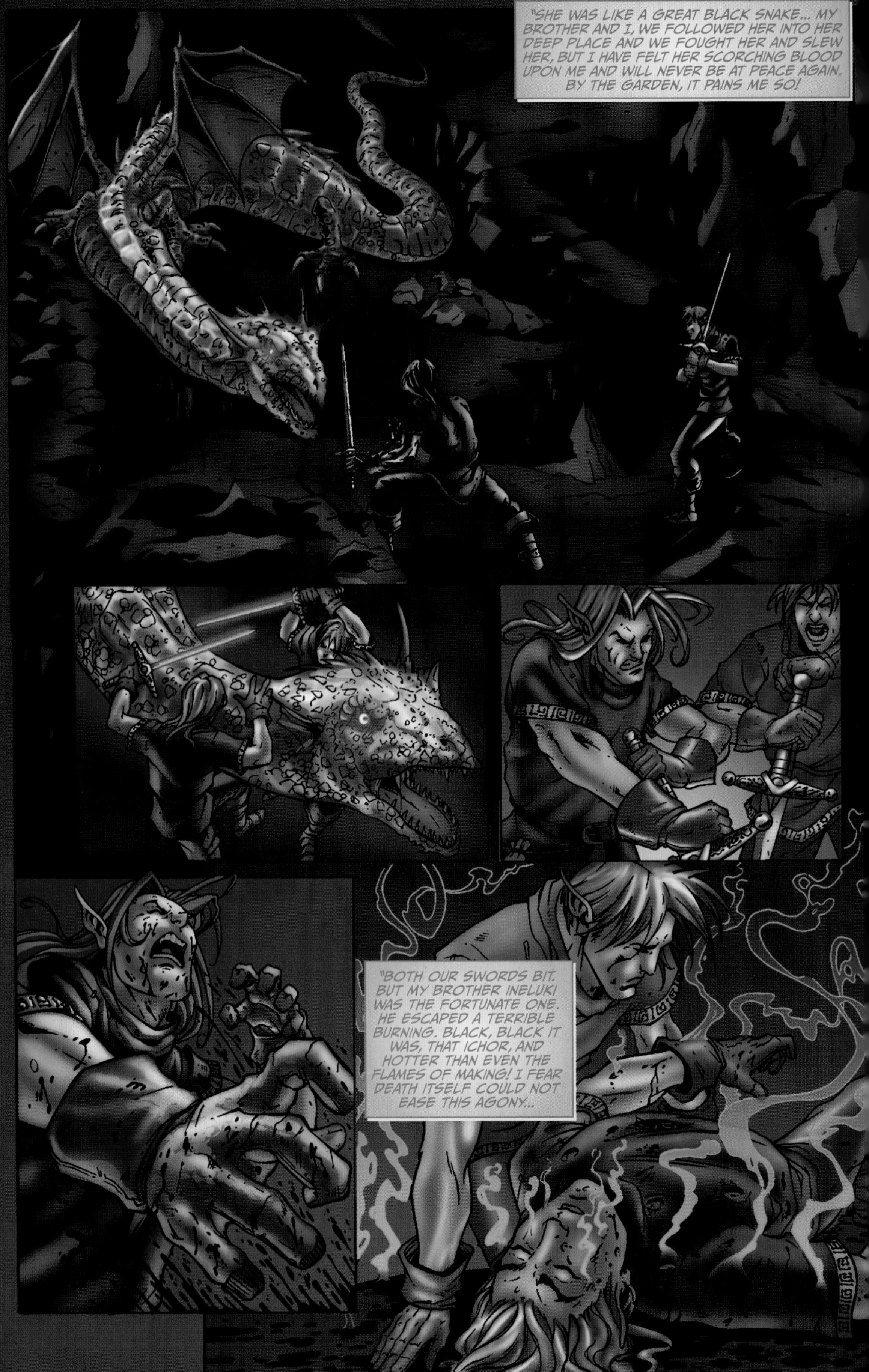
"SHE WAS LIKE A GREAT BLACK SNAKE... MY BROTHER AND I, WE FOLLOWED HER INTO HER DEEP PLACE AND WE FOUGHT HER AND SLEW HER, BUT I HAVE FELT HER SCORCHING BLOOD UPON ME AND WILL NEVER BE AT PEACE AGAIN. BY THE GARDEN, IT PAINS ME SO!
"BOTH OUR SWORDS BIT. BUT MY BROTHER INELUKI WAS THE FORTUNATE ONE. HE ESCAPED A TERRIBLE BURNING. BLACK, BLACK IT WAS, THAT ICHOR, AND HOTTER THAN EVEN THE FLAMES OF MAKING! I FEAR DEATH ITSELF COULD NOT EASE THIS AGONY...

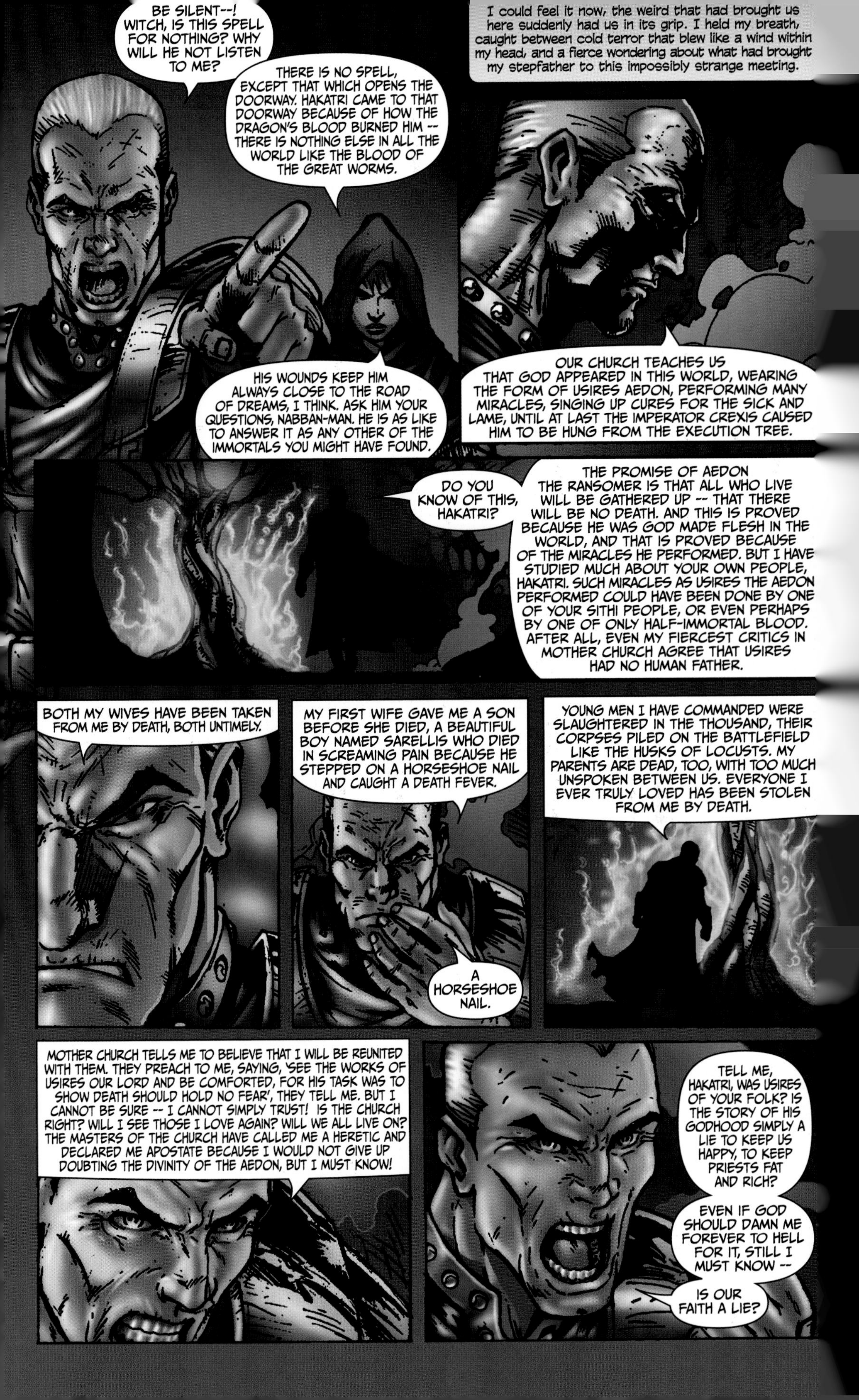
BE SILENT--! WITCH, IS THIS SPELL FOR NOTHING? WHY WILL HE NOT LISTEN TO ME?
THERE IS NO SPELL, EXCEPT THAT WHICH OPENS THE DOORWAY. HAKATRI CAME TO THAT DOORWAY BECAUSE OF HOW THE DRAGON'S BLOOD BURNED HIM -- THERE IS NOTHING ELSE IN ALL THE WORLD LIKE THE BLOOD OF THE GREAT WORMS.
HIS WOUNDS KEEP HIM ALWAYS CLOSE TO THE ROAD OF DREAMS, I THINK. ASK HIM YOUR QUESTIONS, NABBAN-MAN. HE IS AS LIKE TO ANSWER IT AS ANY OTHER OF THE IMMORTALS YOU MIGHT HAVE FOUND.
I could feel it now, the weird that had brought us here suddenly had us in its grip. I held my breath, caught between cold terror that blew like a wind within my head, and a fierce wondering about what had brought my stepfather to this impossibly strange meeting.
OUR CHURCH TEACHES US THAT GOD APPEARED IN THIS WORLD, WEARING THE FORM OF USIRES AEDON, PERFORMING MANY MIRACLES, SINGING UP CURES FOR THE SICK AND LAME, UNTIL AT LAST THE IMPERATOR CREXIS CAUSED HIM TO BE HUNG FROM THE EXECUTION TREE.
DO YOU KNOW OF THIS, HAKATRI?
THE PROMISE OF AEDON THE RANSOMER IS THAT ALL WHO LIVE WILL BE GATHERED UP -- THAT THERE WILL BE NO DEATH. AND THIS IS PROVED BECAUSE HE WAS GOD MADE FLESH IN THE WORLD, AND THAT IS PROVED BECAUSE OF THE MIRACLES HE PERFORMED. BUT I HAVE STUDIED MUCH ABOUT YOUR OWN PEOPLE, HAKATRI. SUCH MIRACLES AS USIRES THE AEDON PERFORMED COULD HAVE BEEN DONE BY ONE OF YOUR SITHI PEOPLE, OR EVEN PERHAPS BY ONE OF ONLY HALF-IMMORTAL BLOOD. AFTER ALL, EVEN MY FIERCEST CRITICS IN MOTHER CHURCH AGREE THAT USIRES HAD NO HUMAN FATHER.
BOTH MY WIVES HAVE BEEN TAKEN FROM ME BY DEATH, BOTH UNTIMELY.
MY FIRST WIFE GAVE ME A SON BEFORE SHE DIED, A BEAUTIFUL BOY NAMED SARELLIS WHO DIED IN SCREAMING PAIN BECAUSE HE STEPPED ON A HORSESHOE NAIL AND CAUGHT A DEATH FEVER.
A HORSESHOE NAIL.
YOUNG MEN I HAVE COMMANDED WERE SLAUGHTERED IN THE THOUSAND, THEIR CORPSES PILED ON THE BATTLEFIELD LIKE THE HUSKS OF LOCUSTS. MY PARENTS ARE DEAD, TOO, WITH TOO MUCH UNSPOKEN BETWEEN US. EVERYONE I EVER TRULY LOVED HAS BEEN STOLEN FROM ME BY DEATH.
MOTHER CHURCH TELLS ME TO BELIEVE THAT I WILL BE REUNITED WITH THEM. THEY PREACH TO ME, SAYING, 'SEE THE WORKS OF USIRES OUR LORD AND BE COMFORTED, FOR HIS TASK WAS TO SHOW DEATH SHOULD HOLD NO FEAR', THEY TELL ME. BUT I CANNOT BE SURE -- I CANNOT SIMPLY TRUST! IS THE CHURCH RIGHT? WILL I SEE THOSE I LOVE AGAIN? WILL WE ALL LIVE ON? THE MASTERS OF THE CHURCH HAVE CALLED ME A HERETIC AND DECLARED ME APOSTATE BECAUSE I WOULD NOT GIVE UP DOUBTING THE DIVINITY OF THE AEDON, BUT I MUST KNOW!
TELL ME, HAKATRI, WAS USIRES OF YOUR FOLK? IS THE STORY OF HIS GODHOOD SIMPLY A LIE TO KEEP US HAPPY, TO KEEP PRIESTS FAT AND RICH?
EVEN IF GOD SHOULD DAMN ME FOREVER TO HELL FOR IT, STILL I MUST KNOW --
IS OUR FAITH A LIE?

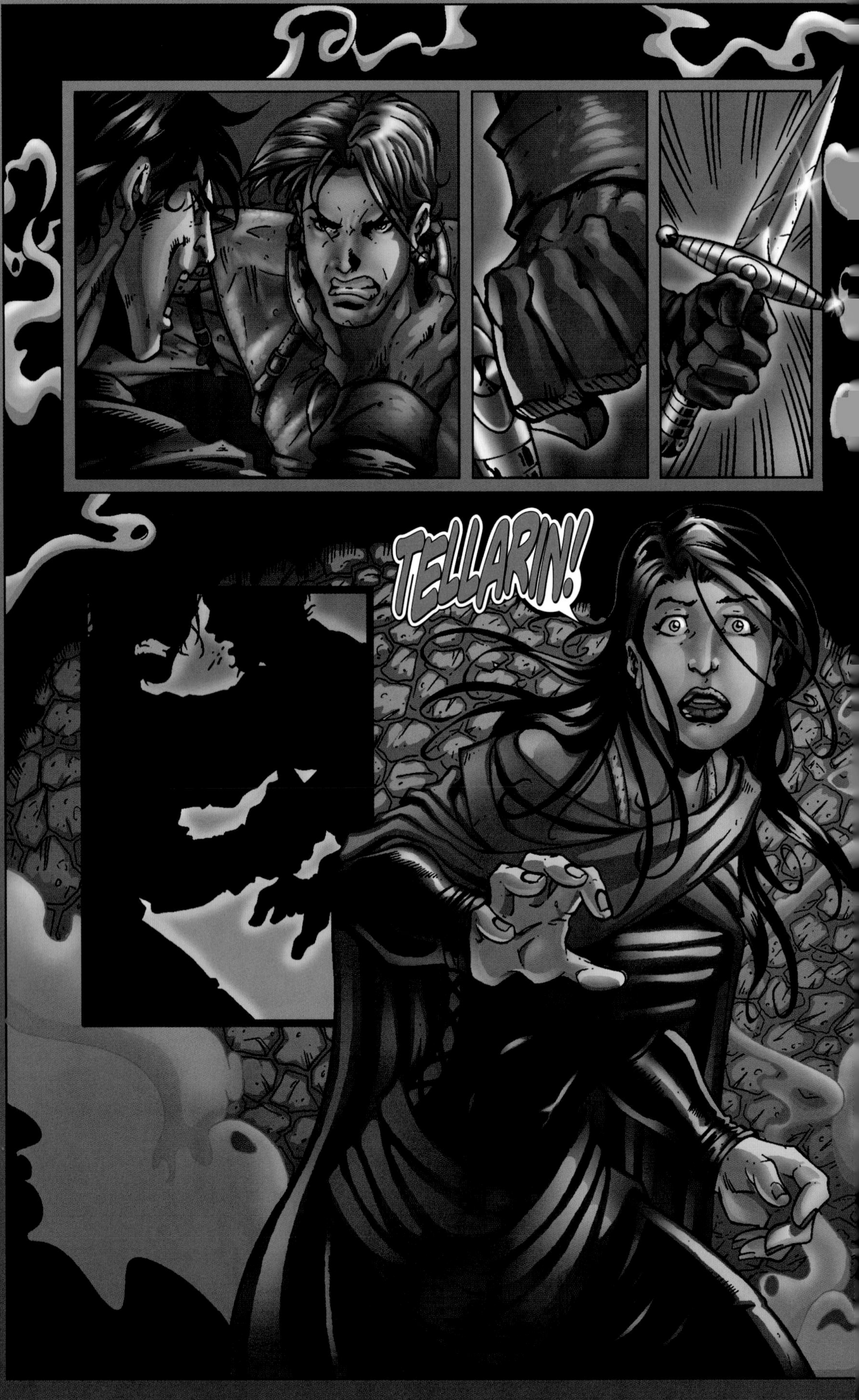
TELLARIN!

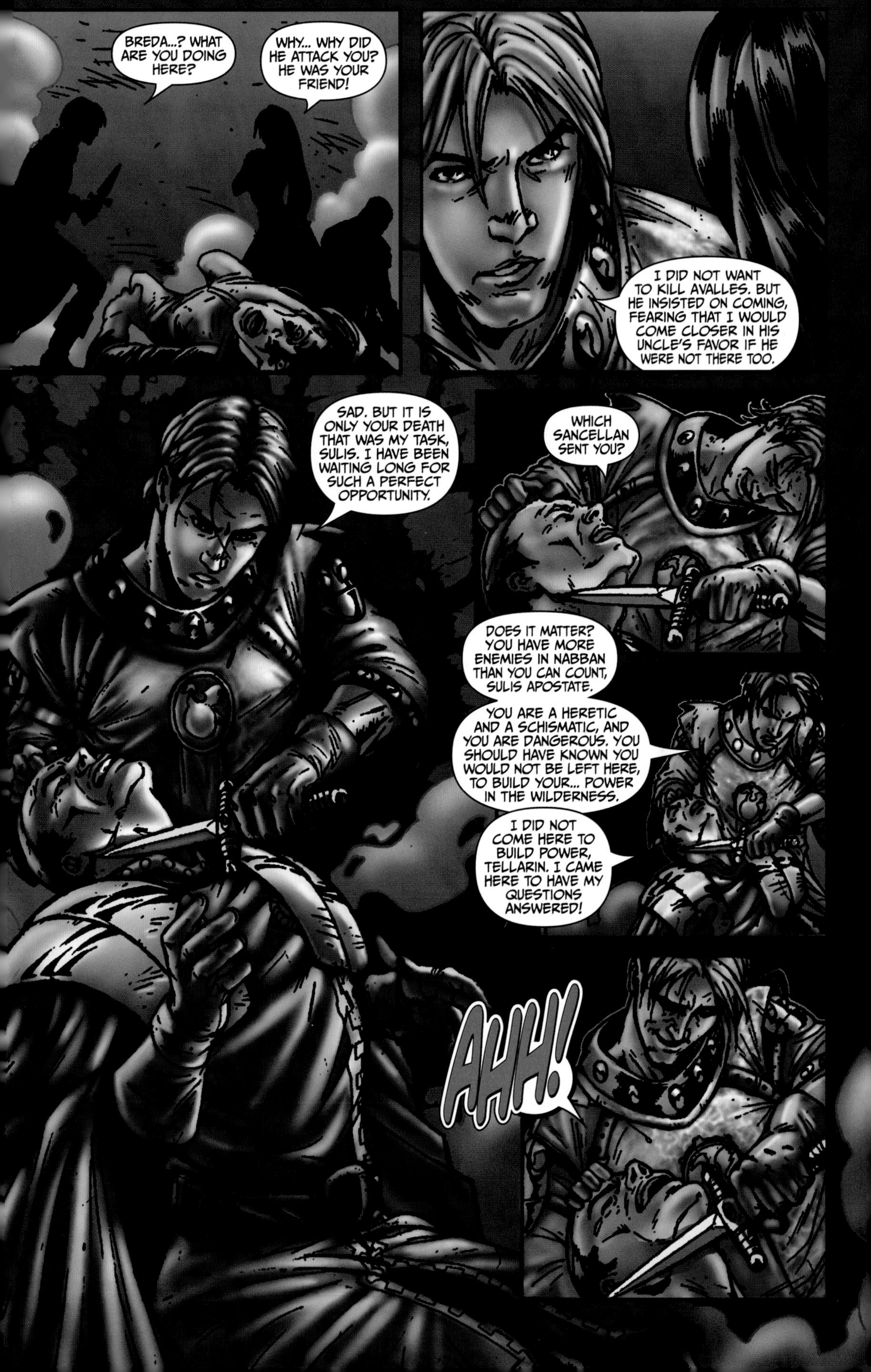
BREDA...? WHAT ARE YOU DOING HERE?
WHY... WHY DID HE ATTACK YOU? HE WAS YOUR FRIEND!
I DID NOT WANT TO KILL AVALLES. BUT HE INSISTED ON COMING, FEARING THAT I WOULD COME CLOSER IN HIS UNCLE'S FAVOR IF HE WERE NOT THERE TOO.
SAD. BUT IT IS ONLY YOUR DEATH THAT WAS MY TASK, SULIS. I HAVE BEEN WAITING LONG FOR SUCH A PERFECT OPPORTUNITY.
WHICH SANCELLAN SENT YOU?
DOES IT MATTER? YOU HAVE MORE ENEMIES IN NABBAN THAN YOU CAN COUNT, SULIS APOSTATE.
YOU ARE A HERETIC AND A SCHISMATIC, AND YOU ARE DANGEROUS. YOU SHOULD HAVE KNOWN YOU WOULD NOT BE LEFT HERE, TO BUILD YOUR... POWER IN THE WILDERNESS.
I DID NOT COME HERE TO BUILD POWER, TELLARIN. I CAME HERE TO HAVE MY QUESTIONS ANSWERED!
AHH!

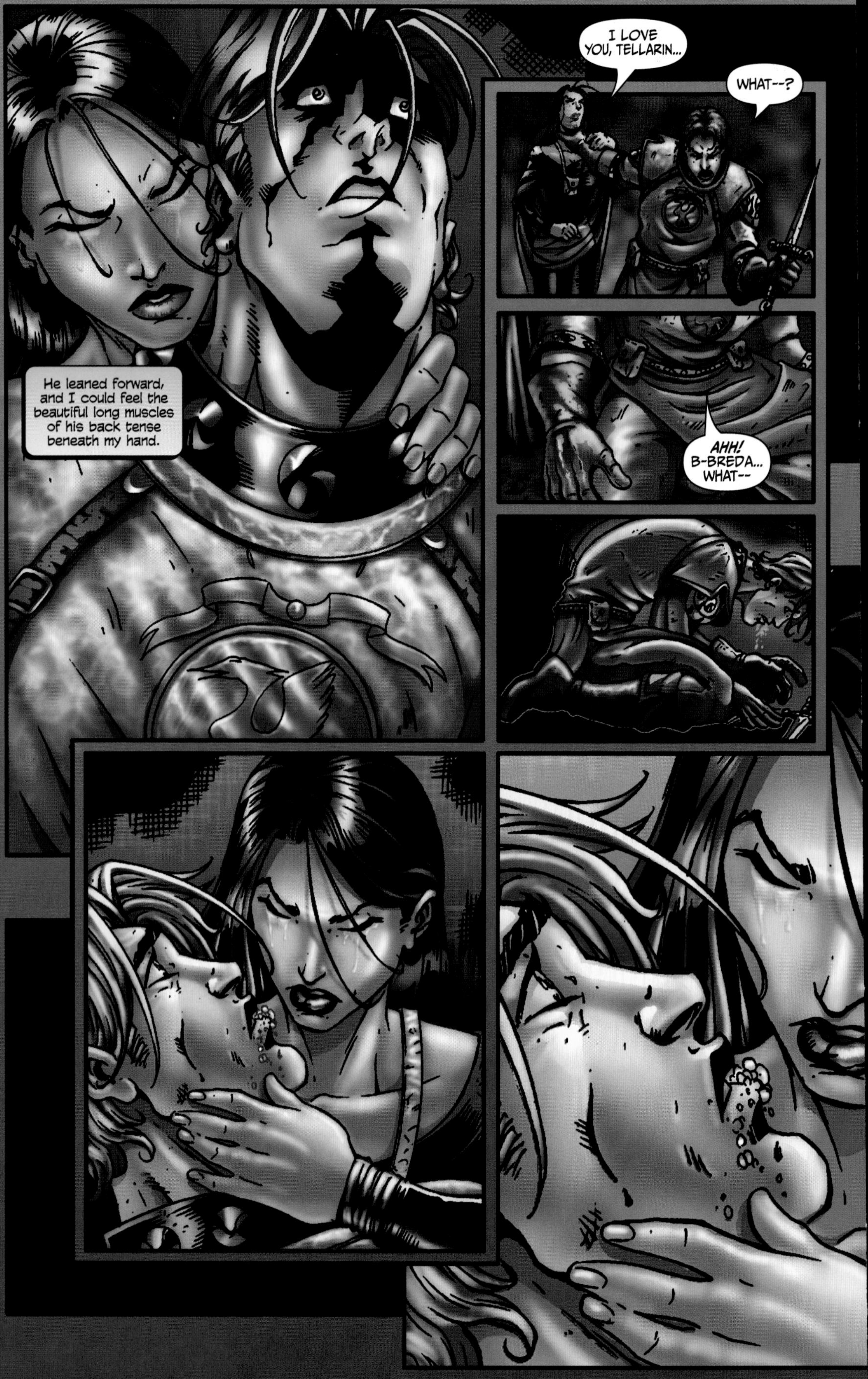
He leaned forward, and I could feel the beautiful long muscles of his back tense beneath my hand.
I LOVE YOU, TELLARIN...
WHAT--?
AHH! B-BREDA... WHAT--

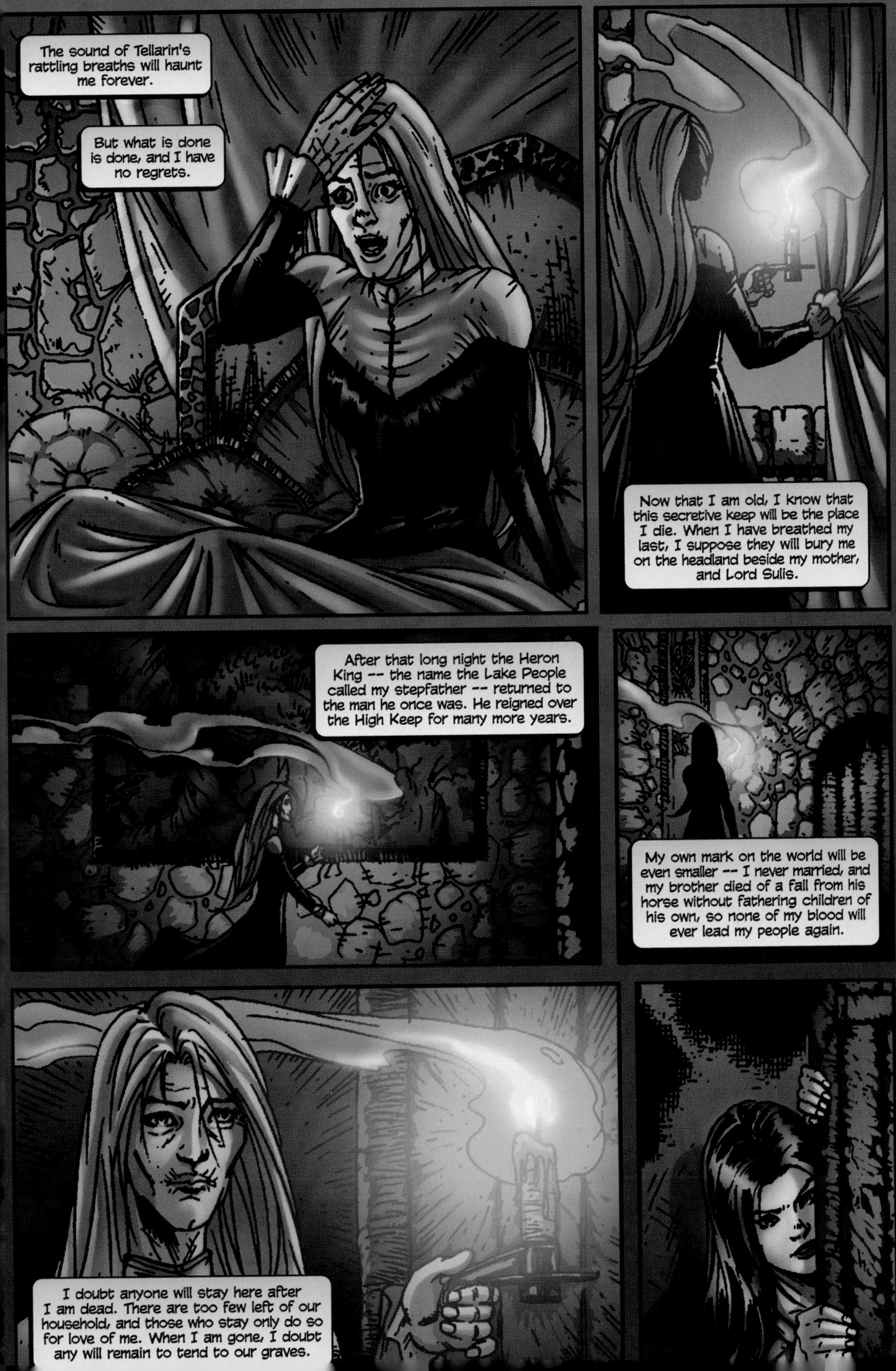
The sound of Tellarin's rattling breaths will haunt me forever.
But what is done is done, and I have no regrets.
Now that I am old, I know that this secretive keep will be the place I die. When I have breathed my last, I suppose they will bury me on the headland beside my mother, and Lord Sulis.
After that long night the Heron King -- the name the Lake People called my stepfather -- returned to the man he once was. He reigned over the High Keep for many more years.
My own mark on the world will be even smaller -- I never married, and my brother died of a fall from his horse without fathering children of his own, so none of my blood will ever lead my people again.
I doubt anyone will stay here after I am dead. There are too few left of our household, and those who stay only do so for love of me. When I am gone, I doubt any will remain to tend to our graves.

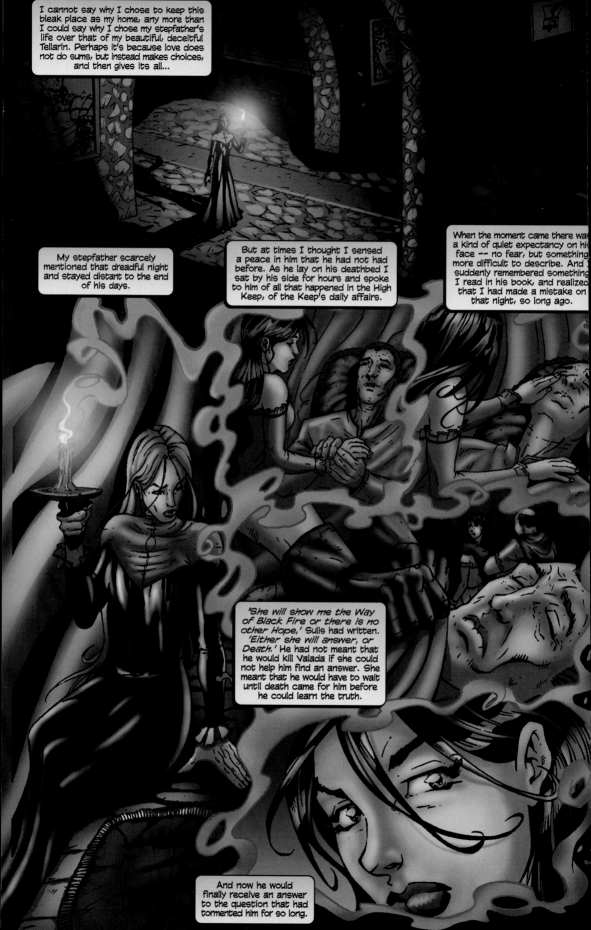

I cannot say why I chose to keep this bleak place as my home, any more than I could say why I chose my stepfather's life over that of my beautiful, deceitful Tellarin. Perhaps it's because love does not do sums, but instead makes choices, and then gives its all...

My stepfather scarcely mentioned that dreadful night and stayed distant to the end of his days.

But at times I thought I sensed a peace in him that he had not had before. As he lay on his deathbed I sat by his side for hours and spoke to him of all that happened in the High Keep, of the Keep's daily affairs.

When the moment came there was a kind of quiet expectancy on his face -- no fear, but something more difficult to describe. And I suddenly remembered something I read in his book, and realized that I had made a mistake on that night, so long ago.

'She will show me the Way of Black Fire or there is no other Hope,' Sulis had written. 'Either she will answer, or Death.' He had not meant that he would kill Valada if she could not help him find an answer. She meant that he would have to wait until death came for him before he could learn the truth.

And now he would finally receive an answer to the question that had tormented him for so long.

Whatever Sulis' answers were, he did not return to share them with me. But now I am an old, old woman, and I will find them soon enough myself.

It is strange, perhaps, but I find I do not much care. In one year with Tellarin, in those months of fierce love, I lived an entire lifetime. Since then I have lived anther one, a long, slow life whose small pleasures have largely balanced the moments of suffering. Surely two lives are enough for anyone -- who needs the endless span of the immortals?

After all, as the Burning Man made clear, an eternity of pain is no gift.

And now that I have told my tale, even the ghosts that sometimes still startle me awake at midnight seem more like ancient friends than things to be feared.

I have made my choices.

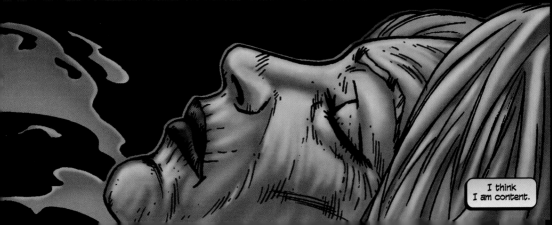

I think I am content.

The Burning Man SKETCHBOOK

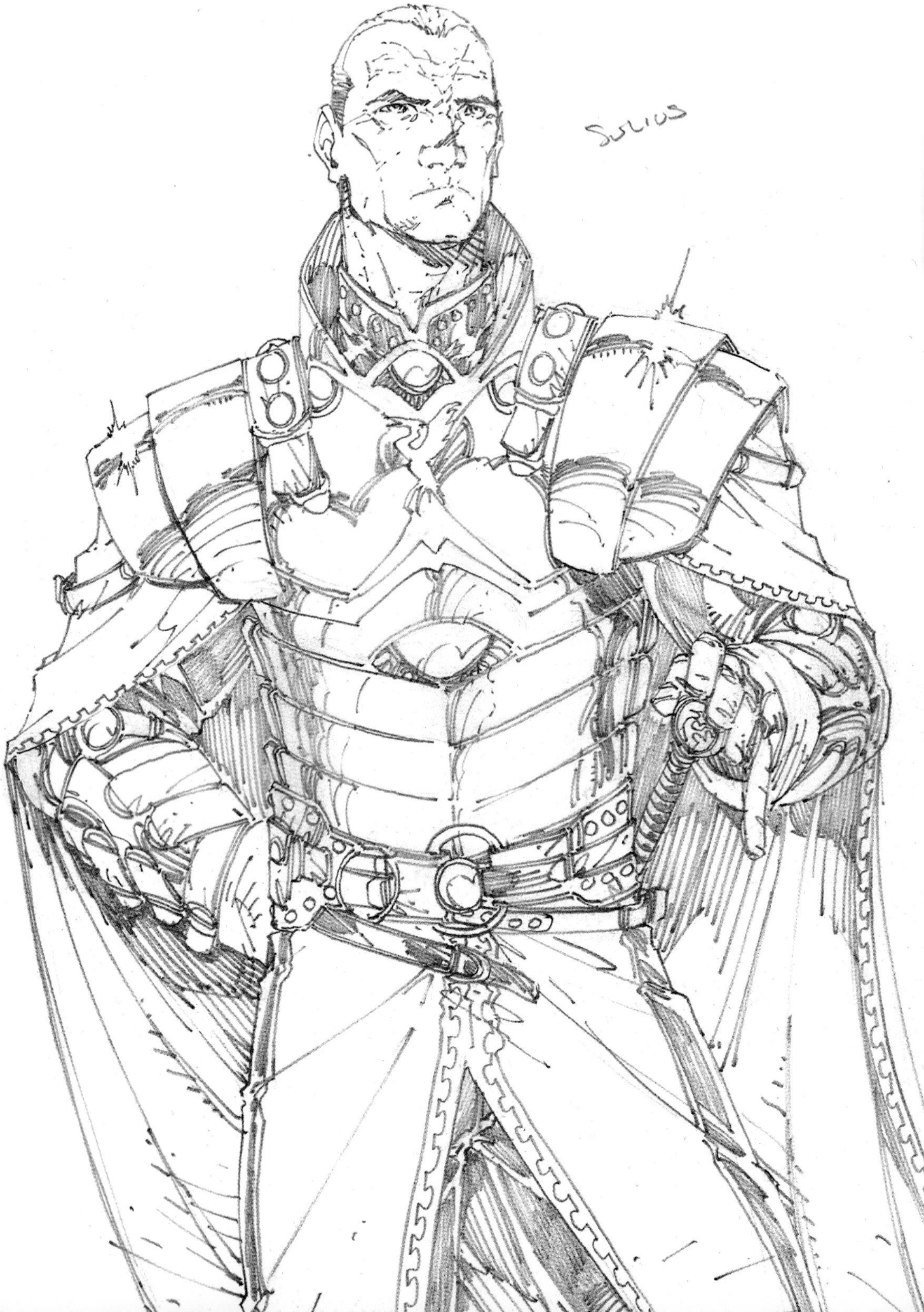
Sulius

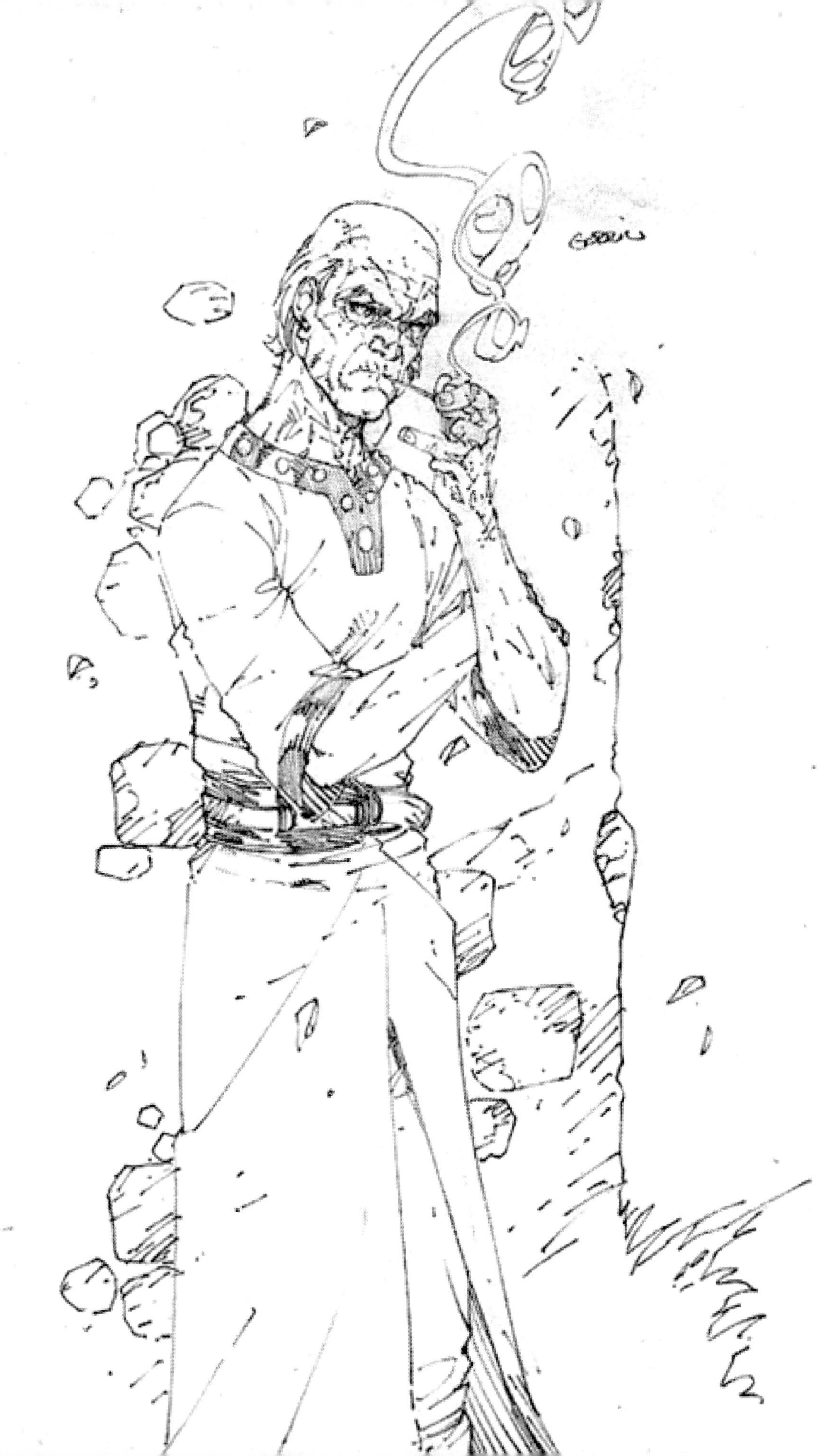

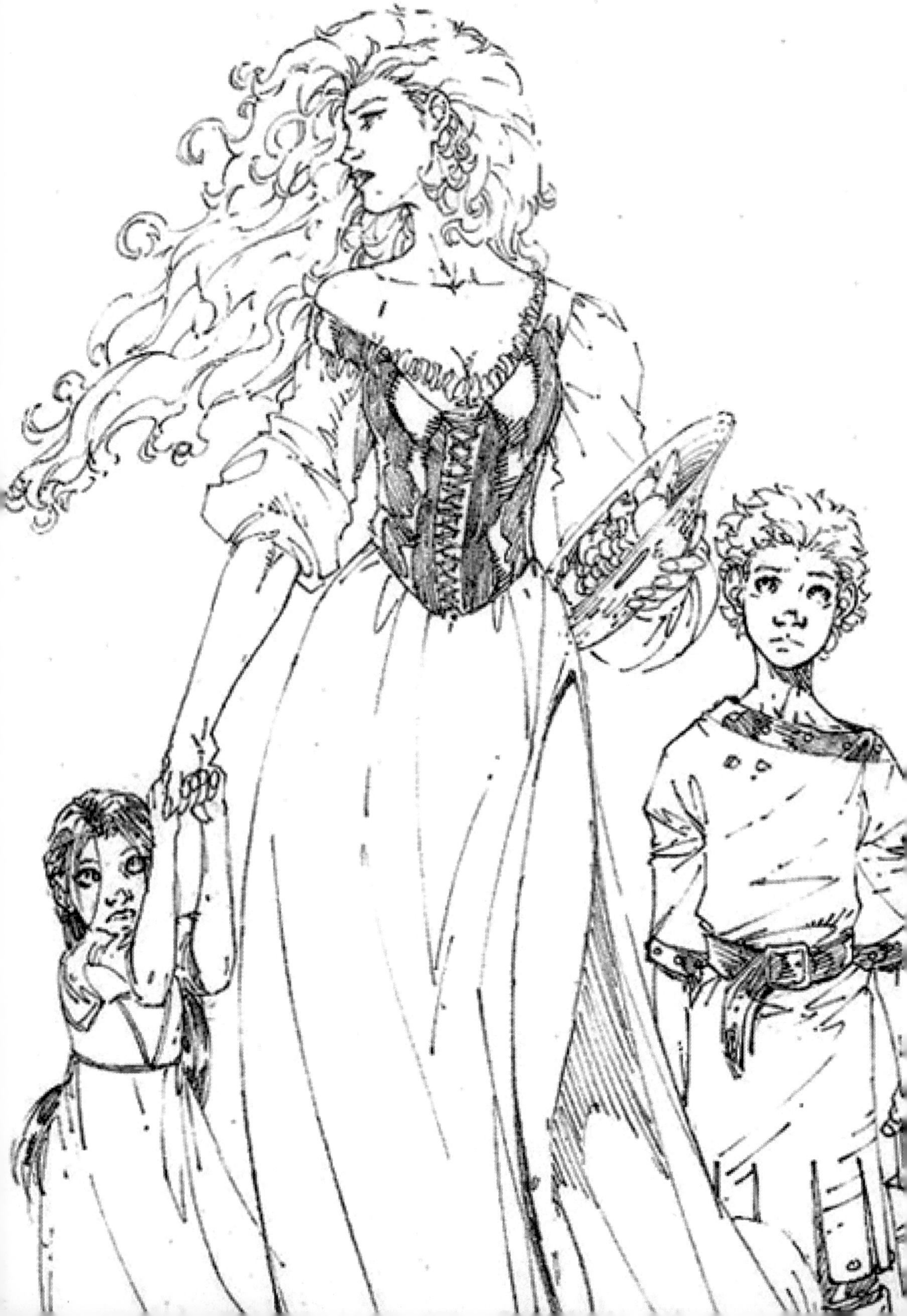

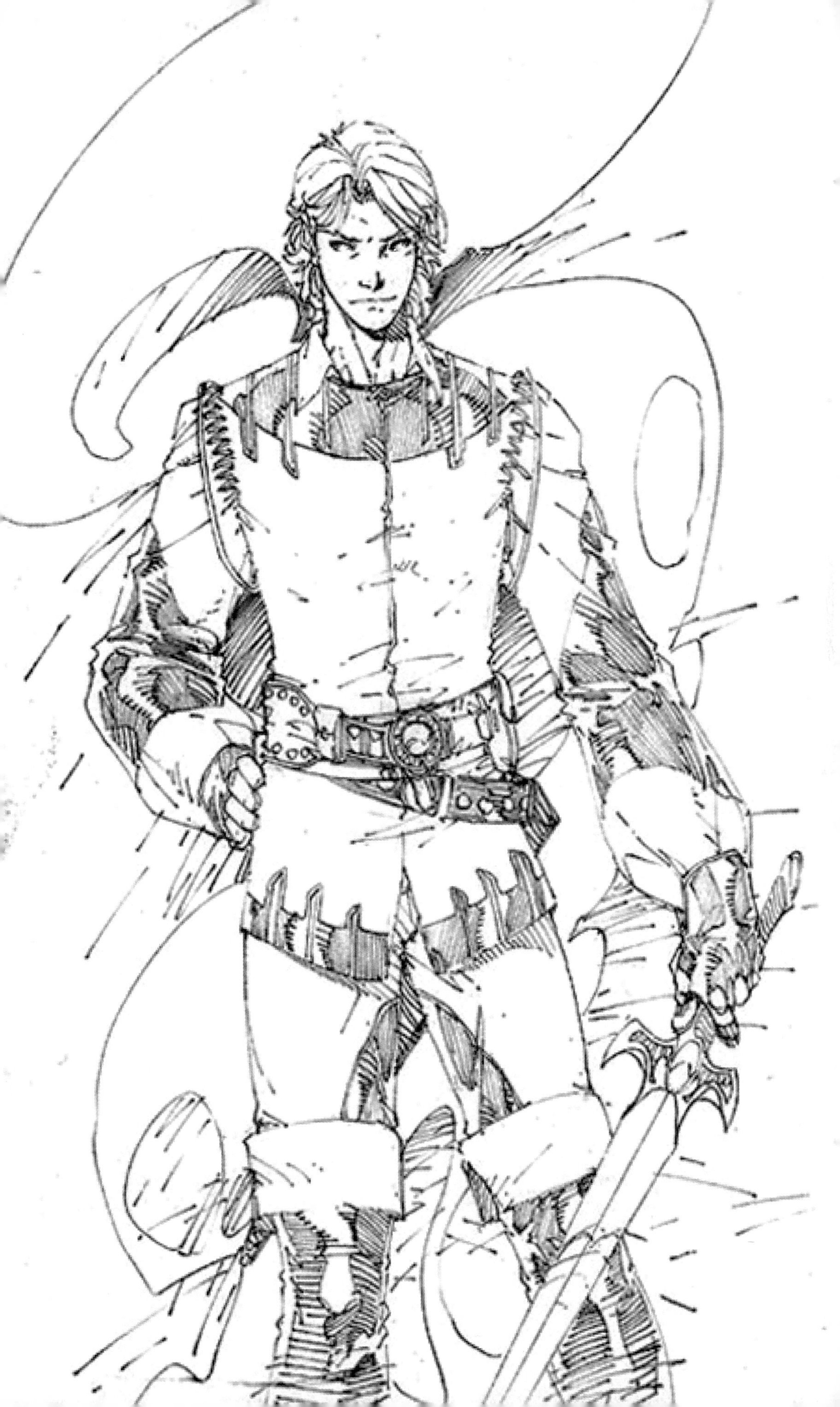

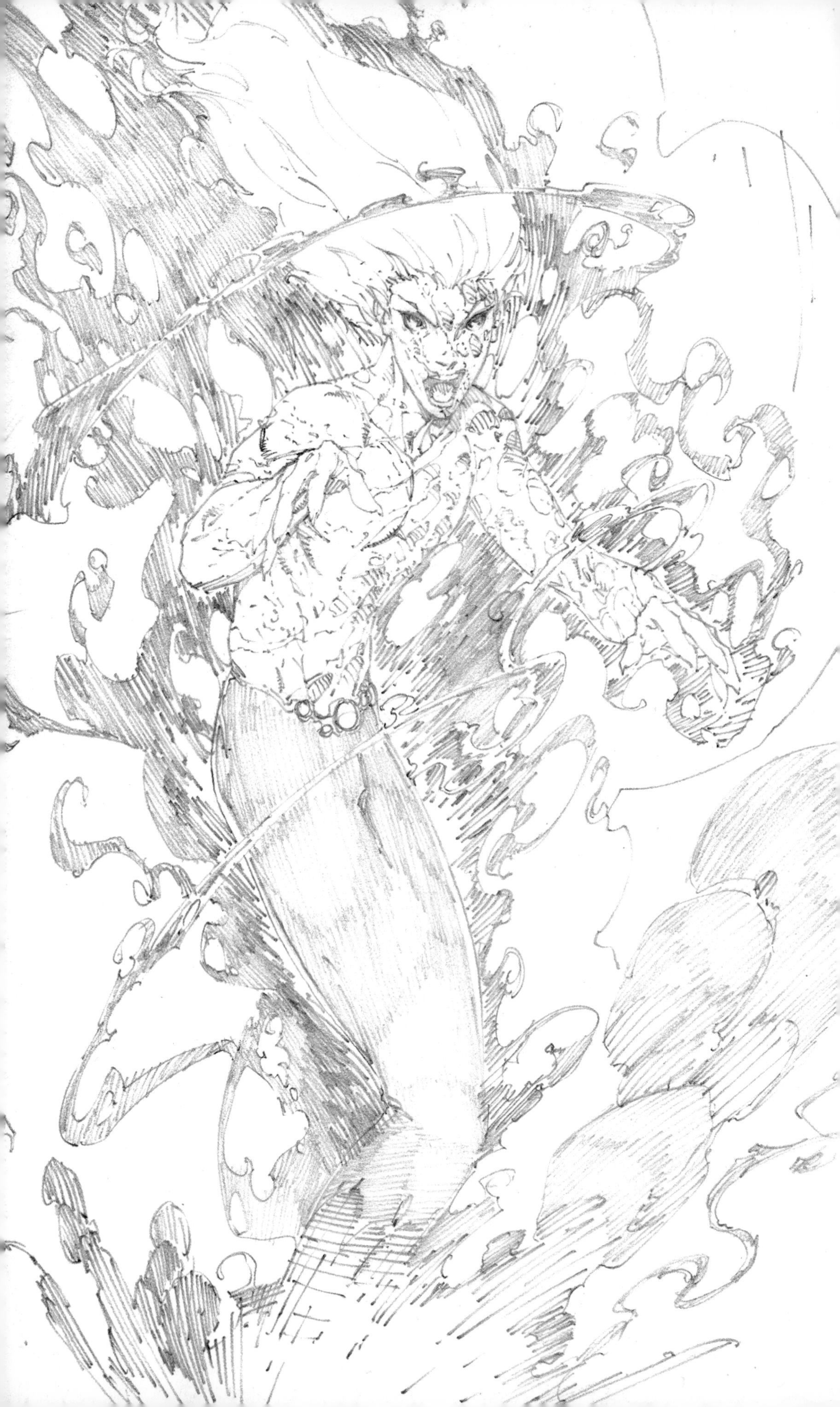

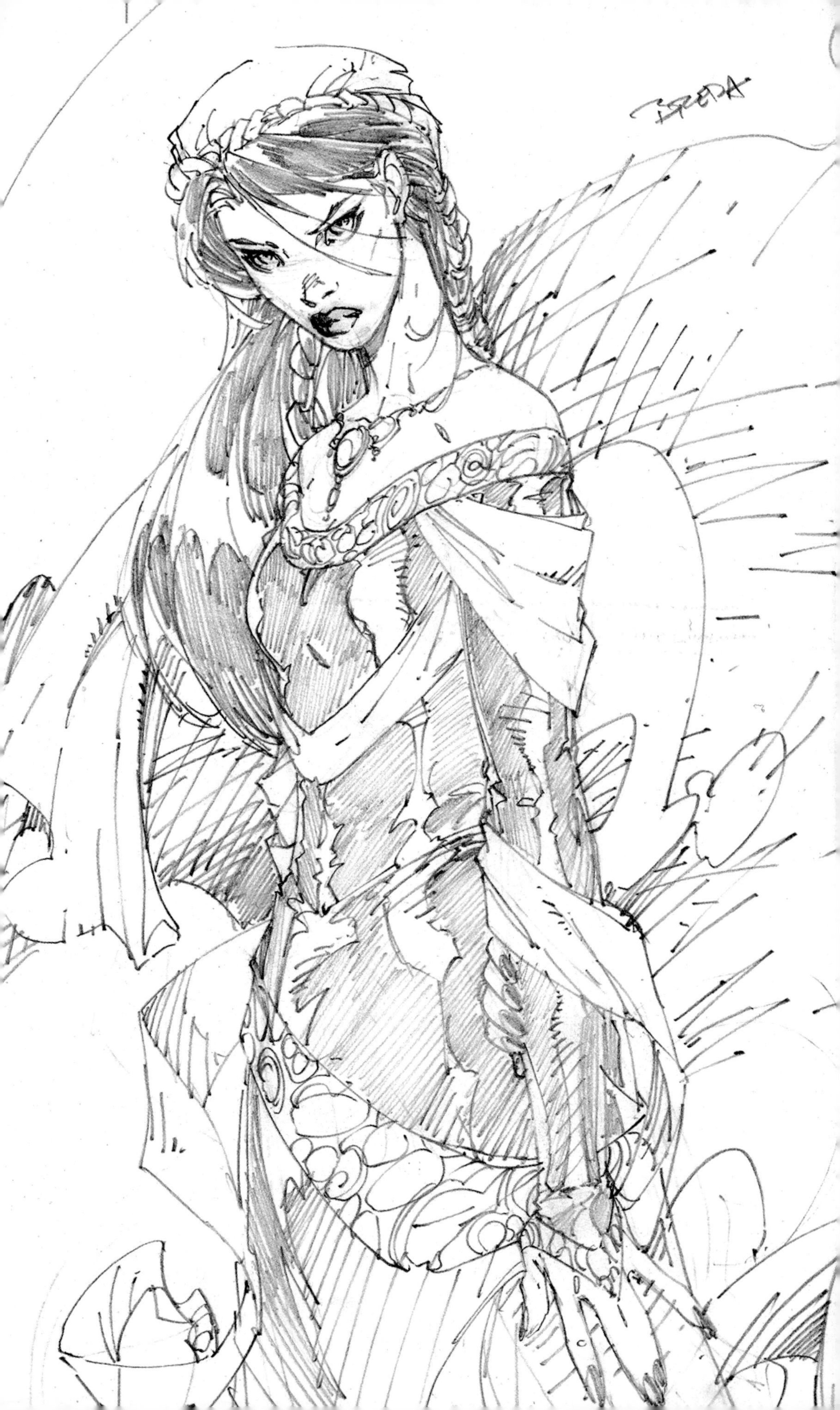
BREDA

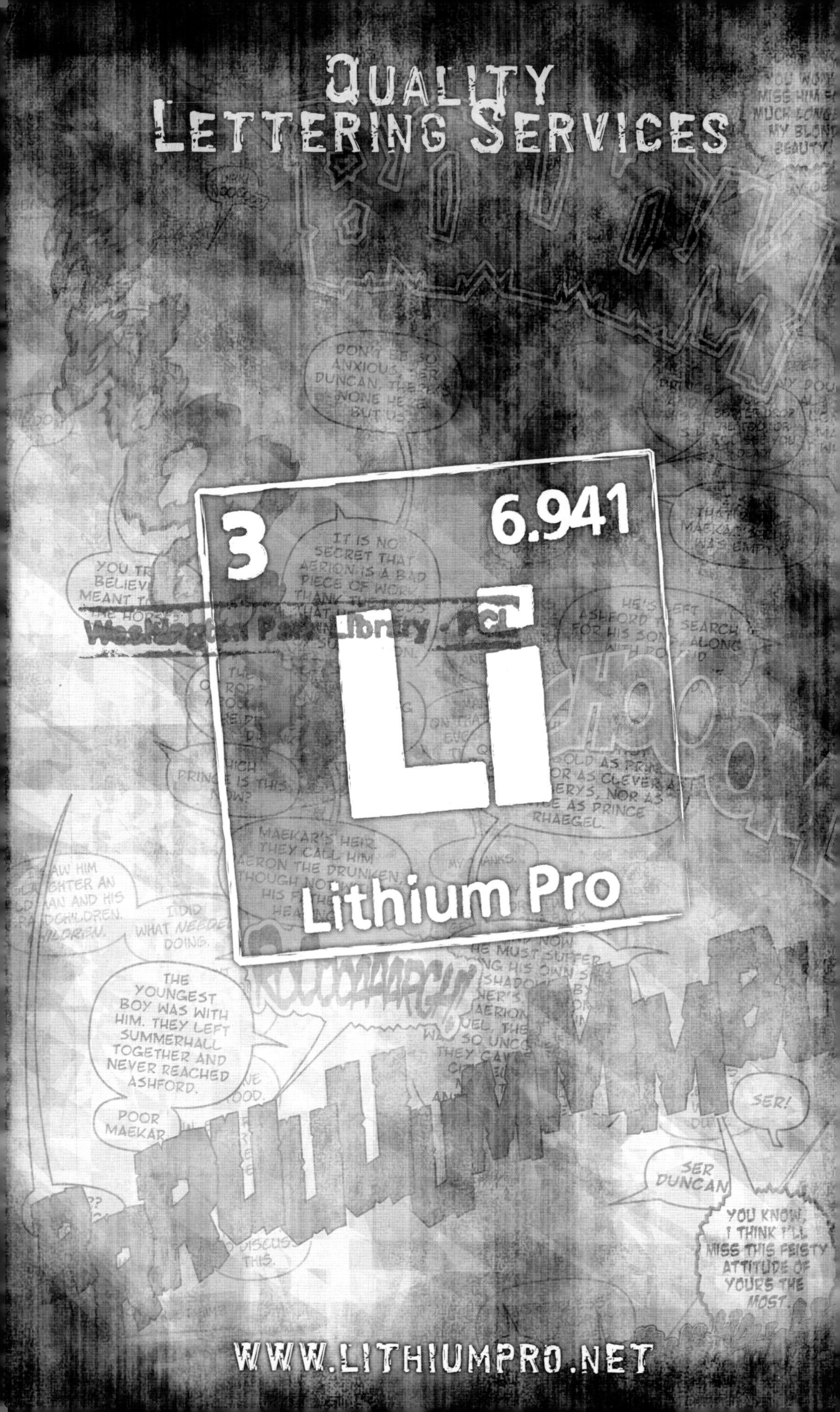

QUALITY LETTERING SERVICES
3
6.941
Li
Lithium Pro
THE YOUNGEST BOY WAS WITH HIM. THEY LEFT SUMMERHALL TOGETHER AND NEVER REACHED ASHFORD.
POOR MAEKAR
I DID WHAT NEEDED DOING.
SER!
SER DUNCAN
YOU KNOW, I THINK I'LL MISS THIS FEISTY ATTITUDE OF YOURS THE MOST.
WWW.LITHIUMPRO.NET